The Relational Self

The Relational Self

Ethics & Therapy from a Black Church Perspective

Archie Smith, Jr.

87-1695

Abingdon
Nashville

The Relational Self:
Ethics and Therapy from a Black Church Perspective

Copyright © 1982 by Abingdon

Library of Congress Cataloging in Publication Data

SMITH, ARCHIE, 1939-
  The relational self.
  Includes bibliographical references and index.
  1. Afro-American churches. 2. Psychotherapy. 3. Social ethics.
  4. Social psychology. 5. Sociology, Christian. I. Title.
  BR563.N4S57   261.8'08996073   82-6733   AACR2

ISBN 0-687-35945-7 (pbk.)

Scripture quotations unless otherwise noted are from the Revised Standard
Version of the Bible, copyrighted 1946, 1952, 1971, © 1973, by the Division of
Christian Education of the National Council of the Churches of Christ in the
U.S.A. and used by permission.

Those noted NAS are from the New American Standard © The Lockman
Foundation; 1960, 1962, 1963, 1968, 1971, 1972, 1973, 1975.

Those noted TEV are from the Bible in Today's English Version. Copyright ©
American Bible Society 1966, 1971, 1976.

Quotations noted NEB are from The New English Bible. © the Delegates of the
Oxford University Press and the Syndics of the Cambridge University Press
1961, 1970. Reprinted by permission.

The quotation noted Phillips is from Letters to Young Churches, copyright ©
J. B. Phillips 1947.

MANUFACTURED BY THE PARTHENON PRESS AT
NASHVILLE, TENNESSEE, UNITED STATES OF AMERICA

In remembrance of my father, Archie Smith, Sr., 1902–1977, and to my mother, Beatrice Skipper Smith, and to my siblings, Margie, Leonard, Joyce, and Geri. They were the first to teach me the most important and lasting lessons about life, love, and forgiveness.

ACKNOWLEDGMENTS

No one produces a book alone. Many kind and supportive people make book writing possible. Without the invaluable criticism, suggestions, and assistance from others, this work would not have been possible. These kind souls must be acknowledged and thanked.

A special word of thanks to Professor Edward E. Sampson, a social scientist, but more importantly, a dear friend and spiritual ally, who read the early draft of the manuscript and gave a conceptual critique of the book that aided significantly to its overall organization. Thanks to Professor James Wm. McClendon of the Church Divinity School of the Pacific, colleague and friend, whose theological and ethical insight and critical discernment is respected and deeply appreciated. His challenges to the theological and ethical themes provided strong encouragement to continue the effort.

Thanks to Professor Robert Ross, sociologist and comrade, who suggested the idea of *the person and the system* some years ago. He read critically the seventh chapter and provided valuable suggestions and corrections and helped clarify certain key concepts. Also, thanks to Professor Jane Morlet Hardie, whose sense of scholarship, concern and criticial reading of chapter 7 helped make this a stronger and easier-to-read chapter.

Thanks to Marion, Sue, and Carl Brodt, who, as perceptive and compassionate laypersons, read parts of the manuscript and made suggestions on how to better communicate my ideas. Doctors Jaylene Summers and Henry Wolstat, both superb therapists each in her and his own right, made significant suggestions and helped clarify some of my ideas on the role of the therapist, therapy, and psychoanalysis. Thanks also to Dr. Frank Sargent who helped clarify the difference between psychoanalysis and family systems therapy.

Thanks to colleague and Professor Karen Lebacqz for her encouragement and supportive feedback on an early draft of chapter 5, social ethics, and the Jonestown chapter, and for providing the opportunity to present a rough draft of the same chapter to Area IV at the Graduate Theological Union in Berkeley. Professor Larry Mamiya must also be thanked for his very helpful insights and suggestions on the Jonestown chapter.

Thanks to my colleague, Professor Charles McCoy, for his early help in developing the idea of the relational self. A special word of thanks to Kelly Miller Smith, Professors Peter Paris and Robert Williams, for the opportunity to present some of my ideas on the relational self to the students and a few faculty at the Vanderbilt Divinity School at Nashville, Tennessee.

Robert Bilheimer, director of the Institute for Ecumenical Relations and Cultural Research, Collegeville, Minnesota, provided the opportunity to study there and helped clarify aspects of this work and in the presence of other scholars. His encouragement and support, as well as that of Sister Deloris, have also been immeasurable.

I wish to thank Professor Cornel West of Union Theological Seminary, New York City, for his suggestion to consult two important sources which proved to be the conceptual backbone for chapter 7, namely, Louis Athusser's *Lenin and Philosophy* and Coward and Ellis' *Language and Materialism*. Dr. Carter Lindberg, visiting scholar at the Ecumenical Institute in Strasbourg, France, provided the opportunity to present an early draft of this chapter at the 15th Annual Meeting of the Institute.

Thanks to my neighbor, Karl Epper, who unselfishly and freely made available the opportunity to reproduce the manuscript. Thanks especially to Ms. Elli Jones, who typed and retyped the manuscript without complaint, and who also edited parts of the manuscript and made helpful suggestions along the way. Her enthusiasm for the project was also a source of encouragement.

Donald K. Grant, a trustee of the Pacific School of Religion, made available financial support, without which the book in its present form would not have been possible. Also, my students who have challenged me and who have contributed their own insights into the problems of relational selfhood have been very helpful in thinking through the concept of the relational self.

Above all, even with financial support, the book would not have been written had it not been for the unwavering support and encouragement of my wife, Jerry, who made the greater sacrifice of time and who allowed me to work long hours until the project was completed. Her love, warmth, understanding, and acceptance were and are the stimulus for continuing to believe in and to affirm the meaning of human-divine forgiveness and reconciliation.

While no one produces a book alone, I alone must bear the full responsibility for the final results.

Archie Smith, Jr.
Berkeley, California
Fall, 1981

CONTENTS

INTRODUCTION

The reality of self is in Relations.
—Bernard Steinzor
in The Healing Partnership

From a biblical perspective Christian discipleship and the moral integrity of a nation are inseparable from justice to the poor and the oppressed. This book is about the church's ministry of liberation with the victims of oppression, the freedom struggles of the oppressed, and the relational or communal nature of selfhood. The biblical challenge to ministry, to church and society is "to loose the bonds of wickedness, to undo the thongs of the yoke, to let the oppressed go free, and to break every yoke. . . . Then shall your light break forth like the dawn, and your healing shall spring up speedily" (Isa. 58:6, 8a).

Allan Aubrey Boesak, in the concluding chapter of *Farewell to Innocence,* wrote:

> Reconciliation requires a new image of humanity (which is why reconciliation without liberation is impossible). But the new image of humanity requires new structures in society—new wine in new wineskins! How new, then, are black persons who move out of their old lines of poverty and dejection into a higher status in the unchanged structures of our oppressive and exploitative system? In other words, the question really is, how do black theologians define liberation?[1]

The need, as Boesak sees it, is for the emergence of new social structures, a new subject in history and liberating relational patterns in society. His concern is to link structural change with psychic liberation; outer transformation with inner transformation; and social criticism with self-criticism. Both outer and inner transformation are necessarily parts of the same process of genuine social transformation.

This book takes the concern of Boesak at its point of origin in that it attempts to identify common ground for keeping together outer and inner transformation. It identifies *relationality* and the communal self as key concepts in emancipatory struggles and liberation ministries. Relationality will be argued as a basis for keeping Christian social ethics and therapy together in liberation ministries which see the connection between spiritual freedom and psychic liberation and social transformation. Relationality means that people are constituted in their relations with other people and within a particular historical context and specific social practice. The relations between people are not only external, e.g. historical, but internal as well. We not only live among other people, but also they live in us and we in them; and we become members one of another through common struggle and identification with the past sufferings and aspirations of a people.

My central purpose is to heighten awareness of the interwoven character of personal and systemic oppression and the importance of keeping an analysis of inner and outer transformation together in liberation ministries. The book is written from a black church perspective, but the message is not limited to the black church.[2] The black church is viewed as a microcosm of the Christian church responding to the liberating gospel of Jesus in a racist society that has denied black people their humanity and a technological society that threatens the freedom and existence of all human subjects.

Specifically, I want to build on the concept of the *relational self* and join Christian social ethics and therapy in a way that renders them useful for a black liberation ministry. Liberation ministry implies a breaking away from *old oppressive structures* in church and society, and seeking new possibilities for the realization of human fulfillment in a new and liberating social order. Liberation ministries must stay alert to the likelihood of old oppressive structures being replaced by new structures of oppression. Oppression is both an external and internal reality, therefore the process of liberation must seek to transform the social and political order and to emancipate the inner life of human subjects from internalized sources of oppression. The reproduction of oppression is inevitable if emancipation of the inner life of the oppressed is not a part of the larger process of social change and transformation. "This, then, is the great humanistic and historical task of the oppressed: to liberate themselves and their oppressors as well."[3] Christian social ethics and therapy need to work together in a liberation struggle where psychic and structural transformation is to be the outcome. To this end it is important to remember what is often repressed or lost to memory under the pressure of contemporary society.[4] The starting point, therefore, is historical.

1.

The black church was born in bondage. It was, from its inception, a servant church embedded and engaged in the anguish and freedom struggles of an oppressed people. Unlike most immigrants who came to these shores to flee religious persecution or poverty, Afro-Americans came involuntarily. They were brought in chains and sold as chattled slaves on the auction block. From their beginnings Afro-Americans were denied acceptance as human beings. They were barred from full participation in the mainstream of social, economic, and political life in America—including church life.[5]

> The black church was the creation of a black people whose daily existence was an encounter with the overwhelming and brutalizing reality of white power. For the slaves it was the sole source of personal identity and the sense of community. Though slaves had no social, economic, or political ties as a people, they had one humiliating factor in common—serfdom! The whole of their being was engulfed in a system intent on their annihilation as persons.[6]

The ministry of the black church emerged *from* and *within* the context of violent oppression. It was a ministry which identified the oppressed condition of black slaves with that of ancient

15

Israel and the liberating gospel and mission of Jesus. The sense of mission was commensurate with the Lord's message and liberating presence in the world.

> "The Spirit of the Lord is upon me,
> because he has chosen me to preach the Good News to the poor.
> He has sent me to proclaim liberty to the captives
> and recovery of sight to the blind;
> to set free the oppressed,
> and announce the year when the Lord will save his people."
>
> (Luke 4:18-19 TEV)

Jesus understood his ministry as one of setting captives free. The black church identified with Jesus, the salvation bringer. Slavery was the evil to overcome. Historical deliverance was the deep yearning of black people in bondage. For the black slave

> Freedom became . . . a real thing and not a dream. His religion became darker and more intense, and into his ethics crept a note of revenge, into his songs a day of reckoning close at hand. The "coming of the Lord" swept this side of death, and came to be a thing to be hoped for in this day. Through fugitive slaves and irrepressible discussion this desire for freedom seized the black millions still in bondage, and became their one ideal of life.[7]

Theirs was a church and ministry and theology often critical of white power and the society that oppressed them. While it is true that many of the Negro spirituals pointed to freedom in a world beyond this one, black slaves did not fail to see the connection between ultimate freedom in the world to come and historical justice and liberation in this life. The connection between ultimate freedom and historical justice is suggested in the Negro spiritual:

> O Mary, don't you weep, don't you mourn.
> O Mary, don't you weep, don't you mourn.
> Pharaoh's army got drownded.
> O Mary, don't you weep.

Mary was a symbol of every slave who in their weeping and mourning could evoke the dangerous memory of God's judgment upon every Pharaoh. Black slaves did not accept the Bible or the gospel of Jesus as it was interpreted to them by their white slave masters.[8] Rather, they rejected the essence of slavery and fashioned, through common struggle, their own interpretation of the gospel of Jesus and the meaning of their own oppression.

> In their minds is the profound belief expressed by the ex-slave Jourdan Anderson, when invited by his former master to return after the Civil War: "Surely there will be a day of reckoning of those who defraud the laborer of hire." That belief in the immutable justice of a powerful and gracious God sustains Black people in their oppression even now. It guarantees that life is still good enough to be enjoyed and celebrated enthusiastically, precisely by the persons thought to be at the bottom of the Western world's pile of powers and possessions.[9]

Black slaves, along with abolitionists, took upon themselves the struggle to endure and to transform structures of oppression. They sought to project their own human values, culture, and beliefs and to liberate themselves and to humanize the social order of which they were a part. The challenge of Christian ministry today is still to liberate and to reconcile the poor and the oppressed; to transform and to humanize society in the conviction that "a powerful and gracious God sustains" the oppressed even now.

Black people and oppressed minorities may be in danger of losing a sense of collective solidarity and common struggle for emancipation in an exploitative society that seeks to incorporate them within its existing ideology, structure, and system of values. Black people and other ethnic minorities may pay the higher price for *integration* into the mainstream of the dominant society. They pay the higher price when they accept, uncritically, the value orientation of modern bourgeois society. Uncritical acceptance of the dominant values of this materialistic society predisposes them to reach for the same commodity pacifiers that the system holds out to so many others, transforming them into cheerful robots without critical recognition of their transformation. The society itself loses in the long

17

run when the oppressed repress and forget their past, and when critical voices are silenced.

The black church cannot afford to be party to the social amnesia that appears to pervade our time. Nor can it afford to turn its back on the innocent victims of oppression without forfeiting the opportunity to proclaim the good news of Jesus' gospel with authority. The black church cannot afford to be silent about exploitative systems that dehumanize its victims and transform them into willing agents in the oppression of other minorities who are also their brothers and sisters.

Many black Americans who have recently become middle and upper income earners appear to have lost touch with this historical mission of liberating the oppressed. The majority of poor black people, especially the black underclass, remain marginal to the mainstream of economic, political, and church life in the United States. Some middle class blacks may no longer see themselves as members of an oppressed group and accept uncritically an exploitative, profit-centered economic and political system which, nevertheless, continues to deny them full humanity. Whether they recognize it or not, the black middle class still belongs to a despised cultural group in the United States. The black church is still challenged by the gospel of Jesus to seek the transformation of an oppressive society as well as to help liberate the consciousness of the oppressed. Spiritual freedom and psychic and systemic transformation and reconciliation must be kept together in the church's ministry. Why?

> Because God's act for man involves man's liberation from bondage, man's response to God's grace of liberation is an act for his oppressed brothers and sisters. There can be no reconciliation with God unless the hungry are fed, the sick are healed, and justice is given to the poor. The justified person is at once the sanctified person, one who knows that his freedom is inseparable from the liberation of the weak and the helpless.[10]

The black church may continue to realize a ministry of liberation and reconciliation to those who are captive to modern materialism, as well as realize a ministry of liberation to the incarcerated, the economically disadvantaged, and the politically impotent and suffering victims.

Black Americans still are among the innocent and suffering victims of our time and are faced with new forms of domination and alienation and bondage in a new age where modern values and technology threaten to transform all human subjects into objects. The mission and ministry of the black church is to help subjects recover their lost humanity and memory. The black church can be a moral agent helping transform structures of oppression as it seeks to be faithful to God, to love one another, and to pray for the liberation of their oppressors. Critical reflection upon the history and struggles of the black church can provide relevant examples of their own and the society's redemption. "To understand such a present past is to understand one's self and, through understanding, to reconstruct. . . . To remember all that is in our past and so in our present is to achieve unity of self. To remember the human past as our own past is to achieve community with mankind."[11] Critical awareness of their common denial as a *black* people was, in the past, a source of strength, because it was a source of communal and *anamnestic solidarity.*[12]

The term *amnesia* means to forget the past or, to block the past from memory. *Anamnesis* has the opposite meaning. *Anamnesis* means to recollect the forgotten past and to participate in a common memory and a common hope. Anamnesis means to call to mind again and again someone or some past event. Ancient Israel, for example, remembered its origins as a people by reciting, in confessional terms, the great events connected with its saving history:

> "My father was a homeless Aramaean who went down to Egypt with a small company and lived there until they became a great, powerful, and numerous nation. But the Egyptians ill-treated us, humiliated us and imposed cruel slavery upon us. Then we cried to the Lord the God of our fathers for help, and he listened to us and saw our humiliation, our hardship and distress; and so the Lord brought us out of Egypt with a strong hand and outstretched arm, with terrifying deeds, and with signs and portents. He brought us to this place and gave us this land, a land flowing with milk and honey." (Deut. 26:5-9 NEB).

Ancient Israel illuminated contemporary events and gave meaning to personal and communal life when it remembered its past. Through recollection "we understand what we remember, remember what we have forgotten and appropriate as our own past much that seemed alien to us."

> When Israel focussed its varied and disordered recollections of a nomad past, of tribal bickerings and alien tyrannies in the revelatory event of its deliverance and choice to be a holy people, then it found there hitherto unguessed meaning and unity. What had been a "tale told by an idiot, full of sound and fury, signifying nothing," became a grand epic; every line, stanza and canto fell into its proper place. The tribal chants, the legends of the unheroic past were not forgotten; they were remembered in a new connection; meanings hitherto hidden became clear.[13]

The forgotten past is recollected and the community can gain a perspective and achieve a sense of continuity. Anamnesis or recollection is a way of keeping alive the dangerous memory of those who lost their lives while struggling for the freedom of others. The Pre-Civil War black church was a community of solidarity remembering its past as it made strides toward freedom and risked its life to achieve liberation and justice. The road to freedom and justice was stony, bitter, and weary. James Weldon Johnson captured this sense of *anamnestic solidarity* in "Lift Every Voice and Sing":

Lift every voice and sing
Till earth and heaven ring,
Ring with the harmonies of Liberty;
Let our rejoicing rise
High as the listening skies,
Let it resound loud as the rolling sea.
Sing a song full of the faith that the dark past has taught us,
Sing a song full of the hope that the present has brought us,
Facing the rising sun of our new day begun
Let us march on till victory is won.

Stony the road we trod,
Bitter the chastening rod,
Felt in the days when hope unborn had died;
Yet with a steady beat,
Have not our weary feet
Come to the place for which our fathers sighed?

We have come over a way that with tears has been watered,
We have come, treading our path through the blood of the slaughtered,
Out from the gloomy past,
Till now we stand at last
Where the white gleam of our bright star is cast.

God of our weary years,
God of our silent tears,
Thou who has brought us thus far on the way;
Thou who has by Thy might
Led us into the light,
Keep us forever in the path, we pray.
Lest our feet stray from the places, our God, where we met Thee,
Lest our hearts drunk with the wine of the world, we forget Thee;
Shadowed beneath Thy hand,
May we forever stand.
True to our God,
True to our native land.

Anamnestic solidarity means a conscious identification with the cause of freedom forged by the innocent and oppressed victims of past injustices who have been destroyed by their oppressors, but who are nevertheless remembered in the praxis of the survivors in the community of the oppressed. Anamnesis is not merely a recollection of past sufferings, it is also a rediscovery of the meaning of the church's task in the present time. *Anamnestic solidarity* can be a basis for hope in the present. It can become a basis for critical reflection upon the structural contradictions under which the black church exists, as well as a basis for affirming their personhood and the personhood of others.

2.

The history of the black church in the United States has been a complex one—as black people sought to adapt to their changing situation. The black church has sometimes been seen as a *complacent* church, passively acquiescing to the status quo. At other times it has been identified as a *moderate* church, neither passively acquiescing nor militantly challenging the status quo. It has been a peacemaker, treading the middle path between passivity and aggressive action. But the black church has also been identified as a *militant* church, a subversive agent, and one aggressively challenging and seeking to radically transform the social, economic, and political order.[14]

Olin Moyd[15] and James Deotis Roberts[16] provide a brief historical sketch of the black church. The black church before emancipation was primarily an underground church. Communality and group spirit and identification and solidarity characterized the pre-Civil War black church. It sometimes expressed itself militantly in the face of white power, as in the case of Harriet Tubman, Henry Highland Garnet, and Sojourner Truth, to mention only a few; and at other times passively or in resignation and sometimes in fatalism. Yet the black church was and is an adapting institution and a source of courage and vitality for resisting dehumanizing conditions. It was the primary and only institution black people had to deepen and to strengthen their spiritual life and to nurture and to practice Christian ethical values, to reconcile and to liberate themselves. In this sense the black church can be viewed as a moral agent as well as a therapeutic community remembering its past as it seeks to combat the demoralizing influences of white power and white racism.

According to Moyd and Roberts, the time between the Civil War and the present can be divided into five periods: (1) *the Formative period*, from the Civil War through Reconstruction. This was a time of exceptional growth for black churches and denominations; (2) *the Maturation period*, from Reconstruction to the beginning of the Great Migration (1914). During Reconstruction blacks were involved at various levels of the nation's political and social life. The black church was the center for social and political activity. Soon blacks were stripped of their rights and places in government. An elaborate system of Jim Crow segregation went into effect in many states thereby wiping out black gains and reestablishing the legal basis for white supremacy which would last midway into the twentieth century. Legal segregation set the pace for race relations until around 1954; (3) *the Expansion-Renaissance period*, from the Great Migration to the beginning of World War II; (4) *the Passive Protest period*, from World War II to 1955; and (5) *the Radical Reassertion period*, from 1955 to the present.

The Expansion-Renaissance period signaled a major shift in the life of the black church as blacks moved from the rural agrarian South to the large, impersonal urban-industrial centers of the North. Black church religion survived, but it did so in new forms and gave rise to black sects and cults, the storefront churches, and movements such as Father Divine, Daddy Grace, the Garvey movement, the Nation of Islam, Black Jews, and the Pentecostal churches. This was a period of great change and adaptation to new and untried conditions.

The Radical Reassertion period was the era of Martin Luther King, Jr. This period can be divided into four subperiods: (1) the Civil Rights/Integration period, from 1954 to 1965; (2) the Black Consciousness/Black Power period, from 1960 to 1972; (3) the Reformist period, from 1973 to 1977; and (4) the present period of political conservativism and response to Neo-Racism. This latter time can be characterized as one of resurgence of new and subtle, and not so subtle, forms of racism and oppression in the labor market, education and political arena on the one hand, and a growing apathetic black bourgeoisie on the other hand. The present has also been described as a dismantleing of the Civil Rights gains of the sixties; the resurgence of white supremacy, anti-Black and anti-Semitic hate groups; and the rise of fundamental New Right religious-political groups.

This brief sketch suggests that the history of the black church is a complex one. Protest and rebellion and moderation and passivity, and resignation have characterized the life of the black church from time to time. Protest and passivity have existed side by side throughout its history. It has often been a church that has kept together spiritual awareness and social political activism as it sought to be faithful to its Lord. It is a servant church that strives to meet the spiritual and material needs of black people. Fundamentally, it is an expression of the black community itself. It now struggles to survive as a servant church, amidst new and complex forms of domination.

Liberation from oppression today requires that the praxis of ministry be joined with critical biblical and theological reflection, and linked with recollection of a forgotten past. The task of a critical theology and ministry of liberation is to recognize and to confess the partial and provisional nature of our theologies, and to seek the continued and unfolding pattern of God's justice and emancipating activity in the concrete history of the innocent and suffering victims of our time. A ministry of liberation may undertake to discern God's self-disclosure and to assist members of the church of Jesus Christ to fashion their moral and ethical life in a manner that is consistent with the manifestation of God's unfolding movement of liberation in history.

The *raison d'etre* of the black church today is the same as it has always been in the past, although it now functions under different and more complex conditions than it faced in its earlier history in this country. Its *raison d'etre* is to witness to God's emancipatory, reconciling, and healing activity in history. Liberation from oppression today requires that theological praxis and ministry be inseparable from criticial reflection upon a society that appears to be committed fatefully to non-freedom in the guise of freedom and to be trapped hopelessly within an ideology that has domesticated the radical and potentially transforming edge of Christian religion—"my country right or wrong!" Civil religion has often supported race domination and the exploitation of women, and it has often served to justify military involvement abroad which has led to the death of many of the world's innocent victims and defenseless people of color.

3.

In the chapters to follow the lessons that were learned from my own ministry are identified, and questions are raised about the role of the black church in its continued struggle for emancipation, reconciliation, discipleship, peoplehood, and redemption in the United States and elsewhere. I will maintain that social science information is an indispensable resource for the black church and for any contemporary church whose consciousness and direction is not only formed by biblical faith, but whose appropriation of the gospel is also shaped in subtle ways by the society in which it ministers. I intend to take social theory and analysis seriously and will endeavor to show the relevance of social and psychological information for the struggles of the Christian church in a sexist, racist, and bourgeois Western society under the domination of modern capitalism. While the starting point is my own biography and ministry, the implications and concerns of the book extend far beyond my own ministry to conditions of oppression and to the church's relationship to societal exploitation. The basis of my own critical consciousness has been the black family, the black church and community in a white racist and materialistic society. Ideally, the black family, church, and community exist in a mutually supportive relationship and together may articulate alternative values which affirm the material and the spiritual, the social and psychic life of the person in the community. Survival of the human subject in the present society and the possibility of transformation in a new and liberating society, to be achieved, is the issue. Survival as black people in the present society is a formidable challenge. The survival of black people has been a challenge in a society that continues to deny them authentic freedom and the material and spiritual basis for dignity and self-conscious selfhood. The survival and welfare of black people in this society is inseparable from the survival and well-being of all people.

The argument for keeping together the outer and inner dimensions of reality in emancipatory struggle, within a critical theological framework wherein the forgotten past is remembered, implies a critique of social science theories which claim to be value neutral, but which nevertheless function in the service of the status quo. Such theories are not cognizant of their own ideological roots, and serve to reproduce limited images of social reality and to further entrench oppressed people in the very structures that need to be criticized and transformed.

Sociologies or psychologies based upon and supportive of modern bourgeois individualism and materialism, or that fail to analyze the system and history of exploitative capitalism serve to delude both victims and social scientists while claiming to be value neutral. Social science and psychoanalysis premised on a different, but historically self-critical and liberating paradigm, will require the support of a different human subject and social order to be effective. In the meantime, the primary role of critical social science, biblical faith, and critical theology is to engage in radical criticism of the existing structures of domination, whether in bourgeois capitalism or socialist societies, without losing sight of those transcending values that can guide a truly emancipatory interest. Psychoanalysis is a potentially radical source for criticism and change. Ideally, its task is to free the inner life of the human subject from repressed fears, neurotic obsessions, and other forms of internalized oppression so as to enable men and women to make more realistic appraisals of themselves and of their world. Yet psychoanalysis itself has not always been free to accomplish its task of radical criticism. Some have argued that it has served to adjust the individual *within* the established norms and structures of society, thereby strengthening the status quo. Martin L. Gross observed:

> The new Psychological Society is not an individualistic one. It is a conformist society in which we are taught not only to think of ourselves and others, but *how* to *feel*. Natural emotions such as outrage, despair, greed, jealousy, suspicion, disappointment and passing depression are made to appear not only undesirable but abnormal. Our striving for psychological equanimity so violates human nature that the only defense against it is emotional blandness, a by-product of the new Society's conforming pressures.[17]

Rather than serve as a source of radical criticism of society, the practice of psychoanalysis has often helped to legitimate established social practices. It has often served to dull even more the potentially critical and emancipatory, reconciling and healing task called for in the suffering of victims. The black church and its ministry have often been the object of a similar charge when they have supported the status quo or withdrawn. It has sometimes been viewed as an opiate to militant action. The black church, as a therapeutic and prophetic community has a vital, yet difficult role to play in today's complex society as the church of Jesus Christ. Its task is to identify with innocent victims, to promote a sense of anamnestic solidarity and to help diagnose, interpret, and transform oppressive structures and conditions. It can undergird liberation struggles and proclaim in what concrete and universal sense God is on the side of the oppressed and innocent victims, and in what sense he is on the side of each man, woman, and child of every race.

Is this implied challenge to the black church unrealistic? Some have already concluded that it is an unrealistic challenge and that it is too much to ask. Others hold out the possibility of such a role for the black church in today's society. The black church as the spiritual face of the black community and as a durable institution should not be underestimated. *Meeting the challenge, sometimes in unorthodox ways, is consistent with its history.* Its own survival and that of the community it serves, as well as the moral health of the society in which it is situated, depend, in part, on meeting the challenge of social and historical criticism and transformation. *The black church as a therapeutic and prophetic institution is crucial to the moral struggle for outer and inner transformation.* It can play an important role in the realization of a new and liberating society to be achieved.

One assumption I make is that ethics and therapy can find common cause in liberation struggles among oppressed groups that seek to build a sense of solidarity and respect for life where issues of self-contempt and demoralizing relational patterns are common. Both Christian social ethics and therapy are complementary when set within the context of liberation, reconciliation, and the relational self—expressed in the age-old African proverb: "One is only human because of others, with others, for others."

"Ethics and therapy" may sound as if one is trying to mix apples with oranges. This would be a justified criticism if ethics and therapy were viewed from the standpoints of the discrete disciplines. But from the point of view of liberation praxis, one can discern some underlying affinities; in deed they must be conceptually related in breaking through the bonds of oppression, which I take to be both psychically *and* socially structured.

This book is intended for pastors, professors, theologians, therapists, pastoral counselors, and social activists who share a common concern for liberation and reconciliation, but who often fail to speak to one another. It seeks to establish a reference point for dialogue among those who are situated differently, but nevertheless are engaged in a common struggle. They seldom see that they may be standing on common ground.

The first chapter seeks a recognizable Christian and human starting point by reflecting on my own biography and ministry. It introduces the idea of *relationality* and shows how a relational paradigm, as a paradigm for ministry, began to emerge for me when private troubles were linked with broad public issues. This chapter introduces the ideal of relationality or the *web* as an important and central theme in ministry. It suggests the importance of family roots and tradition in the activist stance of black, or any Christian, clergy. A minister's social outlook and critical understanding of the gospel are rooted in and conditioned by a complex of personal, familial, social, and historical processes. The suggestion is that *ministry is with people who are embedded in social milieus and structures that need transformation.* A relational theme is not readily apparent in a culture that has overstressed self-mastery, autonomy, and individualism, on the one hand, or conformity, on the other hand. This chapter suggests the idea of the web, i.e., the interrelatedness of all life implied in the life stories of men and women. When the biographies of men and women are told and taken seriously, we can better discern the lines of connection between their stories and the wider social history in which they participate and which they help create and can help transform.

The second chapter develops the idea of the relational self as constituted and reconstituted in context with others and rooted in the primal reality of God. The idea of the relational self is argued as the basis for keeping together the outer and inner dimension of reality which ministry also seeks to reconcile and to heal.

Chapter 3 will address the possibility of transcending and transforming the social process that constitutes the human subject. The chapter's main contribution is to identify three sources of transcendence and social transformation.

The fourth chapter identifies one aspect of transformation through "the dialogue called therapy: a black perspective." In it I reflect upon my own experience as a therapist and upon the potentially emancipatory and reconciling role of therapy and therapeutic relational patterns in freeing individuals to critically reflect upon the social and historical processes that have shaped their lives and have contributed toward internalized forms of oppression.

The fifth chapter moves in the opposite direction to address the problem of social structure and the possibility of critical social reflection in "Christian social ethics: a black liberation perspective." It contains a brief description of the task of ethics from a particular relational standpoint and locates the mission of the black church within a Christian ethical perspective.

Chapter 6 considers the challenge to black liberation ethics and therapy when they are put into a genuinely reciprocal relationship and when they are guided by an interest in the emancipatory struggles of oppressed people.

The seventh chapter makes explicit a central, yet implied, thread that is woven throughout this entire project, namely the problem of the relationship between the person and the system, particularly, the role of ideology in the constitution of the human subject. Ideology is defined as false consciousness. False consciousness here means that an individual or an entire group has uncritically accepted the prevailing social practices of society as absolute, complete, or self-evident. False consciousness further means that a *particular* interpretation or social outlook has become an enshrined reality, a closed circle of certainty which preclude recognition of alternative possibilities for humanity. False consciousness functions to distort the individual's grasp of reality and to adjust the person within the prevailing and taken-for-granted outlook of society. The problem of ideology in contemporary society parallels the problem posed by idolatrous faith, namely *the overidentification of the human subject with the existing power arrangements and the confirmation of infallibility, divine or absolute status upon the existing society,* i.e., "this is the best of all possible worlds," or, "my country, right or wrong." This is what the Bible calls idolatry, and it is what Marxist and critical theorists refer to as false consciousness.

The eighth and final chapter applies the preceding in an interpretation of the Peoples' Temple and the tragedy at Jonestown, Guyana, on November 18, 1978. It brings together in this case history the themes of the earlier chapters and identifies some hard questions and poses a central challenge to the black church and its ministry to the innocent victims of our time.

My hope is that this book will help stimulate discussion and critical reflection upon modern bourgeois society and also help focus attention on the need for transformation and for a liberating ministry in church and society. *While the black church and its ministry is the focal point, the message of the book is not exclusive.*

The black church, as a servant church, is treated as a microcosm of the Christian church. It is hoped that critical reflection upon the historical mission of the black church and its current posture in society will be inseparable from the church's sense of faithfulness to the One who continues to call it, in the name of the new creation, to reconstitute itself in a new, alternative future—the kingdom of God.

I.

Theology and Social Science Paradigms in Ministry: Autobiographical and Theoretical Reflections

"A theology which undertakes the limited work of understanding and criticizing within Christian history the thought and action of the church is also a theology which is dependent on the church for the constant test of its critical work."

—H. Richard Niebuhr
in *The Meaning of Revelation*

The historic First Baptist Church of Worcester, Massachusetts, has been described as one of the most beautiful churches in America.

Because of its beauty and impressiveness there are some who have referred to it as "an ecclesiastical country club." Part of the reason for that may be that the lawn is so large that it looks as if it might have a golf course, but I suspect that the major reasons are that the church has two bowling alleys, many of its members are leaders of the business community, and possibly ninety percent of the congregation vote Republican.[1]

Were a young, activist, black minister in the mid-sixties to join the staff of this upper-middle-class, white congregation situated in a predominantly working-class community, tensions would be inevitable. Now I can look back on the struggles that I experienced in this nontraditional urban ministry and examine how it raised questions about racism and social justice, the nature of the self, and the contribution that can be made toward the minister's understanding of human liberation when social science therapy and theology are related.

31

1.

By 1964, the senior minister had initiated discussions within the congregation that eventually led to an appointment of a black person to the staff as the first minister to the community. Although the First Baptist Church of Worcester had a long history of social involvement, this particular appointment caused some uneasiness and discussion within the congregation. Some financial pledges were lost, and some members left.

In the summer of 1966 I began my ministry as minister to the community. This was a time of social turbulence. The national conscience had turned toward racial conflicts in American cities and toward an undeclared (and racially signaled) war in Southeast Asia. Certain experiences in my personal history had prepared me for this new challenge. The following autobiographical sketch will illustrate how one's world view and thought style are rooted in a complex of personal, familial, social, and historical processes.

I was born in Seattle, Washington, in 1939. The older of two sons, the second-born of five children. I am one of the family's first northern-born generation. My parents were from Mississippi, and my father was a follower of Marcus Garvey, who believed that black people would never be accepted as social equals in this society. The experience of growing up as a black male during the early part of this century confirmed his belief that blacks, as a people, would remain marginal to society. There was, in my father's awareness and experience of racial and class oppression, an existential interest in emancipation, but he could not foresee emancipation emerging for black people within a country that practiced genocide, interned and enslaved people of color.

My father believed that a communist country based on socialist practice would offer a better life for black people. So he started out for Russia and got as far as Seattle (which, in the early thirties, was a long way from Fayette, Mississippi). With an eighth-grade education he began life in Seattle, married, purchased a home, raised a family of five, and changed jobs only once in forty-five years. He was blessed with good health throughout his adult life, and I can never remember his missing a day's work due to illness or for other reasons.

My father does not fit the unstable image that some scholars claim to be characteristic of the black male in the United States. A deeply religious man, conscious of the depths of human evil in American society, he wished to help create a new beginning. He wanted to be a minister. But he was also deeply angry, and he admired the courage of such people as Nat Turner, Marcus Garvey, Sojourner Truth, Malcolm X, and the late Honorable Elijah Muhammad. While his religious orientation was influenced by these figures, he faithfully served as a deacon at the Mt. Zion Baptist Church in Seattle.

My mother also came from Mississippi. She grew up there and knew what it meant to fear the whites. With a high-school education, she taught black children in the third grade. My mother and father never knew each other when they both lived in Mississippi. They met through correspondence later in life. When they decided to marry, my father left Seattle to meet his bride and to take her to Seattle. My mother also shared my father's dream of a new beginning. She has always been a hard-working woman and achiever, usually holding down two or three jobs at a time to supplement my father's income. She still found the time to be in church every Sunday and serve as a deaconess. Her identification with the black church is long-standing, and her commitment to the Christian faith is deep and strong.

My early experience in American society was one of ethnic diversity and cultural pluralism. The neighborhood in which I grew up reflected a multiracial, ethnic minority population which included the indigenous peoples, Afro, Asian, Jewish, and Italian Americans. A few Anglo-Americans also lived in our neighborhood and were among the first to leave. During the late forties and fifties my neighborhood became increasingly black, yet the ethnic mix was maintained. I came to believe that that early experience of growing up in an ethnically mixed community later contributed to my ability, in my community ministry, to relate to others across ethnic and social-economic groupings.

Seattle's Mt. Zion Baptist Church deserves recognition here. It nurtured and supported my aspirations for ministry from the beginning. By the age of sixteen I was preaching—with the encouragement of that congregation. While I was in college,

33

they granted me a license to preach, and when I graduated from seminary, they were there in the person of Pastor and Dr. Samuel B. McKinney to ordain me into professional ministry. It was in this church that I first came to understand the meaning of Black Power before the term became politicized during the sixties. "Black Power" was a symbol of communal solidarity. It meant black people caring for one another in struggle and upholding the faith that gave them reason to continue.

I graduated as a philosophy major from Linfield College in rural McMinnville, Oregon, in 1961. Moving to Rochester, New York, I began my theological studies and preparation for the Christian ministry at Colgate-Rochester Divinity School. My general aim was to enter the parish ministry. During the summer of 1963, I first experienced clinical pastoral education at San Quentin State Prison. Working with inmates, especially black inmates, challenged my original objectives to enter the parish ministry. I became familiar with the techniques of interviewing, taking case histories, and learning something of the dynamics of individual and collective behavior. The dominant conceptual scheme for interpreting my prison experiences was derived from theology, which was informed by psychology and psychiatry. A major objective was to integrate these modes of thought into my overall identity as a student of theology. Enamored with this experience, I took additional training at the Detroit Receiving Hospital. (In 1967 it was renamed Detroit City Hospital.)

In the fall of 1965, I entered the Program of Psychiatry and Religion at Union Theological Seminary, New York. My field experience took place at the Rusk Institute, Goldwater Memorial Hospital, and Riker's Island Penitentiary. My awareness and theoretical understanding of the variability of human behavior in sickness and in health deepened considerably. But the focus was clearly individualistic. Looking back, to categorize where I stood then, I would say that both feet were firmly planted in a neopsychoanalytic framework. The central lesson I learned was that human motivation and behavior were rooted in the person's biopsychological structure. The genesis of meaning was to be sought in the individual rather than in the social-cultural or intersubjective context of experience.

2.

I came to Worcester[2] with an individualistic frame of reference and began to apply my clinical and pastoral skills within a community context. My ministry addressed a wide variety of social needs. Although the individual model was informed by depth theories of personality, my orientation was essentially to a neoorthodox theology and pastoral care. My individual model sought to go beyond the identification of pathological states to seek and emphasize individual strengths. I brought to my community ministry not only a concern for individuals and psychological awareness, but also my faith and theological understanding of life.

It was not psychology or sociology that led me to the ministry and sustains my hope for persons and structures of injustice. For me it happened the other way around. My faith and theological understanding of life informs my psychological and sociological understanding. At the heart of my faith is an affirmation of human dignity and commitment to the emancipation of life. My faith, nurtured in a black family, a black church, and an ethnically mixed community, contributed to my recognition of the value of integrating my faith commitment into the humanities and social sciences in an effort to liberate social life. I stand in full recognition that others may organize their perception of reality differently, but this difference heightens the importance of dialogue among the human disciplines.

The important point is that my life experiences became foundational in pushing me beyond individualistic interpretations of reality. Much of what I had learned from psychiatry about building personal relationships and emphasizing strengths was and continues to be valuable. Psychiatric information is indispensable for helping us see how deeply personal life and motivation are influenced by social structural arrangements from infancy to adulthood. By choice, I moved into one of the worst slum areas of Worcester, and I began to listen carefully, sensitively, to what the situation was saying— what the thoughts, desires, and actions of the people seemed to convey—before deciding on a plan of action. My listening posts included my own neighborhood, industry, and the organizations and institutions that affected the lives of my neighbors, such as the black church, city hall, the police department, the public schools, recreation, hospitals, and clinics. I interpreted my role to the religious communities, industry, the police department and human service agencies. Interestingly, the universities and colleges (secular and religious) did not seem to be resources to be utilized at that time. The social science departments would have been the most logical resources.

I had learned from my clinical experience that one must take the time to build rapport and establish trust before meaningful intervention and change can be effected. I was later to learn that this process of building relationships of trust is essential to community organization and change within low-income communities. I was approached outside a bar by a brother and ex-felon who said,

"Hey, Rev., I need some money."

I replied, "No money, man."

He asserted, "Then we can't be friends."

I said, "We can *be* friends, but not on the basis of money."

This brief exchange led to a challenge and an invitation. The challenge was to become a friend by traveling to New Haven with him the next day to meet his estranged family and talk to his probation officer. He was unemployed at the time, and when he was employed, he stayed on the job only one or two weeks. The work he found offered little challenge. The probation officer agreed to let him obtain a driver's license, since commuting to meaningful employment was essential to continued work opportunities. Because of my established contacts with industry, it was possible to find meaningful employment for him with built-in mobility and reasonable pay. He had never worked for $3.50 an hour with a promise of increase in pay after a ninety-day probationary period. (This was in 1966.)

My friend stayed on the job for ten months. This was a kind of success. As I began to have success in placing other ex-felons and so-called young hard-core persons in employment, the word spread that "Rev. Archie can get you a job, man." Through empathy, I was able to move from the personal and unique life situations of others to the social and general levels of understanding.

As a result of working in the area of employment alone, I began to see something I had known, but had not felt deeply before, namely, that problems and rates of employment and dislocation in a community cannot be explained simply in terms of personal character defects or maladjustments, although these explanations may at times appear plausible. The social-economic structure of community and society must be considered as more important factors. Although my friend stayed employed for ten months, he eventually was going to be on the streets again for reasons that transcended his own personality. The Vietnam War made it relatively easy to place him in a job in 1966. The economy was expanding, and industry was looking for "minorities," the civil rights and Black Power movements were pressuring the national conscience to hire more blacks, and some industrialists were responding to these pressures with creative imagination. Years later, as the war began to wind down and inflation began to rise, unemployment among minorities, especially black youth, began to rise also. Some of those whom I had placed in employment were among the first to be out on the streets. And several landed back in prison.

C. Wright Mills, the sociologist, found it useful to distinguish between personal troubles and the public issues of social structure. Personal troubles, he claimed, occur within the character of the individual and within the range of his or her immediate relations with others. Issues, he claimed, have to do with matters that transcend those limited areas of social life which the individual is directly and personally aware of, or can voluntarily change. Issues in their combination form the various milieus in which personal life is enmeshed. Public issues emerge from the social power arrangements within society as a whole, with the ways in which various milieus overlap and interpenetrate to form the larger structure of social and historical life.[5] It is this larger context, the structure of social life, which remains obscure.

The problems I faced in my ministry were greater than the people with whom I worked. I was working with casualties of larger malfunctioning systems whose functioning remained obscure as long as I looked for the explanations to unemployment in the individual context of experience alone. The real lesson of importance was that individualistic and atomized models of reality cannot demonstrate how individual difficulties are related to significant external factors, while a sociological orientation seeks from the very beginning to interpret individual activity within the context of collective experience. It was the context of this ministry that led to a recognition of my fundamental need to apprehend the significance of social structures (milieus) and the functioning of social systems. Those of us who have been trained to think primarily in terms of the individual and of the importance of subjective experience often find ourselves in circumstances in which the interconnectedness of the self and the social order must of necessity be largely invisible to us. The critical point is to recognize how personal life and social structure intersect in society and to heighten awareness of what role the individual can play as a passive subject or an active agent in social transformation and change. By describing the larger economic and political situation and its implications for the inner meaning and external career of the individual, the person is able to transcend his or her private troubles and begin to see them in terms of broad public issues. In this sense, public issues and the social structures that lie behind them become relevant ethical issues.

I worked closely with the Ecumenical Council and secular organizations, and organized groups within the black community around specific concerns. Many of the neighborhood groups with whom I worked became bogged down without significant awareness of their own contribution to failure. I saw the need to help such groups develop their decision-making capacity, identify needs, specify objectives, and implement the means to achieve their stated ends. The objective was community development from the grass roots up by working with neighborhood centers and by helping indigenous leadership to emerge and to find alternatives. Many of these skills were derived from my clinical training as a therapist and became a part of the strategy of community organization.

One priority was to get Prospect House on its feet. Prospect House was a neighborhood center that was run by blacks and served primarily the black community. Another priority was working with various agencies and professionals in the community. I sensed the need to help agencies and service systems change not only their treatment approach, but also their conception of the poor, thereby blaming victims for their problems.

My role became one of enabling potential leadership to develop, rather than becoming the leader myself. I served as resource person, pastor, and advisor to many of the groups, agencies, families, and individuals with whom I had contact. A major emphasis was helping them find ways to handle their own lives successfully. An example was an alcoholic family with whom I worked. Once the father was restored to sobriety after twelve years on the bottle, it was through continued psychic and community support from the community minister and social service and health agencies that he began to emerge more as a father in control of himself. Another illustration is that of a high school senior who was doubtful of his abilities of going beyond high school. Through supportive guidance he entered Quinsigamond Community College; after a year he transferred to Holy Cross College, a four-year institution, and later graduated. He has emerged as an articulate leader and committed organizer within the black and poor community.

As a result of this ministry, I became painfully aware of how inadequately my traditional seminary education had prepared me to work in an urban, inner city context. I had learned much from my community ministry, but I felt the need to broaden my conceptual framework to include an understanding of contemporary society, and to develop the links between transpersonal relationships, social reform, and sociological research.

3.

I learned to work with many of the individual and family problems of Worcester residents. I worked with traditional agencies concerned with individual and family problems. Both my work and the work of traditional agencies can be summed up in what I call Paradigm I.

Paradigm I refers to theories that focus on the individual and suggests that problems are to be understood as personal (or private) troubles. Personal problems can eventually be traced to their origins in psychic, biological dysfunction, or family disorganization. The major objective of Paradigm I is to explain dysfunction in personal or familial terms. Roland Warren (1971) and Stephen M. Rose (1972) have distinguished Paradigm I from Paradigm II in a critical analysis of the Model

Cities and the antipoverty programs of the sixties. Warren utilizes the term "diagnostic paradigm" to indicate that such paradigms carry not only the definition of the problem but also the "explanation" why some people are poor or disadvantaged; what strategies are most appropriate to handle the problem; and what technologies will be required. Warren and Rose respectively refer to Paradigm I as the "individual deficiency" paradigm. Both I and II are considered diagnostic paradigms.

> The one paradigm takes as its point of orientation the particular situation of the individual-in-poverty, emphasizing that his poverty, as well as other attendant problems, is associated with his inability to function adequately within the accepted norms of American society. We call this diagnostic Paradigm I. The other paradigm takes as its point of orientation the aspects of the social system which purportedly produce poverty as a system-output. We call this diagnostic Paradigm II. Looked at from the standpoint of action orientation, diagnostic Paradigm I indicates the need for change in the individual, while diagnostic Paradigm II indicates the need for a change in the social structure.[4]

Paradigm I, as an institutionalized thought pattern, is far more established in American society than is Paradigm II. The assumption underlying diagnostic Paradigm I is that "American society has a certain residual problem population unable to function adequately without assistance; these people must therefore be helped through social service."[5] The difficulties, deficiencies, or handicaps this population faces are attributed to personality defects or individual problems of adjustment which require the services of psychological counseling, psychotherapy or casework, or some mixture of these.[6] The perceived solution, derived from this paradigm, is to strengthen the relevant components in the service delivery system to better cope with and adjust the person to his or her situation within existing institutional arrangements.

Ministries based upon Paradigm I tend to be individualistically oriented, supportive of privatized religion and limited to issues of individual rescue and salvation. Such orientations tend to contain a critique of individual life, but may lack a serious critique of the social order itself. Strategies that derive from

40

Paradigm I seek either to change individual or family dysfunction or attempt to adjust such problems *within* existing institutional arrangements. Paradigm I fails, therefore, to address problems of social structure, both in its theoretical and practical considerations. Society as the object of analysis and change is precluded from this approach to problem solving.

Therapy, within Paradigm I, is seen as one of the techniques for addressing problems of deviance and personal deficiencies. Following Peter Berger and Thomas Luckmann, Warren accepts the definition of therapy as a strategy for resocializing the deviant into the prevailing normative order of things. The heretical challenge that deviation poses to the status quo is annihilated through therapy as the person is adjusted within the existing, taken-for-granted thought pattern of society. If conceptual annihilation is not successful through therapy or similar modes of adjustment, then physical annihilation through repression, oppression, or death emerges as an even more live option. Warren has identified one use to which therapy has been put in such places as welfare, prisons and correctional facilities, and other closed institutions. I do not accept this as the only role for therapy, although it has been a dominant mode of therapy in modern capitalist society. Warren has considered therapy only in its negative and destructive consequences and under the conditions of modern capitalism and bourgeois ideology. In so doing, he has pointed to a specific social practice which supports a power elite and serves to preserve the prevailing order of things. What Warren ignores is the emancipatory potential of therapy and ministry in the struggles of oppressed people.

Diagnostic Paradigm II, the dysfunctional social system paradigm, sides with the victims by identifying the social structure itself as defective. The private troubles of individuals are perceived to be products of malfunctioning institutions, maldistribution of resources, restrictive opportunity structures, and powerlessness. Paradigm II according to Warren,

... is the widely-voiced approach to the problems of the inner city as the product of the American institutional structure. It sees individual deficiencies existing as the systematic products of this

41

structure rather than as individual aberrations. It defines the problem overwhelmingly in terms of the structure.[7]

Warren goes on to point out that Paradigm I, with its emphasis on individual adjustment, is so entrenched, even in the minds of victims and their advocates, that attempts to redefine problems of the inner city within the framework of Paradigm II inadvertently slip back toward Paradigm I-type solutions. A part of the problem resides in the depth of the internalization of this paradigm, the comparatively undeveloped technology within Paradigm II and power resources to effect social structural change. Hence, the strategies and structure to bring about change within the framework of Paradigm II are incomplete. "Participatory democracy" and "power to the people" were significant sentiments and directives in social structural change, but the mechanisms to translate these sentiments into concrete reality in many situations were underutilized or undeveloped.

> Once the disadvantaged poor concede that the interests of "society" are more important than their individual interests, they throw in the sponge on the location of the highway which will raze their homes. Once they concede that their income levels must remain low because of the necessary high expenditure for national defense, they are lost. Once they acknowledge the professional legitimation of the poverty-relevant agency to define the problem and set the administrative and technical constraints within which a solution must be sought, they "have had it."[8]

As we shall soon see, the role of "mediating structures" (Berger and Neuhaus, 1977) is of paramount importance in addressing structural and personal problems of isolation, alienation, and powerlessness. The primary function of mediating structures is to empower people, to strengthen and nurture their capacity to participate effectively in society and influence the direction of change.

Karl Marx, the pioneer, would be an example of a theorist within Paradigm II. He believed that the root cause of contemporary social problems emerged out of the economic structures of Western society. Marx was perhaps one of the first social scientists to focus attention on existing social institutions as problematic.

Marx identified the economic factor as the foundation for the development of modern industrial society. And it is both science and technology that have important effects upon institutional arrangements, face-to-face encounters, and patterns of thought in modern society. Ministries based upon this second paradigm tend to be politically aware, social action and systems change-oriented. Such orientations tend to contain a critique of society, but may lack serious critique of the individual as agent.

Paradigm II was not addressed in any significant way in my ministry. Much of my work focused on rescuing the victim. Nevertheless, there was, in this ministry, the potential for bridging the gap between a Paradigm I type ministry and a ministry based upon Paradigm II. My point is this: face-to-face relationships provided for the emergence of structured social relationships, as well as the seeds for social change. Awareness of the social situation and solutions for social action had their origins in face-to-face relations. I came to believe that the Worcester black community (young and old, churched and unchurched) would respond positively to goal-oriented leadership that provided them psychic support, opportunities for reflection and growth, and development of their own leadership capacity with self-confidence.

A process that values and supports the individual agent is fundamental to the emergence of creative social relations, social alternatives, and the larger, more conflictive process of community change. Leadership needs to have built into it a sense of authority born of confidence. Perhaps for community-based ministries, the issue is not pastoral counseling (Paradigm I) or community organization and structural change (Paradigm II), but rather an unfamiliar mixture of both processes with the aim of controlling the disruptive effects of institutional arrangements on face-to-face relations, and enabling groups to find creative alternatives to the status quo.

Around the third year of my community ministry, the neighborhood anti-poverty programs were established. I worked closely with the staff of several neighborhood anti-poverty centers, sharing my resources while learning from them. I met on a regular basis with members of the staff of the Piedmont Opportunity Center, a local anti-poverty center, where my wife Jerry was the director. This provided an opportunity to meet and train some volunteers who, in their turn, served as advocates for other community residents. Some neighborhood residents came to the center in search of housing, others came with questions of an economic or political nature, and a few came with questions about meaning in their lives or with concern about loneliness. I helped the staff and volunteers appreciate the role of pastoral care in their work when addressing these questions. They could better appreciate the need for psychic support, while they also advocated social change.

After three years of consistent and intensive community involvement, creative leadership was beginning to emerge in the black community. A social structural approach was developing as I began to link critical awareness of personal and family troubles with the structure and meaning of life in the larger social system.

The shift from Paradigm I to Paradigm II can be seen as bringing the ministry closer to the prophetic vision of social justice and to the biblical understanding of God's liberating acts in history. Paradigm II may help us see what concerned the prophets of Israel—the depth of human injustice and the structures of evil in their time and in our time.

Paradigm II directs urban ministries to systemic injustice, the system of domination and oppression, and seeks to interpret individual problems in this light. This paradigm further implies that urban ministries need to work with groups that seek alternatives to the status quo based on an analysis of the larger system of oppression and its supporting institutional structure.

Traditional forms of ministry rooted in Paradigm I, with its emphasis on the individual, preclude an indepth analysis of social structures and serve to maintain existing power arrangements. In light of Paradigm II, Thomas M. Gannon[9] has seen the importance of the church and local neighborhood as durable units of solidarity. Gannon argues that in the context of advanced industrialism, the church, neighborhoods, the family, and voluntary associations become even more important in helping people order their lives, realize their personal goals, dignity, and self-esteem, and in strengthening a sense of participation, belonging, and attachment within their communities. The church as an empowering and mediating structure links the individual to his or her neighborhood, the larger society, and provides the context for meaningful interaction and critical interpretation of both individual and collective experience.[10]

Peter Berger and Richard Neuhaus define "mediating structures" as "those institutions standing between the individual in his private life and the large institutions of public life."[11] The process of modernization, sometimes referred to as secularization, brings about an historically unprecedented dichotomy between the public and private sphere. In such a society, the individual's capacity to control or influence the big ups and downs of the society diminishes his or her sense of belonging, while increasing a sense of alienation and powerlessness. Mediating structures, then, are of paramount importance, contributing to a sense of belonging and empowerment. "Their strategic position derives from their reducing both the anomic precariousness of individual existence in isolation from society and the threat of alienation to the public order."[12] The church, rather than being an outmoded institution, is being refashioned, and it is of central importance to the ongoing life of the community. "In fact," Gannon argued, "in a democratic society, with the advent of advanced industrialism and urbanization, family residential communities become more central to social and political participation, and religion serves as a constitutive component of the identity of these communities."[13]

Berger, Neuhaus, and Gannon have identified an important function of the church as social institution. The church is a gathering place, and it mediates a sense of belonging and serves as a link between private and public life. It must also exist as a prophetic community, calling into question the very economic and social structures, values and practices of the wider society that create alienation. To ignore this prophetic dimension of the church's total ministry is to deny the church its moral and political significance, while justifying existing dehumanizing conditions. Berger and Neuhaus' emphasis on the church as a mediating structure is in harmony with the historic role of the black church within the black community. It has been a gathering place and a basic source of identity in a society that excluded them. But to ignore the black church's relationship to the wider society is to overlook its long moral and political struggle against the inhumanity of white racism, segregation, and discrimination.[14]

The question is whether local congregations and urban ministries, especially the ministry of the black church, can help build strong communities of solidarity in the future. At the same time, they must not lose their critical prophetic voice and must continue to radically challenge the structures and practices that perpetuate social injustice in the wider society. Black clergy and the resources of the black church must work with other community institutions and continue to be a key mediating structure that supports the moral vision and aspiration of black people, while empowering them to transform and humanize social structures.

> Not only are religious institutions significant "players" in the public realm, but they are singularly important to the way people order their lives, values at the most local and concrete levels of their existence. Thus they are crucial to understanding family, neighborhoods and other mediating structures of empowerment.[15]

The church can function not only as a source for transcendent values, but also as a mediating structure, linking persons to the wider society, while it functions as a nurturing community throughout the life cycle. But as we shall see in subsequent chapters, the black church, as a prophetic institution, has an even more critical role to play in social change at the community and societal levels.

The Worcester community ministry afforded me an opportunity to set current social events in theological and biblical perspective, and to utilize those perspectives to interpret the drama of community life. There were other available interpretations of current community events. For example, the results of sociological surveys helped interpret the housing situation or solutions to other social problems. The results of health and mental health surveys and statistics helped interpret the physical and mental status of the community. But I saw the added importance of interpreting these same events from the perspective of theological and biblical ethics, and of discerning what God was and still is calling us to become and to do, once we've identified our social problems and mental status.

The community ministry provided me with an unusual opportunity to view our common community from a variety of standpoints and to interpret to churches and synagogues what I thought were the implications for the religious and moral life of the community and society as a whole. There was the opportunity, early in this ministry, to substitute for the Protestant chaplain in several of the city's major hospitals and to observe firsthand the delivery of health care on the wards and in the emergency rooms, and to observe the ways in which staff and ethnic minorities related. This experience later became valuable as I served on a committee that evaluated proposals to do research on human subjects, and as I had the opportunity to teach at the medical school of Worcester, while on the faculty of Clark University. Serving as chaplain to juveniles provided the opportunity to work closely with the courts, the police department, the public and private schools, other agencies, and families related to the juvenile justice system. These contacts extended to the larger criminal justice system and provided the opportunity to establish and support the links between incarcerated people, their families, and places of employment.

There were increasing opportunities to minister in situations of tragedy and great loss as the bodies of young black men began to be shipped home from Vietnam and the reality of the war was realized; as young black talent and lives were wasted on drug and alcohol abuse and drug overdose; as employment opportunities for black teen-agers were limited; and as the cycle of poverty manifested itself in the second and third generation of particular families in special sections of the city.

Through all of this it became important for me to raise critical questions about the typical ways in which poverty, drug abuse, and crime were explained and the kind of activity explanations justified. These issues were interwoven and joined in the same social structure. I sought to raise meaningful questions about the social structure and to do it in such a way that critical social issues could be linked with prophetic biblical faith and actions. Questions of meaning were implicit in the structure of social life itself. I tried to make some of them explicit by interpreting events in the light of biblical faith. Sociological information can deepen the minister's understanding of the symbolic structure of the society to which he or she has been called. The drama of social life also expresses religious symbols whose expression is essential to an explanation of the meaning of life in a particular community.

We live in a milieu that suggests that our relatedness to modern society is determined primarily by social structure, an economic system, politics, advanced technology, urbanization, and secularization. Much can be said about the interaction between these phenomena and emerging symbolic forms of social life as clues to social consciousness and forms of collective action.

> In symbolic analysis of social drama we (can) ask: In the struggle for power . . . who evokes what symbols of authority? In what kind of action? By what means? Under what conditions? And, in the name of what transcendent power is authority legitimized?[16]

Finally, sociological information can contribute to the minister's understanding of social action and projections. The social sciences are not able to capture the spontaneous unpredictable flow of experience itself. Social science is able to reconstruct and categorize an experience only after the fact of its happening. Intentionality, the creative side of human behavior, is understood retrospectively. Social science, then, is able to state retrospectively the prior conditions of a particular social phenomenon and can predict, to a certain degree, what is likely to happen in the future should certain conditions prevail. Gibson Winters argued,

> The scientist projects a typical pattern of activity or meaning to the future on the basis of an interpretation of the past; he has no "control" over this pattern, since he cannot manipulate the processes of meaning in which these patterns are held within the society as the way things should be.[17]

Social science, then, may bring forth awareness of certain relevant conditions that are important for therapy, ethics, social action and change, and social policy. The danger is that the minister, like the social scientists, in previsioning the future on the basis of past information, may impute to the future certain imposed interpretations. It is also important to keep in mind that the future is an open horizon, not totally predictable. For example, social scientists never predicted the rise of Martin Luther King, Jr., in the mid-fifties.

4.

Sociological information and social analysis have not played a strong enough role in preparation for ministry. There has been an emphasis on "personal" and privately corporate (the body of Christ, for example) relationships, private reflection, and the development of one's personal relationship to God and the personal forgiveness of sin. Rosemary Ruether argued:

> The individualistic concept of sin ignores this social-cosmic dimension of evil. A concentration of individualistic repentance has led, in Christianity, to a petty and privatistic concept of sin which involves the person in obsessive compunction about individual (mostly sexual) immorality, while having no ethical handle at all on the great structure of evil which we raise up corporately to blot out the fact of God's creation.[18]

Individualism and individual salvation have been a pervasive theme in American Protestantism. True, there have been strong advocates of a social gospel orientation. But the social dimension has been a minority position within mainline Christian denominations and has been effectively countered by a very strong individualistic strain in American Christian life.[19] The black church in the nineteenth century and during the twentieth-century civil rights struggles emerged in contradistinction to this trend. But a strong conservative trend toward noninvolvement can be found in black churches as well. The privatized orientation of the new Born Again Christian movement and many of the new religions is only the most recent expression of this theme. As social life becomes more complex and stratified, the tendency is to resort to individualism. Urban industrial society presents new challenges to the church, calling for new, untried responses.

In societies not marked by rapid change, individuals are united through communal solidarity. Personal, familial, and communal ties are the basis of evaluation. But in an industrial

49

society life becomes more rationalized, that is, application of impersonal and objective standards in the regulation of face-to-face relations.

The church has had difficulty adjusting to this new complex pattern of urban life, which in many ways is alien to its stress upon community. As a partial response, the church has protected the individual from a sense of disintegration. It has been for some a shelter in a time of storm. That is important, but it has limited the commonly understood range of personal religious commitment.

The church has had difficulty in relating individual religious experience to social responsibility. When we think in terms of individual experience alone, the interconnection of the most intimate features of personal life and the social structure is largely obscured.

The overwhelming tendency in America has been a pull toward individualism. Whether there is an individual soul or a social soul that ought to be the object of reform and liberation continues to be debated. Nevertheless, the assumption that the way to improve social or communal life is through the saving or salvaging of individual souls or psyches woefully ignores an analysis of social structures and existing power arrangements which contribute to social dislocation and alienation. Religious and secular strategies that seek to alter individual consciousness and behavior through individual change strategies alone may be doomed to failure, since they ignore the collective influence of society.

5.

Paradigm II, like paradigm I, has its limitations. A major difficulty with paradigm II is that the self and its dynamic relations to other selves do not stand out as reality apart from social structure. Paradigm III considers the dialectical relationship between the self, society, and culture. In reality, these three spheres are fused; they are separable only when considered analytically. Paradigm III conceptually links the individual and society. I call paradigm III the *relational paradigm*. Paradigm III sees the importance of keeping together Paradigm I and

Paradigm II, because its interest is to link personal transformation with social transformation. A societal perspective is the frame of reference for addressing questions of social relations and the nature of the self. Within this paradigm, the focal point for social analysis is the interconnection between the self and society.

Rather than posit an either/or between the insights derived from Paradigm I (individual analysis) or Paradigm II (social structural analysis), it is of paramount importance to stress the dialectical relationship between the two. There can be no true understanding of the self or self-conscious selfhood apart from the web of relations and historical circumstances in which individuals are embedded. This is another way of saying that there can be no true sociology apart from psychology, and no true psychology apart from sociology and history. Communal life and individual biographies stand in a dialectical relation within an ongoing historical process. The structure of social life, and images of the self, may be conceived as an emergence from an ongoing social-historical process.

Relationality is the key concept. It is a way of speaking of the indwelling presence of others in our own concrete reality and of our presence in theirs. Relationality also implies that we can respond not only to the intentions and actions of others, but to our own self as well.

A creative, novel side of human reality is rooted in the world of commonly shared symbols but it transcends the natural standpoint and patterned responses of everyday life. The common language is there, but a different use of it is made in every new contact between people. This is to say, the individual is not to be understood as a mere puppet or robot, or a mere creation of the social process. Individuals, as subjects and as members of society, are capable of doing more than merely reflecting the social systems and culture in which they are embedded. Rather, human reality is complex, evolving, and perspectival. Human reality exists in perspectives that interrelate and that confirm and disconfirm the dominant and taken-for-granted view of reality. No one sees exactly as another. Humans need to engage the perspectives of others, especially the oppressed from other cultures and ethnic backgrounds, so that their own understanding of their society

51

and their position in it can evolve beyond where it is presently constituted. Human beings are preeminently questioning, deliberating, and responding beings, capable of deviating from the taken-for-granted reality and forging alternatives to the existing arrangements of things. Pauli Murray borrows the term "conscientization" from Paulo Freire, to refer to a process "through which people come to a self-awareness that helps them to shape their own personal and social history and learn their own potential for action in shaping the world."[20]

Hence, individuals are capable of thinking, objectifying, and criticizing the plausibility structures of their own society and culture while still in it. Through discourse and reflective thought, imagination, and action, they can, and often do, make a difference through common struggle. Transcendent religious symbols and values are ways in which individuals can become self-critical. Through conscientization and the power of religious symbols they may be empowered to go beyond their individual standpoints, transcend themselves, and move themselves and others, through action, toward a new vision of social life in which agape, mercy, and justice are the guiding themes. A source of creativity in social life is rooted in the self and in empathy with other oppressed groups and through recognition of the common structure of oppression that binds them.

The actual form my ministry took was shaped and steered by my biographical situation and the historical context in which I found myself. Both my biography and the times came together in the life of a particular community—all contributing to the direction my ministry took. What began as a community ministry developed into a way of doing theology by relating faith with action. The dialectical tensions between inner and outer realities, social structures, and individual consciousness can be maintained in awareness of their interconnection. Awareness of this interconnection in ministry can broaden one's theological orientation and can deepen one's faith and understanding of the social world. Theologically I believe the transcendent God is the ground and power of newness and source of creativity in all concrete structures of life. This means that God can be known in the actual lives and struggles of oppressed people straining to break free from the real and powerful structural forces that dominate and portend to undo them. Theirs is the biblical God who acts with them and on their behalf in, through, and beyond oppression. This God *sees* the affliction of people, *hears* their cry, *knows* their sufferings, *promises* to be with them and to deliver them from bondage. My theology attempts to understand historical life and individual biographies as always being constituted in the freedom of God and in concrete structures of oppression in human communities that continually need to experience vulnerability as a basis for faith and forgiveness and to live in self-transcendence before a just God.

Paradigm III has a vision of human liberation. The goal of liberation is to free the human spirit by enabling individuals to form communities that value all life; to share their resources responsibly; to view themselves as valued participants within the larger drama of life; to enable individuals, families, and communities to live creatively with tension, anxiety, and death; to be conscious of the contributions to justice they can make in the broader social process; to see themselves as sources of responsibility, grace, creativity, and healing; and to become self-conscious of their propensity and contributions toward injustice and destructiveness in the world.

The challenge that emerged from my ministry was the need to begin to explore and confront explanations that preclude a relational, social, or communal understanding of the self as a constituent member of the web of life. Ministries based on this paradigm will emphasize the web of life and social-intentional character of the agent as determinant in structuring justice within the life of the community and society. Within the perspective of this paradigm, the individual does not create his or her destiny as a solitary individual, but as a member of society. Openness to the future is necessary. Our destiny and faith are not fixed by the past. We do not know what kind of communities people will create in the future. Urban ministries can be helpful in pointing the way to a future that is responsive and creative. Urban ministries can be grounded in a theology that seeks to keep the insights of social science and theology together. The Christian ministry in an urban context is at a crossroads where a number of interdisciplinary concerns intersect. Social science information can enhance one's conception of ministry and help make one's theological understanding of the social world alive. A theology and social imagination that seeks to strengthen awareness of the interconnection between the self, society, and the religious dimension of culture will recognize the system of domination and oppression that exploits weakness; will emphasize the necessity of continued repentance, transformation, and grace; and will establish structures of justice as authentic foundations for social life. Life in society from this perspective is not something that the individual creates for herself or himself alone, but comes through identification with suffering and as a result of common struggles and in solidarity with *the wretched of the earth*.

Structures of justice are not created automatically. They emerge from common struggle and out of reflexive self-conscious appraisals of present realities and social criticism. One way in which ministry may help guide society toward human liberation is through social change and humane social policies that reflect the creative, relational character of social reality. Social science has played a significant role in the determination of social policy; the clergy, especially women and minority clergy, has not. Social scientists, as scientists, have understood and captured an important aspect of human reality, but they have not worked at the center and on the outskirts of human hope. The clergy have. If social policy may be defined as a "blueprint" for structural change and the future fulfillment of human possibilities, then the clergy, especially black and ethnic minorities, women and laity, with their rich and diverse empathic experience with human suffering and hope, have much to contribute to the direction of structural change and social policy, the quality of life and the future. To achieve an open and just society calls for recognition of the web of life and the communal or relational character of selfhood. The human self will be identified paradoxically and ideally as communal and individual, as determined and yet somehow free, as dependent and yet independent. The self can exist as a relational and responsible self in a creative tension with other selves.

II.

The Relational Self:
Grounds for Ethics and Therapy

One is only human because of others, with others, for others.
—Allan Aubrey Boesak

*"And seek the welfare of the city where I have sent you into exile,
and pray to the Lord on its behalf; for in its welfare you will have
welfare."*
—Jeremiah 29:7 (NAS)

Any discussion about the human self may begin with a
confession, namely that the self cannot be grasped or known in
its totality, but only in its fragments. The self is always
fragmented in its roles, functions, and appearances. All such
roles and appearances express the relational character of the
self. People are eminently relational beings. In order to be selves
people must *ex*-press or *ob*-jectify their selves in order to come to
know themselves through others. Hence, the social nature of the
self will be emphasized.

1.

The decade of the sixties has been characterized as a time of
social ferment, liberation politics, and militant protest (S.
Carmichael and C. V. Hamilton, 1967), social activism (E. E.
Sampson, 1967), and revolutionary change (R. Perrucci and M.
Oilisk, 1971; J. Skoinick and E. Currie, 1973). By contrast, the
decade of the seventies has been characterized as a change of
mood and a time of private withdrawal and resignation, the

unlinking of cultural and political values, a return to traditional values (D. Yankelovich, 1972, 1974), a growing interest in new forms of religion (J. Needleman, 1970; Zaretsky and Leone, 1974; T. Roszak, 1975; Glock and Bellah, 1976; and Needleman and Baker, 1978), and a new emphasis on narcissism (C. Lasch, 1979).

The sixties appeared to emphasize social solidarity and the necessity for external and social structural change, with a deemphasis on emotional development and inward change. Yet there was within the decade of the sixties the emergence of a counterculture that turned inwardly and was privately oriented, i.e., highly individualistic, "do your own thing." Although some of these themes became more salient as we moved through the seventies, they were also a part of the phenomenon of the sixties, with its accent on social structural change. In many ways, the sixties was a decade in tension.

The seventies appeared to subordinate an emphasis on social justice and structural change and accent, emotional security, and inner change; and it tended to be more supportive of private withdrawal and a renewed stress on individualism. The dichotomy between private and social concerns became clearer as privatism and the desire for personal change began to replace a more active concern for political and social structural change.

If these highly generalized statements have any merit, then perhaps the challenge facing the decade of the eighties is to heighten awareness of the interrelated and dialectical nature of personal and social life.

2.

This chapter will establish the idea of the relational character of the self as the ground for keeping together in awareness psychological reality and social structure, and for joining the concerns of therapy and Christian social ethics in ministry. This can be done when theology, sociology, and psychology are brought together in ministry. The concept of the relational self is derived from the work and thought of George Herbert Mead, who understood *mind, self,* and *society* to be inseparably linked and dialectically interwoven.[1] There are many thinkers who have contributed to the idea of the human self as eminently relational or communal in character since Mead, including: John MacMurray (1957, 1961), H. R. Niebuhr (1963), Gibson Winter (1966), P. L. Berger (1967), E. Goffman (1967), H. Blumer (1969), Alfred Schutz (1967, 1970, 1971, 1973), Stanley Hauerwas (1974), Bernard M. Loomer (1976), and Allan A. Boesak (1977). In the pages ahead, we follow the lead of George Herbert Mead and his interpreters, who paved the way for the concept of the relational self. It was Mead who emphasized communicative interaction as the primary basis for the emergence of the social self and for the rise of new social structures within society.

The idea of the relational self developed in this chapter differs from modern liberal perspectives, which view the human self as ahistorical and hence independent of any particular society or historical epoch. In short, the human self can be grasped as an abstraction. The ahistorical self may further be characterized as a self maker and solitary figure and thinker, *independent of time and place.*

In modern liberal interpretations, the individual is a member of a community and society and depends on others for the actualization of life, but the individual is portrayed as innately and autonomously possessing a self already at birth. In this perspective, the human self unfolds independently and naturally, rather than socially, i.e., as rooted in a social process and constituted in specific encounters with others, and within a particular social and historical context. The portrait of the individual as naturally unfolding is, in a way, analogous to Aristotle's acorn—born with innate, latent possibilities which develop over time into an adult oak tree. Experience with others is the occasion for the actualization of innate endowments and latent possibilities. In this perspective society is an organization of essentially interdependent, self-reliant individuals who actualize their inborn potentials within their social contexts. Relationality is seen as a by-product of human association, rather than the fundamental datum constitutive of human existence.[2]

My position, by contrast, seeks to establish the social, historical, contextual, and, hence, the relational character of the self. The notion of sociality or the underlying relatedness of reality is the web which is the primary constitutive condition out

57

of which social and personal reality emerges, and it thus becomes the basis for critical reflection. The idea is that reality is fundamentally interrelated and social and perspectival or plural in character, and it is ever differentiating and evolving. It is this idea that sets the tone for exploring the connections between the self, therapy, and Christian social ethics.

It was suggested in the last chapter that one's location in a particular society can heighten awareness of the dangers of individualism, so ingrained in Western thought. Awareness of one's minority position in society can also help one identify the importance of seeking connections between one's own experience of suffering and the suffering of others. This is most meaningfully done when the relationship between self-understanding and social transformation are connected in awareness and from a posture of strength. By *posture of strength,* I am referring to the important point made by Thomas Merton, when he wrote:

> The monk belongs to the world, but the world belongs to him insofar as he had dedicated himself totally to liberation from it in order to liberate it. You can't just immerse yourself in the world and get carried away with it. That is no salvation. If you want to pull a drowning man out of the water, you have to have some support yourself. . . . There is nothing to be gained by simply jumping in the water and drowning with him.[3]

A critical distance from the world as it stands is a necessary part of transforming it. Inner transformation and critical reflection are related to social transformation. They are dialectically interwoven. Awareness of the interconnection between inner and outer transformation is of paramount importance in liberation praxis. The relational self joins awareness of these two dialectical moments. Awareness of the interconnection between inner courage and outer (i.e., social) transformation was crucial in the life of Dr. Martin Luther King, Jr. He found in this linkage the courage to continue his struggle for social justice in the face of fear and despair. He wrote in a personal communication:

> It seemed that all of my fears had come down on me at once. I had reached the saturation point. In this state of exhaustion, when my

courage had almost gone, I determined to take my problem to God. My head in my hands, I bowed over the kitchen table and prayed aloud. . . .

At that moment I experienced the presence of the Divine as I had never before experienced him. . . . My uncertainty disappeared. I was ready to face anything. The outer situation remained the same but God had given me an inner calm.[4]

For Dr. King, faith in a just and compassionate God and the experience of prayer was linked with action in the struggle for freedom. "The outer situation remained the same" but he had found the inner strength to continue the struggle for social structural change.

My emphasis on the relational self presupposes its ultimate grounding in an underlying relatedness and an all-embracing process, as suggested in the first chapter. This reality may be personally experienced as the reality of the presence of God. The reality of God struggles in and through social processes and is the ultimate source of hope and ground for the emergence of the self and its relations with others. True that this was not the view espoused by Mead. This chapter nevertheless will draw on that idea of God and on Mead's view of the self as constituted in its social and historical relations. It will build on the relational paradigm introduced in the previous chapter.

3.

The Relational Self: A Meadian View

The basic insight of Mead's position on the human self is that the self is eminently social in origin and *reflexive* in character. Communication is prior to the emergence of the social self and the essential condition of its appearance and development. "It is the social process itself that is responsible for the appearance of the self; it is not there as a self apart from this type of experience." According to the Meadian view, the social self is not given at birth, but originates in activity and in a social process, and unfolds through interaction and communication and reflection.

The self has a character which is different from that of the physiological organism proper. The self is something which has a

59

development; it is not initially there at birth but arises in the process of social experience and activity, that is, develops in the given individual as a result of his relations to that process as a whole and to other individuals within that process.[5]

Consequently, there will be many different self expressions answering to many different aspects of the social situation. What this implies is that the human person is an addressing and an answering being. People do not merely react to stimuli, but rather they become aware of themselves as interpreting and answering to different aspects of their experience. People become conscious of their capacity to use symbols to address and to call out responses in others as well as in themselves. For example, an infant soon learns that crying usually elicits a comforting response from a caring adult. The adult in turn must interpret the meaning of the cry. The adult may respond by picking up and holding the infant, feeding, or singing softly, or by any other number of ways, based on an interpretation of the crying in a particular context.

According to Herbert Blumer:

Mead's picture of the human being as an actor differs radically from the conception of man that dominates current psychological and social science. He saw the human being as an organism having a self. The possession of a self converts the human being into a special kind of actor, transforms his relation to the world, and gives his action a unique character.[6]

It is through the agency of the self that the human organism can have a double relationship to the world. On one hand, the human organism is *in* a world which predates his or her birth. We are "always already in a world" which is determined by a particular mode of productive activity and by the relational patterns of our predecessors. This already lived-in world will have a determining effect on what the infant or the individual will experience. On the other hand, the world into which the individual is born is a world that is open to and influenced by his or her activity.

The human organism must *create* a world that is meaningful for himself or herself. The term "human organism" refers to the body or the biological constitution and instinctual structure of the individual. The self cannot exist apart from the body and yet it is not identical with it. The self is distinguished from the body in that it is a social product, an emergent reality. It emerges from dialogue and develops through continuous interaction with others. It is essentially reflexive. The social self may be understood as the totality of the individual's *ex*-pressions or objectifications and reflexive intelligence.

It is through continuous activity and in response and reflection that the self arises, unfolds, and differentiates in experience and under specific historical conditions. "In asserting that the human being has a self, Mead simply meant that the human being is an object to himself."[7]

People become self aware (i.e., become an object to their self) by taking the role of other people who are implicated in their activity. In this way people are able to see the meaning their activity has for others and hence, for themselves. People come to self-knowledge in the social process by viewing themselves and the meaning of their acts through the eyes of others. The following illustration is an example of this concept. While serving as a student chaplain intern in a downtown Detroit city hospital, I had the opportunity to follow a patient through her experience from admission to a hospital ward to her release from the hospital. Her condition was critical when she arrived. She took a turn for the worse midway in her stay at the hospital and had to be rushed to surgery. The patient was given a fifty-fifty chance of surviving the operation. She asked if I would go with her to the operating room. I had doubts about my ability to minister to her need at that point. I thought, "How can I comfort her? What can I say, do, or be to her to give the support she needs?" She was very frightened, and I was uncertain of myself, but it was to her fear which I chose to respond. I recalled how frightened I had been in a hospital when being prepared for surgery. I remembered how comforting and encouraging it was just to have Pastor Lloyd present prior to my surgery, and afterward to have him help me talk about and integrate my experience. I was enabled to vicariously place myself in her position, to take her role, and to sense what was needed at the time through empathy with her in her fright. Through identification with Pastor Lloyd's role, I was able to minister to her similar to the way he had ministered to me. In this experience, I was able to come back to myself from another perspective, that of the patient's and of the pastor's, and to move beyond my own questions of inadequacy and self-doubt. This experience provided an opportunity to view myself in the role of the frightened patient and in the role of the potentially healing pastor who was ministering to a very frightened woman. She later shared how comforting it was to have me present as she slowly regained consciousness. Days later she walked out of the hospital with her sister who had come from Chicago to be with her. This experience was seminal for learning how to learn from my own experience (deutero-learning). By taking the role of others, the agent is able to transcend his or her own standpoint and come back to himself or herself. This capacity for reflexive thought, memory, and imagination is the basis for the development of self-conscious selfhood. The self that returns to itself in imagination and through the response of another is not exactly the same self that originated the act. In other words, the self not only unfolds and differentiates in experience, it may also become a more universal self as it acts and reflects upon its relations with others and integrates the past with the present. The self evolves through discourse and continuous activity and reflection in the process of role taking.

> It is just because the individual finds himself taking the attitudes of the others who are involved in his conduct that he becomes an object for himself. It is only by taking the roles of others that we have been able to come back to ourselves. . . . It is further true that the self can exist for the individual only if he assumes the roles of the others. The presence in the conduct of the individual of the tendencies to act as others act may be, then, responsible for the appearance in the experience of the individual of a social object, i.e., an object answering to complex reactions of a number of individuals, and also for the appearance of the self. Indeed, these two appearances are correlative.[8]

The self is constituted through a reflexive process with other selves who are implicated in the activity of the actor. The self, then, is not merely a passive product, or a victim reacting to external stimuli upon it. The self is an *agent,* an "I" acting toward his world, interpreting what confronts him, deliberating and organizing his actions on the basis of the interpretation.

> The process of self-interaction puts the human being over against his world instead of merely in it, requires him to meet and handle his world through a defining process instead of merely responding to it, and forces him to construct his action instead of merely releasing it. This is the kind of acting organism that Mead sees man to be as a result of having a self.[9]

The concept of relationality is implied in Mead's understanding of the human self. Again, the social self is constituted through communication and in relationship with others. It cannot arise in isolation, and it does not exist apart from the communicative praxis of action and reflection within a community of persons. Relationality implies the indwelling presence of others in our concrete experience and our indwelling presence in theirs. We only exist in and through others, in concrete situations. People produce a world *together* through mutual interaction, and their resulting products, in turn, shape them. In this way, people are both *self*-determined (i.e., free) and determined and limited by what is given in the objective social order.

> Selves can only exist in definite relationships to other selves. No hard-and-fast line can be drawn between our own selves and the selves of others, since our own selves exist and enter as such into our experience only insofar as the selves of others exist and enter as such into our experience also.[10]

Relationality implies that the agency of the self, the "I" as a conscious center of activity and creativity, of unity and power can be recognized.

> The unity of the self is constituted by the unity of the entire relational pattern of social behavior and experience in which the individual is implicated and which is reflected in the structure of the self; but many of the aspects or features of this entire pattern do not enter into consciousness so that the unity of the mind is in a sense an abstraction from the more inclusive unity of the self.[11]

The idea of "unity of the self" implies that both continuity and discontinuity is constitutive of the self. Unity does not imply harmony or a self free from conflict, contradiction, or tension. There is a tension within the self between a particular manifestation of the self and its many relational *ex*-pressions. We can say with the apostle Paul, "For I do not do the good I want, but the evil I do not want is what I do" (Rom. 7:19). There is tension between the actual self and the self as idealized; a tension between the self and the social situation. There is also a tension between the self and its plurality or its many self expressions.

Relationality further implies that the social self is also a spectator,[12] an onlooker and a beholder and observer of events. This is the self as passive or receptive of himself or herself and the world. The socialized self is one who is capable of inner conversation, imagination, and synthesis. The self is capable of reflection and criticism and one can become the author of one's self. But one's self is also determined and limited by the given situation. In the hospital experience described earlier, I was able, through inner dialogue, imagination, and synthesis of roles, to view myself from an ideal perspective, and then to integrate that ideal into my concrete situation. The hospital situation revealed both my limitation (i.e., my fears and doubts) as well as the possibility for self-determination. Through imagination the idealized other (Pastor Lloyd) was appropriated into myself and I was able to be the pastor the patient needed at the time. Relationality means that one can recognize the other in one's self and one's self in the role of the other. This is a method of empathic participation that pastors and therapists use in their own ministry and practice. It is a form of deutero-learning or learning to learn from one's own experience.

John MacMurray related the two aspects of the active and the reflective side of the self by suggesting its unity. "The Self that reflects and the Self that acts is the same self."[13] Arthur W. Munk has argued for keeping these two capacities of action and reflection together in a relational understanding of the human self.

This basic fact cannot be overemphasized. In trying to understand agent and spectator then, we must never conceive them as abstractions. As meaningful concepts, together they really comprise the self in all of its fullness. Without either, the latter would be poor indeed. Without its capacity as spectator, it would lack receptivity and perspective. In short, to be fully human and fully creative, the self needs both capacities.[14]

Edward Sampson[15] identified the "I" with the agency of the self. The "I" is the unfolding of activity itself. It is the source of creativity and newness. The "I" is unknown in its spontaneous unfolding. We do not come to know the "I" until after it has acted and become *ob*-jectified, and we have come to reflect upon the act. The "me" is that part of the self that has become objectified in a role or in many roles. In childhood, the "I" and the "me" are fused and only becomes differentiated as the child grows and begins to answer to the various parts of his or her environment—in family, church, school, and play.

It has been argued that totalitarian trends are at work in modern technological societies; that modern technology itself is ever increasing its capacity to mold the consciousness of its members. In this view the self at variance with its milieu becomes an exception, since the dominant social process is one of massification and domination. "The process of massification takes place not because the man of today is by nature a mass man, but for technical reasons. Man becomes a mass man in the new framework imposed upon him because he is unable to remain for very long at variance with his milieu."[16] In this kind of society the capacity of the individual for critical reflection upon the productive processes of the society is diminished. The self, the "me," may appear to be a mere mechanical reproduction of the social order, and the creative side of the self, the "I," may appear to function to preserve the status quo. In this view and under these conditions the self is like a captive in Plato's famous cave allegory. Under this condition people may not be able to identify or to recognize, name, or to analyze the nature of their domination.

It has also been argued that in a society under the impact of industrial technology, the objective order itself tends not so much toward massification, but toward increased differentiation, specialization, and fragmentation. With increased differentiation and anomic conditions in the social structure comes a corresponding sense of fragmentation, powerlessness, and loss of meaning in the social self. In this view, the "I" and the "me" undergo a kind of splitting, and the experience of isolation, alienation, and self-estrangement becomes prominent.

> The I feels "normless," for there exist few standards or guidelines for the presentation of the self in life's many situations. The I feels "isolated," for most others address to him only in terms of his "me" that vary too frequently and too certainly from situation to situation and from person to person. Others cannot be of help in one's search for the "I" as the integrator of the self's me's. One also feels itself estranged from itself, for the "I" and the "me's" are not reconciled.[17]

In this later view of the world, the self becomes self-estranged as society itself calls out different and conflicting responses from its members. The integration and harmony of the self, then becomes a particular problem for modern society.

On the one hand, the individual has sought refuge by withdrawing or retreating into a private world or sought retreat under the sacred canopy of religion, as an attempt to protect or to integrate the self. The self may also attempt to limit itself within a particular cognitive community of interest. On the other hand, the self may become a self over against the society as in the cases of Sojourner Truth, Martin Luther King, Jr., or Malcom X by affirming values that either transcend or deviate from the prevailing outlook and self-understandings of the society of its time.

In the ideal situation to be achieved, the social self is an active, evolving being capable of producing meaningful changes in one's self and in the social world. The person, as a social and historical being, is capable of inner conversation and self-authorship and self-transcendence through role taking. It is in taking the role of another and coming back to one's self that the individual can address and observe himself or herself. This is made possible because of the reflexivity and the relational character of the self. People are able to step back and think (i.e., reflect) upon the social process itself. They can re-present it through language, synthesize experience in thought and imaginatively reconstruct or construct new possibilities. This is an interior dialogue. It is through inner dialogue, action, and reflection *in context with others* that people transcend the very social processes that constitute them. We now turn to a fuller treatment of these ideas.

4.

Human reality is fundamentally social. As social scientists have long noted, the socialized individual lives in society and society lives in the individual. This observation is not only a datum of sociological literature, but it was in Greek philosophy, particularly the platonic tradition, and in the great Hebrew-Christian tradition. The full impact of this statement, "the socialized individual lives in society and society lives in the individual," is often missed. It posits the social world and the language used in everyday life as the prior condition for the emergence of the social self. The self is constituted in its concrete relations with others. Bernard Loomer stated this when he said:

> These constitutive relations are the means whereby the realities of our world are objectively present within our own lives. They are present in us as part of our very being. In being present in us, in the process of entering our lives, they create us. This is how the community "lives" in us.[18]

The community not only lives in us, we live in the community and help shape and transform it, through continuous activity. The reality of the community itself lives and has its being only in the relations between the people who constitute it.

Social reality is perspectival or relative. Although people together contribute to the maintenance and continuation of society, they nonetheless occupy a particular relational or relative standpoint within the society as a whole. Although human experience is individuated within the totality, it does not unfold independently of the social and historical processes that constitute it. Rather, it unfolds and is shaped in response to others and within a particular social and historical context. Individuation of the social self is a by-product of personal, systemic, and historical forces. No one views the world in exactly the same way as someone else.

> Each individual has a world that differs in some degree from that of any other member of the same community, that he slices the events of the community life that are common to all from a different angle from that of any other individual. In Whitehead's phrase, each individual stratifies the common life in a different manner, and the life of the community is the sum of all these stratifications.[19]

Like wearers of different lenses, individuals and groups will perceive the social totality from different angles and will mirror a different consciousness of the community as a whole, however slight or great the difference may appear.[20]

George Herbert Mead was greatly influenced by Einstein's views on relativity, and in some ways, Mead anticipated Einstein. For Mead there is, in the natural and social worlds, nothing that can be considered self-determined or self-sufficient entities.[21] Nothing brought itself into existence under its own power alone. There is always some prior or underlying constitutive relationship through which events or things come to be what they are. In this light, all reality at any given point in time is an achievement. Each situation owes its existence in part to prior, continuous activity. Social reality is a complex emerging process which is mediated through a plurality of perspectives. The uniqueness of the social self is in its capacity to occupy a perspective within a social milieu, to give it its own unique stamp, and to enlarge its own particular standpoint by organizing within its own perspective the standpoint of others. In this way people learn not only to share a world in common with others, but also to enlarge the capacity for love and justice when they empathically participate in the concrete experience of others, especially the sufferers.

The solitary side of human experience also arises in the social process. It is from this solitary position in context with others that people construct different perspectives on the total social process and come to self-knowledge in it. From their individuated standpoints they can analyze the response of others in ways that are meaningful to them.

In the foregoing statements, it has been suggested that reality is constituted in particular encounters between people within a particular social and historical context. The world into which the individual is born is given and perspectival in character. From a particular standpoint people make specific contributions to the continuation of this world through action and reflection in context with others. Both Alfred Schutz[22] and Gibson Winter[23] have helped develop the idea of perspective in the concept of the we-relation. The we-relation includes all face-to-face encounters, both an I-thou or I-it encounters in one-to-one or in group relations.

The We-Relation. In the we-relation, the face-to-face encounter, the individual comes to know who he or she is by being present to another person, an alter ego. Here, the alter ego can be a resource for enlarging the individual's self-understanding. It can also be an occasion for the tragic exploitation of others, and hence diminish the genuine possibility of establishing nurturing relational patterns.

> The other's speech and our listening are experienced as a vivid simultaneity. This simultaneity is the essence of the intersubjectivity, for it means that I grasp the subjectivity of the alter ego at the same time as I live in my own stream of consciousness. In these terms, it is possible to define the alter ego as "that vivid present." And this grasp in simultaneity of the other as well as his reciprocal grasp of me makes possible "our" being in the world together.[24]

The "lived-in" world is an intersubjective world. It means that I, in face-to-face encounters, can grasp the subjective meanings of the other person at the same time that I become aware of my own meanings. It is this experience that makes possible self-conscious and self-critical reflection and is the occasion for the appearance of a new perspective. The meaning that I catch from another person is taken in by me, reflected upon, and, by synthesis, becomes an integral part of my own experience and frame of reference.

Alfred Schutz suggested that in the we-relation, there is a sense in which the knowledge that one has of oneself is transformed by the knowledge one is getting as he stands in relation to another.

> Although I know infinitely more about myself than I do about the other, there is a crucial respect in which the knowledge I have of

the other transcends my self-knowledge. In reflection I can grasp myself only in my past acts. The very act of reflection is possible only if the object of reflection is part of the past, even if it is the immediate past. This implies . . . that the "whole present" . . . and also the vivid present of our Self, is inaccessible for the reflective attitude. We can only turn to the stream of our thought as if it has stopped with the last-grasped experience. In other words, self-consciousness can only be experienced *modo praeterito* in the past tense.[25]

When I was teaching at Clark University, I experienced this kind of we-relation with one of my students in a seminar on Symbolic Interaction. After a half hour into the new semester, a student strongly expressed his dissatisfaction with the way the class experience was going. We had hardly gotten beyond introducing the course outline and reading assignments when his dissatisfaction emerged. There seemed to be little empirical ground to support the strength of his dissatisfaction. The student was not very clear when I asked him to state his complaint. It became evident that his complaint, vaguely stated, was directed at me and not at the course content. After class I asked him what was going on in the classroom. He was not sure he could explain it, so I asked him to think about it. Midpoint into the semester he told me that he was really quite angry with another professor in another department at the university. He had never admitted to that professor or to himself just how deep his anger was. It was when I confronted him about his anger in the classroom and later invited him to think about it, that he was able to consciously reconstruct his experience. Through reflection he was able to make the connection between his repressed and unresolved anger toward the other professor and his displaced expression of it in the new situation. Together we were able to form an affective bond and to identify a dimension of experience that was inaccessible to reflection until it came to light in a we-relation.

We come to the full knowledge of the meaning of our own acts only after others have responded and we have reflected. In reflection we have both the act and its meaning and can anticipate the future from predictable leads from the past. It is the other person's response to our act that confirms our being-in-the-world together. We catch ourselves in response and reflection. We never fully catch ourselves in the vivid present. We come to know ourselves, *modo praeterito,* in a reflective attitude as we turn back to the performed action. But our reality is apprehended by another in the "live-in" moment, before we are aware of the meaning of our acts. This mutual interdependence and interchange of subjective meanings suggest the priority of the social in the emergence of self-awareness. Schutz makes the point in his concept of "mutual tuning-in." Tuning-in is a "reciprocal sharing of the other's flux of experience in inner time, by living through a vivid present together, by experiencing this togetherness as a "We."[26] Meaning arises as each participant in the situation enters into and becomes a part of the living expression of the other.

The we-relation, then, is fundamental to the emergence of self-conscious reflective activity and is basic to the transformation of social reality and alternative possibilities in society. Critical reflection upon the constitution of the self and the productive processes of the society are inseparable from the moral community and, therefore, from human action. Through reflection upon the we-relation and through internal dialogue, the activity of the self is brought under the reflective control of the individual. People can bracket the flow of experience, take it apart, analyze it, and present it to themselves in a range of different alternatives. In this way, the self gets distance on its own experience and praxis, through reflection, self, and social criticism. Then the individual can reconstruct his or her activity in terms of new possibilities. Both ethics and therapy, in their different modes, attempt to bracket experience, analyze it, and identify a range of different alternatives. The process of communication puts the reflective intelligence of the individual at his or her own disposal. In reflection people may find new possibilities for an alternative plan of action.[27]

Social ethics and therapy. Since society and the self are interrelated and interwoven realities, both social ethics and therapy may be seen as part of a praxis that understands social transformation and psychic liberation to be inseparable. Social ethics and therapy employ a reflexive, self-critical methodology which seeks to free human life from fetishism and idolatrous forms of faith and to enable people to reconstitute themselves in

71

light of new self-understandings of a just and liberating social order.

On the one hand, social ethics has been viewed as systematic or rational reflection upon the normative character of society. It has tended to be concerned with issues of *virtue* or character, i.e., What ought I to be? *action,* What ought I to do? and *goals* or *ends,* What kinds of communities ought we to have? On the other hand, therapy has enhanced self-understanding, emancipated the self from internalized forms of oppression, and enhanced a sense of self-worth, a fuller expression of responsible freedom, and developed the capacity for critical reflection. The task of both ethics and therapy is to free the creative, spontaneous side of the relational self (the "I") and to help transform a world and social processes that have become solipsistic, alienative, and oppressive. Gibson Winter[28] based his approach to social ethics on the principle of the we-relation and emphasized the intentional and relational character of social existence. He maintained that ethical reflection can be viewed as a science of human intentionality.[29] The task of ethics is to ask about the adequacy of a model for the everyday world; "to clarify the moral claims and rights of the social world and their proper ordering in the structure of social organizations"; to decipher the meaning of the past; and to consider the moral possibilities that will enable society to move toward the future goal of human fulfillment.[30] Ethical reflection is intentional activity which takes place in a social world.

> Ethics seeks to clarify the logic and adequacy of the values that shape that world; it assesses the moral possibilities which are projected and betrayed in the social give and take. Ethical reflection may take one or another abstract perspective to clarify the moral order, much as social science abstracts from the everyday world, but the criterion of adequacy for ethical interpretation is to be found in the "lived" experience of the social world.[31]

Winter's ethic looks to the future and inquires, "What must people do" now in order to bring about the good society? At another point he states:

> Social ethics is also reflection on doing, but it focuses upon the moral qualities of willing, social relationships, social structures,

72

and cultural ideals; it is reflection on value in social process. Whatever the ultimate source of its valuative perspective, social ethics views man and society in their intentionality; it evaluates the adequacy of doing in relation to man's nature and fulfillment. *Thus, social ethics is evaluative interpretation of the intentional character of practice.* Social ethics asks about the "goodness for what and whom" in societal process.[32]

Relationality in Winter's approach to ethics implies that people participate in a fundamental, primordial, and comprehensive and creative source of redemption and reconciliation. "This redemptive power is the source of reconciliation and renewal by which all we-relations are nurtured."[33] Relationality is a pregiven structure of being which, in the ideal situation, moves people toward universal values, empathic sharing, and a deeper experience of their humanness in their historical context. He maintains that the basic approach to ethics rests upon an underlying structure of sociality, which he calls the "we-relations." The "we-relations" is implied in the structure of being itself, and it is the source of sociality. Implied is the idea that human beings are not self-sufficient, they are unfinished. They must continually fashion and refashion a world for their fulfillment. "Dialogical communities furnish a crucial, relational structure for such transformations, though ultimately the transforming interpretation has to alter the institutional networks in community, works, politics, and other realms of activity. The special character of face-to-face relations derive from the self-transcending power of personhood, the otherness of I, which generates tensions and dynamic transformations in life."[34] The human self, then, is not a fixed form, but a dynamic and relational reality that unfolds historically in dialogue and through conflict, tension, negation, and challenge. Fundamentally, then, people are questioners who can never find the answer to their being alone in themselves. "The self that man searches for is eminently social. This means that man is searching not for his idiosyncratic, private self, but for what is truly and universally human."[35]

According to Jerome D. Frank,[36] the primary function of therapy is to combat demoralization which may result from certain relational patterns. Therapeutic relationships attempt to address internally or externally induced stress such as feelings of impotence, isolation, despair, damaged self-esteem, failure, or a loss of meaning in life. The task of the therapeutic relationship is to bring about self-understanding and to help effect change so that individuals and groups may be empowered for self-determination and to establish or to reestablish a sense of connectedness or integration with self and within one's group. Moreover, the therapeutic relationship may strengthen or enlarge the individual's and group's capacity for self-critical discernment, imagination, warmth, empathy, and sense of justice and vitality, and it can help deepen the capacity for hope and love.

Both social ethics and therapy may be concerned with strengthening awareness of the relational patterns in which individuals and groups are enmeshed. Both social ethics and therapy may be seen on a continuum, as shown below:

Therapy
and
the Therapeutic Relationship

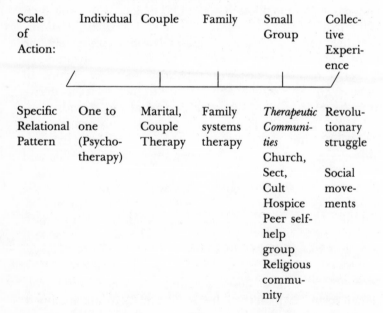

Scale of Action:	Individual	Couple	Family	Small Group	Collective Experience
Specific Relational Pattern	One to one (Psycho-therapy)	Marital, Couple Therapy	Family systems therapy	*Therapeutic Communities* Church, Sect, Cult Hospice Peer self-help group Religious community	Revolutionary struggle Social movements

Social Ethics

Scale of Action:	Small Group	Community Action (local level)	Large Group
Specific Relational Pattern	Church social action-reflection groups	Boycott, Strike, etc.	Mass protest, Mass forms of resistance Reform movements Revolutionary struggles

The term *therapeutic relationship* refers to the link established between two or more people with the aim of effecting a change, or furthering a curative process that relieves suffering. Usually the "therapeutic relationship" shall refer to a change in oppressive relational patterns which relieve the suffering of the oppressed and may result in constructive and supportive relations in society. This implies that people are agents who can participate cooperatively in socially redemptive processes. By serving or helping a fellow or sister sufferer, or by helping change the systemic character of injustice, they can further the redemptive work of Christ in the world (Matt. 25:39-40).

Therapy may take the form of psychotherapy[37] or one-to-one talk therapy (as in the dialogue of therapy) with a professional help-giver or a friend. It may take the form of marital or couple therapy or family systems therapy. It may come through participation in a therapeutic community as in a worshiping community, or in a religious community (i.e., a religious order); or it may come through revolutionary struggle as oppressed people unite in solidarity and collectively confront an issue, such as colonialism or racism, that one person alone could not change.

The church as therapeutic community is perhaps the most prevalent social form of therapy in black communities. W. E. B. DuBois referred to black worship and revival as "intense excitement." Some of the key therapeutic elements he saw were: strong preaching, singing of spirituals, gospels, and jubilee songs, dancing, shouting, and fervent prayer. He described shouting as the one element more devoutly believed in.

> Finally the Frenzy or "Shouting," when the Spirit of the Lord passed by, and, seizing the devotee, made him mad with supernatural joy, was the last essential of Negro religion and the one more devoutly believed in than all the rest. It varied in expression from the silent rapt countenance or the low murmur and moan to the mad abandon of physical fervor, and the stamping, shrieking, and shouting, the rushing to and fro and wild waving of arms, the weeping and laughing, the vision and the trance. All this is nothing new in the world, but old as religion, as Delphi and Endor. And so firm a hold did it have on the Negro, that many generations firmly believed that without this visible manifestation of the God there could be no true communion with the Invisible.

Revivals *were* social and psychological therapy for the participants. It *is* a form of psychic release and healing, social cohesion, and a sense of communion with the Divine. "Back of this more formal religion, the church often stands as a real conserver of morals, a strengthener of family life, and the final authority on what is Good and Right."[38] Worship and revival in the black church tradition was the most characteristic expression of African character linking therapeutic expressions with the moral life.

Traditionally, the black preacher was the community therapist, par excellence.[39] He or she continues to be a bringer of glad tidings, a spiritual and psychological healer, the interpreter of the Unknown, the comforter in times of sorrow, the one who gives voice and picturesquely expresses the longings, disappointments, and resentments of a stolen and oppressed people.[40]

This form of therapy may be linked with liberation praxis which seeks to involve people in changing a society that has systematically excluded and denied full humanity to the poor, and people of color, especially blacks and Native Americans. The Civil Rights Movement and the ministry of Martin Luther King, Jr., may be viewed as an attempt to link the therapeutic resources of the black church and the gospel of Jesus with liberation praxis.

Social ethics may take place at the level of the local church as in a church-related social action-reflection group; or at the community level, as in a local demonstration or protest such as a boycott or strike; or at the societal level such as a mass demonstration like the 1963 march on Washington, or Vietnam Veterans' march on Washington, or the Native Americans' walk from the West Coast to the White House in Washington, D.C.

At all of these levels people may engage in action and then step back to reflect critically upon what they have done, or they may engage in rational analysis to clarify the nature of their obligations or duty to society. From the perspective of black communities struggling to be free from external and internal forms of race and gender exploitation and class oppression, ethical reflection must emerge out of the day-to-day struggle for freedom and embrace the values of communal responsibility and solidarity.

The task of *Christian* social ethics, according to H. R. Niebuhr, is to understand the self as a questioning and answering being before God and having responsibility in society and history. The human self is shaped by its responses to action upon it. Christian social ethics can be viewed as response-ethics. The questions then become, What is God doing? What is the fitting response to the action of God upon us? "Responsibility affirms: God is acting in all actions upon you. So respond to all actions upon you as to respond to his action."[41] In this view, the responsible self is a relational self which understands that God is the one ultimate action who addresses us in our many self-expressions and through the many actions upon us.

Christian social ethics must take Scripture seriously. It cannot ignore the Scriptures or the folk traditions and praxis of the faith communities of the oppressed who sought, in their time, to be faithful to God in the face of suffering, injustice, and cruel oppression. Reflection done from this standpoint and in light of God's self-disclosure in Jesus and continued liberating activity "to set captives free" may be termed Christian social ethics and may be seen as a way to discipleship. Forms of freedom, justice, power, and love are rightly focal concerns for Christian social ethics. The Scriptures and the faith of our predecessors live on in memory and in contemporary expressions as the communities of oppressed peoples today evolve their understanding of what it means to be a faithful people reconstituting themselves in the promise of a redeeming or liberating social order.

Both Thomas R. Bennett[42] and Robert C. Leslie[43] attest to the central importance of sharing and nurturing as essential elements which help to sustain meaningful activity in small groups within church and society. Apart from group support, the building of trust, and the experience of reconciliation, it may be impossible for groups or the individual Christian to sustain effective action and critical reflection or to see clearly their mission as God's agents of renewal and redemption in the midst of change. "The local church can be a source of preparation and support to enable the laity to be the people of God at work in the world."[44]

The interest of therapy is self-understanding and emancipation through psychotherapy or pastoral counseling, family therapy, or through participation in a therapeutic community, or in struggles for social justice. When individuals, families, or groups are relatively powerless, i.e., politically impotent and members of oppressed communities too, then the role of therapy and therapeutic relationships may be a means for empowerment to promote effective action and personal integration as a resource for transforming communal life.

But therapy alone cannot transform social reality; nor can Christian social ethics do it alone. Neither strategy by itself or together is the ultimate truth. They are provisional strategies that must undergo critical reflection and may be judged in light of God's liberating activity on behalf of the oppressed, and all people.

The relational self suggests that social reality and psychic life, like public and personal existence, are interwoven. Therefore, the emancipatory interest of Christian social ethics and therapy may be kept together as part of an effort that seeks to transform the social processes that constitute us. But before we apply the idea of the relational self to therapy and to Christian social ethics (to be redefined as "a black Christian liberation ethic"), we must address a question implied in our view of the self as primarily relational, that is, the social self that is constituted in its relations with others.

III.

The Relational Self
and Social Transformation

"Our past is our present in our conscious and unconscious memory. To understand such a present past is to understand one's self and, through understanding, to reconstruct."

—H. Richard Niebuhr
in *The Meaning of Revelation*

If the relational self emerges out of a particular social process, even if that process is an oppressive one, does this imply that the self is hopelessly trapped within the language systems and social processes that give it rise? Since we are formed by our society as much as we form it with others, are we not trapped by it to the depth of our being? If the concepts with which we work toward change and the structures of consciousness are formed by the society of which we are a part, then how do we forge alternatives since our own biographies, values, and beliefs are largely determined by the very social processes we hope to change?[1] In short, how do people transcend their social origins?

1.

It would be a mistake to think of our past and our various social origins as having a fixed or forever unalterable meaning. Our social origin, as well as our selves, are social and historical creations which continue to unfold and change. Our social origin is part of a continuous unfolding process which is, in principle, incomplete and open to interpretation and revision

79

from future standpoints. We may note here that the principle of interpretation (hermeneutics) becomes enormously important for liberation struggles, for the church's ministry, for ethics, and for therapy. Since this concern is carried in subsequent chapters, I only mention it in passing here.

We never capture the past as it actually was. Rather, we recall, construct, and reshape it from a present perspective which is surpassed by interpretations from a future standpoint. As long as new viewpoints arise, the meaning of the past is altered and enters into and becomes a part of the unfolding story that takes on an enlarged and even richer meaning. The meaning of our social origin is comprehended in relation to the unfolding present and is open to revision and to new significance. We are embedded in an underlying and continuous social process which constitutes and reshapes us. At the same time, we can affect the processes that determine the kind of selves we become. If it were not for the capacity for transcending awareness, human subjects would be reduced to nonpersons, prisoners of their own activity and trapped in their biography and history without conscious recognition of their captivity. The purpose of this chapter is to identify sources for liberation from domination and freedom for potential creative transformation of the social process and the human subject.

2.

What are the resources for transcending our social origins? Three possibilities are suggested: (1) the novel side of human experience which Mead associated with the biologic "I," the spontaneous and undifferentiated unfolding of experience itself; (2) the self as objectively knowable and reflexive. Reflexivity is the capacity for role-taking, reflection, and critical self-consciousness; and (3) the role of reflexivity at the group level in intentional communities. This third resource links the collective will of the group with an interest in emancipation. These three elements are interrelated in a potentially creative transformation of the social and historical context and of the individuals who live in that context. These three resources for transformation must be kept together in liberation praxis. None of them alone sufficiently addresses the problem of transcending our social origins and transforming the social context.

The Novel Side of Human Experience

The novel side of human experience is perhaps one of the more difficult and fascinating of Mead's concepts to convey. Novelty here refers to spontaneous and unpredictable activity that moves us beyond the familiar or ordinary boundaries of our experience, and introduces us to new horizons.

A few years ago, while vacationing in St. Thomas, I met a young medical doctor who challenged me to go scuba diving. Without thinking about it, I said, "Sure!" I surprised myself with my spontaneous acceptance of his challenge. I have a fearful respect for the ocean and tend to be very careful not to venture far from shore, especially in unfamiliar water. I had the evening to think about what I had gotten myself into, but I also felt that I could not back down. Somehow, I had gotten myself into this agreement to dive sixty feet in unfamiliar ocean water with scuba equipment and with someone I hardly knew. I had no prior experience with scuba diving. I was unfamiliar with the use of scuba equipment, and I was venturing far beyond my experience and the safe limits I normally set for myself when it comes to ocean swimming. The next day I went to the beach, put on scuba gear, and dove to a depth of sixty feet in ocean water.

We have all had the experience of surprising even ourselves through spontaneous activity that departs from our normal and commonsense routine. If asked why we take a certain, uncharacteristic course of action, we might reply, "I don't know!" But then begins the process of reconstructing our experience in order to get hold of its meaning for us. Spontaneity in the moment, without thinking about it, so serves to push the human subject a step beyond the safe limits in which he or she would customarily stay. To cross the threshold to a new experience is to acquire a new dimension of freedom and a new horizon in which the self is reconstituted.

The spontaneous and unpredictable side of the human self can be referred to as the experience of the *biologic* "I." Mead used the term *biologic* "I" to emphasize the "living" process and to distinguish it from later reflection. Later reflection brings back the lived experience for interpretation and meaning. The "I" appears in our experience in memory. It is only after we have acted and reflected upon our activity that we know what we have done.[2]

Mead identified the "I" with the life process. It is the unfolding of activity itself, creating new possibilities for human subjects. The action of the "I" is a primary source for transcending our social origins and for creative transformation and liberation. The action of the "I" belongs to the future. It is the avenue through which the subject's activity can help shape a new future.

Mead did not explore the theological implications of his thought. His interest was that of a secular humanist. He sought to explain the social origins of the self and society from the perspective of social psychology and philosophy. He did not make explicit the theological assumptions implied in his treatment of the self and its relationship to the world. The later task has been taken up by some of his interpreters whose interests were more theological. They sought to interpret human activity and freedom in light of God's liberating activity in human life. Rubem A. Alves argues from a theological perspective:

> In the context of the politics of human liberation man encounters a God who remains open, who has not yet arrived, who is determined and helped by human activity. God needs man for the creation of his [man's] future. . . . God's freedom was appre-hended by the community of faith from the activity that made freedom and life possible, so man's freedom is to become a praxis, an activity that makes the world different. Man's freedom, therefore, is not only a dimension of his subjectivity; it is power to transform the world, to create a new future.[3]

Theologically speaking, the human self and human freedom participate in an ultimate and creative reality that is for, not against, the human subject. From a biblical perspective, God sides with the oppressed and gives meaning and hope to their liberation struggles. The language of hope is intrinsically related to the emancipatory activity of the dispossessed whose interest in ultimate salvation is inseparable from historical justice and liberation. The action or agency of the "I" is its language, a language to be deciphered in a later moment of reflection. Through the action of the "I," the human subject can discover that he or she is not a monad, not a closed microcosm, but is an open horizon that participates in a transcending reality. To paraphrase the apostle Paul, "But we have this treasure in earthen vessels, to show that the transcendent power belongs to God and not to us" (II Cor. 4:7). This "transcendent power" is not an alien force, but is constitutive of selfhood. This transcendent power from which the self derives its own agency is the ground of creative transformation. It is the reality of God that struggles on behalf of the downtrodden in and through the social process. The reality of God influences and is influenced by human suffering, freedom, and activity. It is this God who identifies with the downtrodden and whose will is consistent with their historical struggle to be free.

Mead distinguished between the biologic "I" and the social "me" in his idea of the self. The two are dialectically related and only analytically separable. These two aspects represent different moments in the life of the self and are interwoven in experience. The biologic "I" is prior to the social "me." The biologic "I" is the active and initiating, impulsive, and creative side of the self. It is the source of novelty and ground of self-transcendence, and it is essentially unknown, spontaneous, and unpredictable. The "I" does not get into the limelight of experience (e.g., we talk to ourselves, but we do not see ourselves talking). Only after we have acted and responded, that is, after the "I" has become a "me," an object or a taker of roles, can we know what it is. If you ask, then, where directly in your own experience the "I" comes in, the answer is that it comes in as an historical figure. It is what you were a second ago that is the "I" of the "me."[4]

The essential point is that the "I" is elusive. It cannot be caught in its unfolding. It is the actual process of acting, thinking, and reflecting. Mead's "I" involves a paradox: "on the one hand it represents freedom, spontaneity, novelty, initiative; on the other hand, it is blind and unconscious, a process we become aware of only when it is a fait accompli."[5]

In contrast, the "me" is that part of our experience that is knowable and predictable. It is the "I" objectified in experience. The world in which the "me" exists is the routine world of everyday life where our *doubt* concerning its reality is suspended. The world in which the "me" exists is taken for granted as it appears to us. "The 'me' does call for a certain sort of an 'I' insofar as we meet the obligations that are given in conduct itself, but the 'I' is always something different from what the situation itself calls for."[6] The "I" asserts itself as the source of novelty in its action upon one's own experience, and as action over against the social situation. The "I" is not entirely bound by convention, and it is never completely calculable. It is that part of every social act that never gets directly into reflective experience. It is through this spontaneous, unpredictable, and unsocialized side of our experience that new perspectives emerge and new possibilities for personal and social transformation arise. It has been argued that the self exists in a creative tension with reality. It is paradoxically in two worlds: the world of the biologic "I" and the world of the socialized "me," one created and one in creation.[7]

The relational self is conditioned and free; caused and cause; victim and victor. Two possibilities forever confront the human subject: one, to adjust one's response to fit the normative and taken-for-granted patterns of society; or two, to move beyond them through recognition that spontaneous and unpredictable activity contains possibilities for placing the taken-for-granted world in question. Both dimensions of experience constitute the human subject. The second possibility is a resource for transcending our social origins by acting in the society that shapes us. But, the self-actualization of the "I" in itself is not sufficient to bring about social transformation. Another element in its constitution must be recognized, namely, reflexivity.

The Self as Objectively Knowable and Reflexive

The self has an objective side and a subjective side. The objective side of the self, the "me," exists in certain concrete relations to other selves (i.e., as infant with mother or father), and it occupies a particular position in the social structure. The self exists in particular roles, for instance, pastor, parishioner, employee, student, friend, enemy, and so forth. This is the self objectified in the social process and in a particular social and historical context. This differentiated side of the self is objectively knowable. The ability to know one's self as others know comes from the capacity to become an object to oneself. This is the human capacity to achieve *self*-consciousness, and not just consciousness. Self-consciousness means that one can grasp one's self from the standpoint of others.

On the other hand, the subjective side of the self emerges through thinking, reflection, and internal conversation. It evolves as the individual stops and thinks about his or her continuous relationship with others, the environment, and the world. The self is a dynamic process and a center of consciousness. It not only emerges from its relations with others, but also arises in relation to itself and through the use of language, imagery, and memory. In this sense the self is a resource for getting hold of its social origins in the act of reflection. The self that emerges in this way can construct and reconstruct its own experience.

Reflexivity within the social process is a key concept for addressing the problem of our relationship to the social context in which we live and out of which we continue to emerge. Reflexivity is the process by which the individual becomes self-conscious in communicative relations. "It is by means of reflexiveness—the turning-back of the experience of the individual upon himself—that the whole social process is thus brought into the experience of the individuals involved in it."[8] It is through this communicative process of taking the role of another that people are able to step outside themselves, so to speak, and look back at themselves and thereby intentionally transform the social context.

It has been suggested that people transcend their social origins through recognition of their participation in a primal and transcending source of freedom that underlies their struggle, and through reflexivity as an individual act.

Through reflexivity, the human subject is able to come back to himself or herself. People can recall past experiences, relate memory to the need for action in the present, make choices, take risks, make mistakes, think, and reconstruct their activity. People may be able to transform themselves and their concrete situations through this reflexive process. On the basis of new information and through critical awareness, people can initiate new lines of action that lead toward new patterns of relationships, which in turn contribute to an alteration of the social context. The changed context, in its turn, brings into appearance a different self, although it may not be the self imagined.

One of the boyhood lessons that has stayed with me happened one day when a neighbor, a good friend of my father's, greeted me warmly and wanted to give me a nickel. I refused the nickel saying, "Oh . . . no, Mr. Riley. Thank you, but I can't take that." My father, who observed this exchange and recognized what it was, spoke, "Take it, Son. Mr Riley *wants* to give it to you. Don't refuse him." I did not recognize that I had refused Mr. Riley in refusing a nickel. I overlooked the meaning of my neighbor's kind gesture in the moment of refusing. It was not until after my father gave permission and objectified the situation could I understand that it was not the nickel that was important, but my neighbor's expression of his affection to both my father and to me. To give a nickel was the one spontaneous thing he could do at the moment. To refuse the nickel was to thwart a genuine show of friendship. Only when I was able to see through the eyes of the other people in my situation, was I able to come back to myself and gain a new and enlarged perspective on what it means for persons to show affection through the giving and receiving of a small gift.

Reflexivity is the condition through which people can gain awareness of themselves acting in the situation that forms them. They can become aware of themselves acting for good or for ill in their social context. But reflexivity and self-consciousness at the individual level are not sufficient enough to alter underlying social processes, although they are an important part of it. Reflexivity at the individual level is only one ingredient in the total process that contributes toward transformation of the context and the people in it.

A third possibility is reflexivity at the general level of the community. Here, the group as an intentional community can develop the capacity for self-critical reflection and can direct the collective will of a people toward human emancipation. This third possibility suggests that freedom from domination of structural oppression requires collective and revolutionary struggle and the capacity for self-critical reflection upon its own praxis.

Reflexivity and Intentional Communities

By intentional communities, I have in mind groups that have emerged from historical struggle, that seek to remain faithful to the imperatives of social justice and to the continued need for the transformation of sinful social structures. The historic black church and contemporary religious groups engaged in freedom struggles of the people and struggles against forms of domination are examples of intentional communities. They act with the intent of interpreting and criticizing their own praxis in light of transcending values and with the intent of creatively transforming the historical context.

From this perspective, reflexivity identifies the human person as an agent in context with others and as valued participants in liberation struggles. This perspective identifies the individual as a thinking subject, capable of self-address and initiating activity that is consistent with the groups' historic interest in emancipation.

When they struggle collectively, oppressed people are able to effect changes in the social structure that the lone individual cannot. They can transcend the social histories that have kept their struggles separated when they recognize their common humanity and the common sources underlying their oppression. They can transcend their social histories when they empathically enter the struggle with other groups that are oppressed by the same forces of domination. New selves are called out and shaped through the process of reflection, criticism, and revolutionary struggle within the context of group struggle. However, in actuality, the changed situation may not be the one desired.

Critical reflection at both the individual and group levels are interdependent and necessary parts of a process of social transformation. Critical reflection begins by uncovering the social and historical roots that lie behind our emergence as conscious subjects. We are self-conscious when we become critically aware of the material forces that constitute us in our relations with others. Self-conscious reflection can enable us to comprehend the relationship between self and society as a dialectical, rather than as a mechanistic or frozen, moment. Human subjects are enabled to transcend their context, to break through the dogmatism of false consciousness and limitations of the past, and to reconstitute themselves in a new and open future. They can transcend their context through the internal connection of reflection, criticism, and action, and in an ideal speech situation.

The ideal speech situation[9] is a dialogue that is not yet a reality, but ought to be. It therefore anticipates a future state constituted in freedom from domination. The ideal speech situation is Habermas' way of indicating (verbally and non-verbally) what *ought to be* the telos, the goal, of verbal and nonverbal communication, namely human emancipation. Actual dialogue contains the elements of domination, repression, and ideological distortion embedded in our human praxis and from which we continually strive to emancipate ourselves.

> No matter how the intersubjectivity of mutual understanding may be deformed, the *design* of an ideal speech situation is necessarily implied in the structure of potential speech, since all speech, even intentional deception, is oriented toward the idea of truth. This idea can be analyzed with regard to a consensus achieved in unrestrained and universal discourse. Insofar as we master the means for the construction of an ideal speech situation, we can conceive the ideas of truth, freedom, and justice, which interpret each other—although of course only as ideas. On the strength of communicative competence alone, however, and independent of the empirical structures of the social system to which we belong, we are quite unable to realize the ideal speech situation; we can only anticipate it.[10]

The "ideal speech situation" will always remain an ideal, to be *achieved*. Concrete speech situations, in actuality, can only presuppose, anticipate, and approximate the ideal speech situation.[11] Any speech situation in which two or more people are present to each other will not guarantee the achievement of this reflexive, transcending awareness. In a concrete speech situation one person may "win" in the conversation and the other person(s) may not learn anything except that they are still the loser(s). The ability we have of reflecting, in light of an ideal, on the very process that has constituted us, is one way of taking hold of it and attempting to transform it.

3.

These three levels, the unpredictable and novel side of experience, the individual capacity for reflective activity, and reflexivity at the communal level are a part of the same process of change and are dialectically interwoven in experience. I have further suggested that the normal coming together of people does not guarantee that they will approximate an ideal speech situation. There must be some ideal speech situation that can be described and revealed in their coming together, *truth*. Truth here means a dialogue in which the interacting parties together transcend the dogmatism and ideological distortions implicit in their individual standpoints and become aware of the social origins that underlie their outlooks.

A new situation can emerge through the desire to change and through revolutionary struggle with others who are also seeking to break the enslaving bonds of the past. People evolve together through common struggle and reconstitute themselves in a new relationship to their environment or context. But this requires self, social criticism, and a distancing from the false consciousness of the past, as well as a vision of the kind of future toward which the collective group is moving. Without awareness of the past, persons may be hopelessly doomed to replicate it and to fail to recognize how their current activity and mode of reflection serve the interests that enslave them. Hence, intentional communities are needed for the practice of the activity that will evolve them in new directions and help bring to light the subtle and structural forces of domination that currently oppress them and circumscribe their reality. The social process in which people are embedded and through which their reality is constituted must evolve the possibility of a different perspective in the light of a new vision. The new vision must contain a genuine alternative to the one that currently prevails in the society providing the framework for their own thinking. This can come only through a process of revolutionary struggle and critical reflection upon things as they stand at the group and individual level. Bracketing the taken-for-granted reality and subjecting it to rigorous criticism in light of an alternative and ideal vision of what could be are necessary in an emancipatory struggle that enables people to transcend and transform the social contexts that shape their reality.

4.

An illustration is in order. For it, I draw on a recent experience at the Theology in the Americas (TIA)/Detroit II Conference, August, 1980. One of the most significant moments of the conference occurred when the indigenous and ethnic group participants came together to explore the possibilities of, and then to form, a coalition within the TIA. The opportunity to recognize and create a process for addressing the common structure of oppression emerged. This newly formed coalition, the Inter-Indigenous and Ethnic Peoples' Project, represented the coming together of several groups and projects: the Black, Indigenous, Hispanic, Asian-American and Pacific Island Peoples' Projects. A desire was voiced within the Black Theology Project to establish dialogue with the other minority groups present. This desire was shared by the other minority groups as well. What helped stimulate the coming together of the various ethnic groups in the first place was the calling into question and the bracketing of the context and process in which they were conducting business. The need for joining together was expressed by individuals who were aware that the structure of oppression, though complex, was one.

Prior to this coming together, the primary concerns of the individual members of the various minority groups reflected different levels of awareness of the history of struggle and suffering of their own people as well as awareness of the history of the struggles of the other minority groups. But these concerns remained at the level of *individual awareness,* and the reflective process was on the level of in-house dialogue. The reflexive process at the group level, that is, the process of incorporating the shared standpoint of the other groups into the perspective of each of the groups for collective struggle, had not yet become a reality. It was in the coming together of the various minority groups to share their experiences and explore that it became possible to evolve the social process to a new level of collective struggle and intergroup structuring. A new context for collective struggle among racial minorities could not have been achieved had the various groups remained apart. Now each could appreciate even more the intricate nature of the experience of oppression; each could see in new ways, the complexity of the structure of oppression.

Within this new context and through this process, the various groups were able to evolve beyond previous perspectives to a new standpoint which was now far more complex and richer because it incorporated the previous standpoints of each group. This newly constituted standpoint is now an added resource for collaboration and for projecting beyond the earlier standpoints and perspectives that constituted the individual groups. This added dimension to reflexivity permitted each group to come back to itself and to gain a new perspective from the context as a whole and push the struggle for liberation to a new level.

The various groups saw the importance of keeping intact their own projects and their unique groups as the fundamental intentional communities in which action and reflection took place, and out of which dialogue and decisions emerged. Interindigenous and ethnic structuring did not mean the abolishing of the individual projects and the melting of particular minority groups into some kind of universal community. The particular groups, as intentional communities, were recognized as even more important in their role as historic communities, remembering and celebrating the history, the victories, defeats, and resurgence of the peoples. Each group had its own unique culture as well as its own history and structure of oppression which both diverged from and converged at points with the historical experience of all the other groups present.

This experience of "uniting" may serve as a paradigm for an ideal speech situation which respects the autonomy and interdependence of other national and ethnic groups, and yet is conscious of the common structure that underlies their oppression. The structure of oppression is one, although it is complex, and the experience and response to this common structure of oppression will vary from group to group. The various groups found common ground through recognition that a new collective was possible. Together they can struggle more effectively against the forces that dehumanize them. The cooperative situation is not guaranteed by the mere coming together of the various minority groups.

At one point in the conference when the indigenous peoples and ethnics were exploring a possible coalition between them, we got bogged down about how, or whether, to proceed toward coalition. For example, we asked, do we confront the real substantive issues between us head on and run the risk of early polarization and alienation, or should we first share our stories and experiences of oppression, thereby building rapport and a genuine respect for the struggles of others and a base for working together before confronting the more difficult and potentially volatile issues facing us? A spokesperson for the indigenous peoples confronted the ethnics around the issue of land. He pointed out that the land on which we ethnics live and have some of our businesses belongs to them! As their numbers increase and they step up their demands for their land to be returned, where will we, the ethnics, be on this issue? Will we side with the capitalists or will we support the indigenous peoples in their claims? An Asian brother turned to ask the members of the Black Theology Project how to proceed on coalition building, since black people have had long experience in dealing with methods of confrontation and negotiation and sacrifice. So several shared from their experience what they thought would be the best way to proceed. Each group went back to its gathering place to consider the objectives and methods essential to each group. Then we returned to share with the others the goals that had come out of our individual group sessions. We found that our concerns and our goals were very similar, if not the same in many areas. There were differences also. The differences that emerged did not preclude, but favored, the building of an interindigenous peoples and ethnics coalition. This experience is but one way in which a collective political will can emerge and provide a new basis for the possibility of social and individual transformation.

The reflective and imaginative capacity of the individual is an important and often underestimated source of novelty in liberation praxis. It was sensitive and self-conscious individuals who first imagined the possibility of a coalition, before it became a reality. It began as an ideal to be achieved. But the individual, for all his or her richness, needs the collective group for the achievement of the ideal; and the group needs the reflexive capacity of the individual. The group makes relational or mutual recognition possible. "Mutual recognition, the act of seeing oneself in others, extends each individual's awareness to cover the whole human race; he realizes that the actions of others have aims similar to and even connect to his own."[12] People need others because it increases their capacity to think critically and to act collectively to influence the more powerful structures that oppress them. The group needs the individual because of the unique contributions he or she makes to the life of the whole. The individual is the self-conscious center of creative activity and novelty, of love and justice and mercy, and these are mediated through structures of sociability.

Individuals acting alone usually initiate changes at certain levels of the social structure. But these changes are limited in their effects. The majority of individuals just do not become the great figures in history, effecting major changes. Perhaps, we should be thankful for that. While the reflexive capacity of the individual is significant, one alone is not sufficient to effect fundamental social structural change. In most instances when it is the person against the system, the system wins. But when the individual acts in concert with others, he or she has a greater power to effect beneficial change.

The relative isolation of racial minorities from the mainstream of U.S. society may give them a special critical standpoint from which to view the working of society. Their special standpoint can be a source of critical reflection upon the nature and forms of oppression and suffering when they remain identified with their history and cultural heritage and when they keep alive the traditions of the people and their communities. Racial minorities, acting in the context of their groups and out of awareness of the history of the people, have a basis for critical reflection on which they can draw and get an effective hold on the very processes that dehumanize them. This critical capacity is enlarged when oppressed groups come together, share, learn from their differing standpoints, and take collective action.

People can get hold of the ideological distortions that would fix their mental outlooks within a limited horizon. They can effect meaningful change through continuous and collective struggle and critical reflection upon their constitutive context. Together they can transcend the context that keeps them separate and pitifully trapped within the systems and thought patterns that will guarantee their continued enslavement.

I have earlier suggested that the social process in which people are embedded and through which their reality is constituted must itself evolve a genuine alternative to the one that currently prevails in the society. It is important to state what is that prevailing view and then to sketch briefly what an alternative might look like. The prevailing view is that the United States is fundamentally a just, free, open, and democratic society for all; that it is "the land of the free"; that anyone who wants to make it to the top can do so through individual effort, for "God surely helps those who help themselves." Failure to achieve success, according to this view, can be attributed to individual deficiencies. This prevailing outlook has functioned to obscure awareness of the structural contradictions of an exploitative economic, political, and social system. It is incapable of correctly analyzing the depths to which race, sex, and class oppression have been institutionalized.

A vision of a new society must be capable of correctly diagnosing the systemic character of oppression and of fostering relational patterns that liberate human life. The vision of a new society is one in which ethnics are free from race oppression and economic exploitation and free for self-determination. It would be a society in which European-Americans are free from being the oppressors and free to be white—not white

94

overlords and masters—but white as one ethnic entity that comprise the mosaic in the family of God.[13] As long as European-Americans, as a ruling group, dominate and exploit nonwhite peoples, they are not yet white in the sense of being one entity among the many. They are still the oppressor.

A new society can be a liberating one that is conscious of its own history and unique version of oppression. The old society that subordinates an interest in the wealth of a few, with a military that protects its interests, can become a society that is fundamentally interested in the quality of family life and the spiritual and physical welfare of all its people. It can be a society that gives priority to the elimination of structural conditions of poverty, race and sex oppression. This vision of a new society holds that people are not to be used as tools, but are to be valued and loved and enabled to become resourceful human beings capable of fostering relational patterns of love, justice, and forgiveness. This utopian vision must not foster its own tendency toward new forms of domination. It may continue to break every yoke of oppression (Isa. 58:6). This utopian vision points toward a society in which an interest in the liberation of all is the uniting bond.

It has been argued that the human subject participates in a primal source of transcendence and potential transformation. The subject is capable of reflecting upon the social processes that constitute its reality and anticipate future possibilities. The individual can reconstruct his or her experience, enter into it purposefully, and gain a critical perspective on various forms of oppression *because of others*. The collectivity, because of the multiple standpoints implied in its constitution, is the effective source for social structural change and a new society. Within the collectivity, the individual can more effectively act in the interest of transforming the self and its relations in light of new information and new possibilities, and in light of a new image of what the self and the community of persons can achieve. Therapy and social ethics together can be utilized as ways to enable the individual to evolve and become a self-conscious agent in personal and social transformation. Therapies that are not based on an atomized Cartesian view of the self can empower people to help themselves by uncovering repressed sources of a negative self-image and by changing self-defeating activities. This is only one way to liberate the "I" to become more spontaneous. The dialogue of therapy can enable people to see individual action in the social contexts. Ethical action can empower them as moral agents and as members of a community to restructure their priorities and hence their institutions to meet the real needs of the people, thereby enabling society to realize a fuller measure of justice and freedom.[14]

IV.

The Dialogue Called Therapy:
A Black Perspective

*"There is a moral context to all acts of care. We often minimize
the importance of the frameworks of meaning we bring to our care."*
—Don S. Browning
in The Moral Context of Pastoral Care

This chapter reflects upon the experiences of a black therapist
and pastoral counselor. It shall be argued that the color, cultural
background, skills, political interest, and religious faith play
important roles in the dialogue called therapy.[1] These factors
influence the content and the approach to the therapeutic
relationship, whether the patient is white or black.

Once, in a face-to-face encounter, a would-be client told me
that he did not want me as his therapist. He said, "I do not know
any black people. I do not seek out blacks for friends, and I
certainly would not have chosen a black for my therapist!" This
particular client was referred to me by a white therapist who
failed to explore the question of race or racism with him. This
client was unwilling to enter into a therapeutic relationship with
a black therapist, and shortly after meeting me, he terminated
the association. On other occasions I have had potential clients
turn and walk away when they discovered that their therapist
was a black person. The black psychiatrist William Grier wrote:

The therapist's race presents a stimulus from the outset which
evokes a response in the unconscious of the white patient. The
patient may enter into treatment with greater or less alacrity, or

97

may decline treatment altogether, in any case often giving as his reason some anticipated effect of the racial difference.[2]

LaMaurice H. Gardner reports:

Very little has been reported in the literature on the parameters and dynamics of psychotherapeutic interaction when the therapist is black and the client white. There are many reasons for this neglect, perhaps the most significant being that only in recent years have a significant number of blacks become professional psycho-therapists. From the limited literature that exists on the experiences of black therapists in the treatment of white clients, it is clear that the color of the therapist plays an important role in determining the contents of the relationship. Curry (1964) has noted that when the therapist is black, his skin color alone can elicit fantasies and symbolic processes in white clients that may have profound effects on the process of therapy. He suggests that in the treatment of white clients the black therapist will have to deal not only with standard resistance and transference phenomena but also with culturally conditioned resistances stimulated by the fact that he is black.[3]

The other side of the coin is that the black therapist has been consciously sought out because of his blackness and often because of his religious and pastoral identification. Black therapists cannot ignore the culture or social and historical context in which they practice. The context is operative whether the black therapist or client chooses to recognize it or not. There is an emerging body of research literature that focuses attention on the role of race and of the black therapist in therapy.[4]

1.

The dialogue of therapy can be seen as a bi-personal field. It may be described as a two-way interaction, a dialogue, even though the client, his or her history and its meaning for the subject, is the central focus. "Bi-personal field" refers to both the identity of the therapist and the client as significant in the therapeutic dialogue. The background of the individual also plays a significant role in the outcome of therapy, although of course, it is what the client takes the therapist to be, not what he is that is significant at the initial level of the therapeutic relationship. The above exchange between the would-be client and the black therapist implies that the therapist and client who successfully work together are often similar enough in background, values, and social outlook to effect a situation in which therapy may meaningfully take place. Neither therapist nor client enters into the therapeutic relationship value-free. Both occupy a standpoint in the social world and share the capacity to communicate. Together, they effect a curative process.

Therapy, whether individual or group psychotherapy, family systems therapy, group or family group counseling, is usually seen as a therapeutic intervention by a trained therapist into the life processes for the purpose of change, growth, and strengthening of the capacity to love and work effectively with others. However, it has long been recognized that *any communicative context that is characterized by such qualities as openness, accurate and sensitive awareness of the other person's feelings, nonpossessive warmth of deep concern for the person's welfare, without attempting to manipulate or dominate him or her, is therapeutic* and can strengthen the capacity to love.[5] Therapy is a learning or relearning and sometimes an unlearning process. It is concerned with such relational issues as power and justice, as well as the clarification of *inner meaning* for the patient of his or her history and current relationships. The dialogue of therapy can give insight and heighten awareness of one's own self as a resource in healing, and it can strengthen awareness of other people as resources. The salient elements in the dialogue called therapy are described and illustrated below.

Bracketing

A crisis or a problem or a felt and recognized pain in some area of interpersonal relations is what usually causes a person, family, or group to seek therapy. In therapy the assumptive world of the subject is brought into question and under scrutiny for intervention and change. The assumptive world of the individual is the unquestioned, taken-for-granted knowledge and motives that underlie the subject's outlook and interpretation of reality. The crisis or recognized problem throws in doubt the unquestioned and taken-for-granted world of the subject. Something has occurred, or is anticipated, that causes the subject or the family to doubt or to bracket experience and to raise questions about it. The term "bracketing" is borrowed from Alfred Schutz and ultimately from Edmund Husserl. It is a verb, an action word. It implies *conscious activity*. To "put the world in brackets" means to raise it to the level of conscious reflection and to examine critically what has been unquestioned and accepted as self-evident in daily life.[6] The subject is saying in effect, "Something is going wrong or has gone wrong. I do not know what it is, but I (or we) want to take a good hard look and find out more about it and make some changes if it is possible."

By the time the person gets to therapy, he or she has more than likely identified "self" as having the problem. He or she accepted the illness role, i.e., "It is all my fault," or "I caused it to happen; I am to blame." The tendency to self-blame is strong in marital partners undergoing separation or divorce. Children also tend to blame themselves for the breakup of their parents' relationship. Self-blame is especially the case when people are hurting or suffering from a broken relationship which they care about. The resulting frustration, anger, and hurt are often turned inward.

The tendency in psychotherapy and pastoral counseling has been to focus on the meaning the pain has for the subject or family system. This focus is an integral part of effective therapy, but the tendency has been to view the self or family system in isolation from the rest of society rather than in the appropriate context of the web of relations and the social history that underlies it. One of the early tasks in therapy is to view the presenting complaint in terms of its relational context, including the society in which the subject is embedded. This is crucial for the dialogue called therapy.

Reconstruction and Reflection upon the Past

In therapy the individual or family is encouraged to reconstruct past events, to locate one's self in that past, and to recall the connections that have led to the present crisis. The process of reconstruction is not simply a rehash of past events, but rather a bringing of them to light in such a way that alternatives can be seen.

Recalling the past is always selective. Different family members have different versions about what is happening in the family. Each perspective reveals a truth, a small segment of the whole, "the way it looks to me." By returning to the past in the vivid presence of others or another, a person can begin to tap into the unstated or unrecognized dimensions of the present. No single member possesses complete knowledge of the family or of the individual as a totality. Recall is a way to reach back from the vantage point of the present, which permits one to bring forth new insights and interpretations that were not perceived.

> The terms "reflection" and "transformation" are pivotal in this discussion. The former may be defined as the human capacity for taking thought, to stand outside one's own experience and to order that experience by means of reason, recollection, imagination, and anticipation. Logical thought is a form of reflection by which order is imposed upon a problematic situation.[7]

In this sense, the reconstructed past is still a largely untapped reservoir of data that is potentially available to the subject in the dialogue called therapy. Memory of the past, from this perspective, continues to be a powerful dimension of the present as the subject acts toward the future. By reaching back and connecting the past and the present in the dialogue of therapy, people may come to see new things that can inform and liberate them. So reconstruction of the past is not simply a rehash of history; it is a reaching back with a purpose in mind. The purpose is emancipation from debilitating experiences for growth and transformation of the present and future. The process of reconstruction is a bracketing of the past in the vivid present for the sake of charting an alternative future in ways that are more enhancing and more responsive and responsible to self and others.

The past is also a chain to be broken. It contains the repressed fears, the lost objects of desire, and the distortions that play an unrecognized role in the present. The repressed past functions in the service of the present to maintain the status quo. Hence, recall of the past is not only a resource for inner liberation, but it is also a chain to be broken insofar as it serves to adjust the subject to domination and inhibits critical reflection and emancipation. The future need not be an extension of the debilitating past, but a way of visioning new possibilities and generating the hope and courage to act upon new insights in the present. Reconstruction, then, can be a part of a liberating process when awareness of the dialectical relationship between psychological reality and the social context are maintained in the dialogue called therapy.

Listening, Interruption, Interpretation, Resistance

The therapist's own values and use of self is of crucial importance. The therapist may listen to his or her own messages as well as those from the subject. The black therapist must come to terms with his or her own oppression, inner hurt and rage, and status in a white-dominated society. He or she can recognize that the history of black people, in this country, is rooted in servitude and continued oppression and domination. But this history is also marked by a rich tradition of black folk, tutored and untutored, who have suffered and struggled for freedom against seemingly insurmountable odds without surrendering their dignity or integrity. The black therapist, whether recognized or not, is the benefactor of this heritage of struggle and survival of a people. This heritage is a part of his or her social and historical context. Blackness is constitutive of his or her humanity. The black therapist's own work includes recognition of his or her blackness and the way his or her own inner experience, personality, and biography have been shaped by this heritage. It also includes recognition of the resources he or she has used to deal with the dynamics of hostility, rage, self-hatred, and oppression. The black therapist must also have enough insight to recognize his or her own limitations and be resourceful enough to link the subject to other community resources.

The black therapist who is *working through* inner and outer forms of domination may bring to his or her practice an invaluable resource that can enhance the dialogue of therapy. I emphasize the term "working through" because the struggle against insidious forms of race and sex domination continue and assume new form, thereby calling for new and often untried responses. For example,

> Black clients who themselves reject blackness may, through the projection of their own self-hatred, manifest intense overt hostility toward their black therapist. On the other hand, the more militant black client may accuse the black therapist of having sold out to the whiteman, of being incapable of understanding the black experience and of trying to convert blacks to the bourgeois standards and lifestyle of whites.
>
> Black therapists treating black clients must be prepared to experience many of the same tests by blacks that white therapists are put through. Thus it is important that the black therapist come to terms with his own feelings about being black in a society that, at deep unconscious levels, considers blacks dirty, unattractive, primitive and inferior.[8]

The therapist's major task is to listen with empathy to what is being said as well as to what is not being said. This may be achieved through active listening, accurate empathy, clarification of confused messages and distorted self-images and acceptance.

> In every form of psychotherapy several processes go on simultaneously and serially: by listening effectively to what the patient has to say, you may make him feel he has been heard and understood; by summarizing and reformulating what you have heard, you may help him take the first steps toward clarifying and reducing the underlying confusion that complicates his life; finally, by a more objective assessment of his resources and by presenting alternatives, you may help him arrive at a point where he can take action, no longer so helplessly caught in his anxieties and vicitmized by circumstances. These are the essential tasks of both short-term and long-term therapy, in whatever elaborate form it is practiced. Treatment itself is the process through which a patient develops new mental tools so that he can manage his life in a more realistic way, less distorted, less burdened by misinterpretations and repressed emotions.[9]

The therapist listens, interrupts, makes interpretations, for the purpose of directing the subject to areas of unconscious conflicts and to relational or structural issues of which the subject is either unaware or only dimly aware. By interpretation is meant any statement by the therapist that helps connect experience with feelings that had been regarded as separate and distinct or as unrelated to the subject's psychic life. Interpretations help uncover and clarify the unconscious mental processes which underlie the subject's motivation and actions.

> In a preliminary interpretation the analyst may do nothing more than connect one behavior with another ("I notice that you smile when you say that"), but he has an idea that for this patient the smiling and the saying somehow connect in a special way. The analyst surmises that if this is pursued it will probably be seen to have roots deep in the patient's past and touch a pattern of reaction which somehow has a substantial place in the patient's neurotic life. In that respect, "I noticed that you smile when you say that" is already within a larger horizon of interpretation and may even lead to the reconstruction of a major piece of past history.[10]

The therapist's response, "I notice that you smile when . . . ," has the potential for opening up new and unrecognized areas for exploration, thereby enlarging the subject's or family member's capacity for self-critical reflection. An illustration may help clarify some of the material presented here.

One client I saw in therapy was having difficulty valuing other black people and identifying with them, especially black males. He had never met his father; however, he did recall having received a letter from him while serving in the military. His response to his father's letter was indifference: "Why should he write now; he was never around when I needed him." The formative influences in his early life came from the women in his family. He had little contact with other black males as a child.

He married a non-black; he spent most of his life with non-blacks. He did not see any connection, at first, between his feelings of worthlessness and his hostility toward other black people, especially other black males. Through the course of therapy he resisted, initially, my attempts to work with him on the issue of blackness. I raised the issue more directly, "I notice that when you refer to black people you seem to put them down." Slowly he began to raise questions about his own identity as a black person and about his relationship to the black community from which he felt estranged. This began to happen as he became more accepting of himself and more accepting of the identity of his therapist, who conveniently, was both male and black.

It would have been possible to avoid the issue of being black with this client. But in so doing, I, as a black therapist, would have missed a significant opportunity to work with this person on unrecognized sources of self-hatred and inner conflicts highlighted by indifference to his own life and family and by his resistance and negative reference to other blacks.

The issue of self-hatred and the sense of worthlessness in a white and racist society is deeply ingrained in the conscious and unconscious life of black people. From one perspective this black client's self-hatred was normal in a white racist society. The black person who hates himself or herself at the deep level of the unconscious reflects the social and historical context that practices black hatred at every level. In this sense, the subject is only conforming to the dominant cultural pattern in which he or she has been socialized. The task for the dialogue of therapy is to break the inner chains of this internalized form of cultural domination.

Throughout the course of therapy, my client became more self-conscious as a black person and self-critical of his participation in events and relationships in which his deprecation of black people and of himself had been taken for granted. In short, in therapy he was able to bracket his taken-for-granted view of himself and others, which included his sense of worthlessness, and he began to consider some new ways of relating to his life, to his family, and to black people. He took action based upon a new and emerging self-image.

An objective of therapy in the emergence of black conscious selfhood includes acceptance of one's self and others, respect and self-determination, self-initiation, and responsibility for one's own life. This implies affirmation, integration, and transformation of the symbol "blackness," which in this society is still most often used negatively—i.e., the association of blackness with depression, evil and bad luck, sin and death, a character flaw or moral depravity, and so forth. My client was able to reconstruct significant events in his life and to view old patterns in a new light. Through introspection and reconstruction of the past, he was able to reach back and bring into awareness certain relationships that played an unconscious, yet decisive, role in his mental life, current involvements, and social outlook.

Meaning, Integration, and Change

Rarely does psychotherapy transform its recipients into agents of change or revolutionaries. In fact, the therapist is often viewed as a placater, sometimes as an agent of colonization, providing tranquility, while social processes of oppression are strengthened. A therapist such as Franz Fanon, however, would not fit this image of the colonizer.[11] Fanon explained psychic pathology in light of social oppression and the price of liberation. He was aware of their interconnection. Few therapists make the necessary connection between psychic disorders and the oppressive character of social and economic power systems. Conversely, social scientists seldom extend their analyses of social power systems to show the linkage between such power systems and their consequences for individuals in ways that reveal the nature and extent of social oppression and the requirements for their transformation. Fanon wrote:

> Because it [colonization] is a systematic negation of the other person and a furious determination to deny the other person all attributes of humanity, colonialism forces the people it dominates to ask themselves the question constantly: "In reality, who am I?"
> . . .
> The defensive attitudes created by this violent bringing together of the colonized man and the colonial system form themselves into a structure which then reveals the colonized personality. This sensitivity is easily understood if we simply study and are alive to the number and depth of the injuries inflicted upon a native during a single day spent amidst the colonial regime. It must in any case be remembered that a colonized people is not only simply a dominated people. . . .
> Total liberation is that which concerns all sectors of the personality (and social system). . . . This dialectic requirement explains the reticence with which adaptations of colonization and reforms of the facade are met. Independence is not a word which can be used as an exorcism, but an indispensable condition for the existence of men and women who are truly liberated, in other

words who are truly masters of all the material means which make possible the radical transformation of society.[12]

The challenge to the dialogue called therapy is to make further linkages between political interdependence of Third World and oppressed communities, psychic health, and social transformation. Fanon did not live long enough to think through or develop these linkages. In this view therapy has not achieved the implicit emancipatory potential until it helps connect in consciousness the interplay between the biographies of the oppressed, the hegemony of ruling groups in society, and the requirements for structural transformation. Although Fanon's critique raised significant questions, it did not provide a sufficient model for a new and transformed social order, primarily because it tends to ignore the potential transforming power of religious faith among oppressed peoples. We shall return to this point shortly.

2.

When clients or family members have gained insight into their oppression and sufferings, worked through areas of disabling conflict, and feel stronger, it is appropriate to enable them to find meaning through participation in larger networks of change. Often, when it is appropriate, I have suggested reading materials to my clients and identified groups in which they might participate to help confront the systemic and structural sources of the pain that they have come to identify in a personal way. It is also important for the therapist to know when such suggestions are inappropriate.

A former student of mine from the deep South, who attended Holy Cross College in Massachusetts, entered into brief therapy with me during a walkout when the Black Student Union charged the school with racism. I will refer to this student as "Samuel." Samuel had been a conscious victim of racism on several previous occasions. The most vivid was his first day on campus, his first time in a northern city. When Samuel arrived at his dormitory room, his would-be white roommate was already there with his parents. When Samuel appeared in the doorway, he was met with a stunned silence. His white would-be

107

roommate and parents walked out of the room, protesting that he would never have a black for a roommate! Samuel was hurt, bewildered, enraged, and alone.

Two years later, at the time of the black student walkout, Samuel had gained a reputation of "carrying a powerful punch" which he would unleash unexpectedly on white students (and a few black students). He was feared by both white and black students, and he was considered "highly unpredictable" and maybe a little "crazy" when under pressure.[13] He had already been suspended twice for attacking white students. On one occasion, while waiting in a lunch line, Samuel suddenly turned and punched a white student, sending him to the floor. Why? "Because he looked at me funny, like I was strange." A third offense would have led to expulsion from the college. Samuel was already on probation. There was considerable concern among the black students that Samuel might do something "unpredictable" during the walkout and precipitate an escalation of the protest, now in the form of a nonviolent walkout.

I saw Samuel only briefly to establish a clinical picture: to understand his experience of what was happening to him, to help him see how the institutional context was implicated in his situation, and enable him to assume responsibility for completing his education. The basic task was to help him find alternative ways to express his rage without giving up his militant concern for social justice and change. During this time I continued my supportive role as a consultant to the Black Student Union and explored with them ways to involve and work with Samuel. The objective of the black therapist and pastoral counselor was to make a therapeutic intervention that served to clarify for Samuel and certain faculty members, the administration, and the Black Student Union what was going on in the larger context of this walkout, while supporting personal integration within the black student community without weakening the concern for justice and social change.

Several things happened to place me in a working relationship with the black students and the college administration. They may be summarized as follows:

1. The administration, mainly the Jesuit president and vice president of the college, saw clearly the justice issues the black students brought before them, and were sensitive to their

situation. In a real sense, the black students did not walk out on the president and vice president. They were protesting the racism they faced daily in the student body and classroom. They had turned their backs on the system that ignored their reality as black students in a white-dominated environment.

2. In this particular context I, as a black therapist, was in a rather ideal situation to work with black students. Most of the students in the Black Student Union had taken an introductory course on black liberation theologies that I taught and had discussed at length the implication of this for black students at Holy Cross College. Many of the students were Catholic, and an increasing number were becoming Black Muslims. They shared a common faith and interest in liberation, and they dared to believe that the God of justice was on the side of their struggle.

3. My presence in the counseling center was the result of a request from the Black Student Union. Therefore, I had an opportunity to work closely with black students in areas of personal concern as well as on academic issues.

4. There was the black church and pastoral presence, and therefore, the opportunity to help students in their personal faith and direction in life.

My own skills and experience, theoretical understanding of interpersonal and group dynamics, religious faith, and respect for and trust in the black students came together in an effective working relationship. It was not that I possessed a superior wisdom. Rather, a social process had developed over time, so that when the crisis emerged, the rapport and trust to work together had already been established. For all my skill and experience, it would have been to no avail had the community of black folk at Holy Cross not validated me. It was the black community that had entrusted to me and to themselves the gospel of liberation.

Struggling for institutional change became a part of the role expectation of many black college students during the 1960s. Student protest became the way to effect change and a way to place one's school on the map. An assumption was that in order to combat racism and to break through the insularity of academia, forms of disruptive protest were often necessary. By the early 1970s, this communicative style, in the form of disruptive politics, had become a part of the taken-for-granted world view of dissident students. The assumption was: You cannot get what you need through the established channels of discourse.

Samuel shared the outlook of his contemporaries, namely, that much of what happened in academia was irrelevant to the needs of black students and their communities, and that dramatic protest was often necessary to bring about necessary changes. This style of communication became an unquestioned strategy and aspect of the world view of the more militant black student activist. There was, in Samuel's taken-for-granted situation, a presupposed anticipated *ideal situation,* namely, that Samuel and his fellow students could effect meaningful change and bring about a greater degree of justice for black students. It was this anticipated ideal situation that became the norm for guiding self-reflective activity and interest for change. In the therapy there was the latent potential for a reflection process which could emancipate one agent (Samuel) and open him (and them) to new possibilities for action in their particular situation. Hence, the way in which Samuel's situation was framed and interpreted was of crucial importance. He too began to believe that something was the matter with him, i.e., that he was out of control or perhaps, "crazy." Samuel eventually graduated from Holy Cross with a major in physics. At the last report he was employed by a reputable company in the South as a physicist.

Emancipatory struggle must increasingly involve a self-critical dimension, joined with faith in the communicative capacity of humans to create alternative futures. It can involve the self-liberation of persons from a psychology that would entrap them within the distorted perceptions of their own limited perspective. Genuine social emancipation is inseparable from self-emancipation. Both can be a part of the same dialectic in the dialogue of therapy.

Social and self emancipation struggles emerge from the same communicative process that seeks to comprehend and transform what Marx referred to as the material constraints of social relations under capitalism. In a Freudian sense, the task of emancipation is to expose to reason the repressed aspirations toward constructive change and to transform the unconscious motives that would otherwise maintain covert ties to an exploitative system of social relations.

In the ways described above the dialogue of therapy can be understood as an intervention into an oppressive situation which seeks to do several things:

1. Bracket the unquestioned and taken-for-granted world of experience and clarify the individual's, family's, or group's context (as in the case of Samuel and the Black Student Union).

2. Enable the person or family to reflect upon and reconstruct past events in ways that bring the meaning of the past into a working relationship with the present and future. In addition, therapy can help the individual, family, or groups *do* something constructive about the conditions that oppress them, and thereby they can become agents in the liberation and healing of others.

3. Heighten a person's sense of self as a member of a community (and the community's consciousness of the importance of each member) where other perspectives are available for the person's and the community's enlargement, enrichment, and critical reflection.

4. Chart alternative possibilities.

5. Enlarge and free the person's or family's capacity for creative change and meaningful participation in a larger community context in light of a new image and a new whole.

In the dialogue called therapy, new self-understandings and symbolizations can be called forth which enable commitment and action to an open future and a just society.

V.

Christian Social Ethics:
A Black Liberation Perspective

"This, then, is the great humanistic and historical task of the oppressed: to liberate themselves and their oppressors as well."
—*Paulo Freire*
in *Pedagogy of the Oppressed*

"You are like salt for all mankind. But if salt loses its taste, there is no way to make it salty again. . . .
"You are like light for the whole world."
—*Matthew 5:13a, 14a (TEV)*

This chapter is not intended as a thorough examination of Christian ethical questions. It is not even intended as a survey of the entire field of Christian ethical questions or of Christian social ethics. Rather, the purpose is to *identify the standpoint of a black Christian liberation ethic from a particular relational perspective.* Christian liberation ethics is concerned with the transformation of social structures of oppression, the emancipation of poor and oppressed peoples, and the emergence of responsible selves in a liberating society. According to J. Deotis Roberts, "Liberation ethics as well as liberation theology is rooted in an experience of oppression in which a group of people suffer; their suffering may be based upon class, sex, or race. A liberation ethic emerging out of the black experience must be an ardent and uncompromising foe of racism."[1] The ethical task is seen not simply from a "relational" (H. R. Niebuhr) point of view, but precisely from a black liberation theology perspective that issues in a specific relational standpoint. I will briefly reflect upon the

112

ethical position of Joseph Fletcher, H. Richard Niebuhr, and John Swomley, Jr., before identifying the relational perspective of a black Christian liberation ethic. An assessment of the critical ethical problems of violence and non-violence as strategies for revolutionary change, important as they are, will not be taken up at this time.

The purpose, then, is to give a brief description of the task of a black Christian liberation ethic from a specific relational perspective.

1.

Christian ethics may be viewed as rational activity or philosophical inquiry into the rules and principles of morality, of right and wrong conduct, of good and evil as they pertain to the beliefs and practices of the Christian faith in obedience to the will of God. Within the traditions of Western philosophy, ethics has generally meant rational activity or disciplined reflection. It has tended to focus on abstract moral rules and moral justification for determining right and wrong and the good for people. Moral rules have often been abstracted from their concrete social and historical context and have been lifted to the level of theory to serve as normative complements which in turn were deemed universally applicable. Fredrick S. Carney, for example, says this about virtue theory in Christian ethics:

> The moral notion of virtue performs two fundamental functions in theological ethics. First, it indicates the kind of person who is to be rightly considered good, just, faithful, loving, holy, and so forth. As such, it provides both a normative complement to a merely descriptive account of human nature and an ideal of human personhood at which to aim. Second, the notion of virtue offers an alternative to notions of obligation for the discernment of the morality of human acts. It does this not by seeking what is required by some principle or rule obligation, but by inquiring what characteristics or qualities (such as faithfulness, fairness, a loving disposition, and so forth) constitute the goodness of a person, and by designating those acts to be good (or bad) to the extent that they are appropriate to the model of a good (or bad) person.[2]

In the light of this quotation, Christian ethics has its locus in the rational, i.e. thinking, activity of the ethicist rather than in the social-political context where thought is embedded. In this view rules and principles are abstracted from their social and historical context and become the guide for judging and justifying right and wrong. The social context of the ethicist is often ignored as a necessary component of ethical analysis and reflection in this perspective.

By contrast, *Christian situation ethics* seeks to take seriously the social context where decisions are made by applying love or agape as the norm for conduct in each situation. Here love is the highest norm of human action. This is often expressed as doing for the neighbor what love requires, or promoting the good of the neighbor. Joseph Fletcher is the name most commonly associated with situation ethics in the United States. According to Fletcher, "Christian action should be tailored to fit objective circumstances, the situation." Fletcher continues:

> Christian situation ethics has only one norm or principle or law (call it what you will) that is binding and unexceptionable, always good and right regardless of the circumstances. That is "love"—the *agape* of the summary commandment to love God and the neighbor. Everything else without exception, all laws and rules and principles and ideals and norms, are contingent, only valid if they happen to serve love in any situation.[3]

Situation ethics accordingly breaks with the approach to ethics as preconceived rules or principles of right and wrong or as universally binding. The only exception to this is the norm of love. The emphasis is upon the situation. The situation determines the rightness or wrongness of an act. Judgments of right and wrong are relative to the contexts in which actions take place. "Thus it is possible to say that ordinarily it is right to tell the truth, yet in some situations it would be wrong if telling the truth, on balance, had 'unloving' (i.e., bad) consequences."[4] Situation ethics makes individual freedom and personal responsibility and the social context the important determinants of right and wrong. While situation ethics seeks to address the particular social context, it ignores the larger historical context and the systemic character of injustice such as race, sex, or class oppression. The historical context and the systemic nature of injustice are central concerns for a black Christian liberation ethic in a relational perspective.

A relational ethics and responsibility ethics are associated with

H. Richard Niebuhr, among others. In *The Responsible Self*, Niebuhr developed the concept of *responsibility* into a unified and central principle in his ethical system.[5] His work can be seen as an alternative to teleological and deontological ethics. Our task here is not to spell out Niebuhr's entire ethical system, but rather to identify his concept of relationality and responsibility as expressing a fundamental datum about the relationship between God, the multiplicity of human response, and the moral constitution of the subject for community. Here the human subject is interpreted as a *relational self*, a self that comes to exist in response to other selves and in response to the radical action of God. Response and responsibility are the symbols Niebuhr uses to speak about the self in its relational existence.[6] According to Niebuhr, "Our action is responsible, it appears, when it is response to action upon us in a continuing discourse or interaction among beings forming a continuing society." Niebuhr goes on to say, "The idea or pattern of responsibility, then, may summarily and abstractly be defined as the idea of an agent's action as response to an action upon him in accordance with his interpretation of the latter action and with his expectation of response to his response; and all of this within a continuing community of agents."[7] According to Niebuhr, God is the ultimate one who confronts us in the many finite actions upon us. The task of Christian social ethics, then, is to respond in faith and obedience to the one ultimate action of God in all the many responses to finite action.

While Niebuhr stressed relationality, he did not apply his concept of the responsible and relational self to an analysis of systemic injustice and to an interpretation of the freedom struggles of poor, black, and oppressed peoples. Relationality and liberation ethics were not linked in his ethical system. John M. Swomley, Jr., on the other hand, identified liberation ethics as activity that continuously seeks the fundamental transformation of society and the replacement of systems of violence through non-violent revolutionary measures. A link between relationality and liberation ethics can be found in Swomley's *Liberation Ethics*. Swomley argues that genuine liberation must seek the emancipation and humanization of the whole society and not a limited segment of it. "Liberation ethics holds that the goal of history is the liberation of man." The accent is on transforming systems and structures of violence such as monopoly capitalism, racism, and poverty, rather than on individual decision making in face-to-face relationships. According to Swomley, "Liberation is an impossible goal so long as men seek freedom for their own group at the expense of others." The true test of emancipatory struggle is whether or not the poor and powerless and the oppressed are being set free from domination and free for self-determination. Swomley suggests that liberation ethics is concerned with the transformation of entire social systems and the emancipation of various oppressed groups from powerlessness and from the common structures which enslave people, deny them fundamental respect as human beings, and restrict their opportunity for self-determination. Swomley argues that the goal of liberation is inclusion in the beloved community where no one is a slave or a second-class citizen. Love and respect of persons rather than the possession and control of people must become the motivating force in a new liberating society. The evil that results from the possession of persons is not only rooted in social systems and structures of dominance, it is also located in human sinfulness or finitude. The stride toward freedom then must always address these interrelated sources of human enslavement—individual *and* systemic. "Liberation ethics recognizes the great power of evil in the world and in ourselves and therefore acknowledges that there is no easy strategy to make men happy or to set them free."[8] Swomley continues:

> Everyone is to some degree corrupted by sin, which is the acceptance or willing of such unfreedom. Liberation ethics does not accent the transformation of systems on the ground that new men free from sin will emerge. That is a Marxist error which asserts that a particular organization of society will make perfect human beings.

Since no current operating society, whether capitalist or socialist, embodies this liberating ideal, emancipation of whole societies must be seen as a continuous struggle, a progressive revolution, and the responsibility of all persons—especially those who are committed to human freedom and dignity.

> The goal of liberation ethics is community rather than any particular political or economic system. By community is meant a

116

unity of persons around the idea that each is important enough to be respected and loved by all. It means that I want every other person to be as free and as loved as I want to be. Liberation then, implies a quality of life that asserts the importance and worth of persons in such a way that they are free from poverty, from control by more powerful interests, from superstition, fear, hostility, or from anything that enslaves them.[9]

To summarize, liberation ethics is rooted in revolutionary praxis. It is concerned with transforming systemic injustices and the conditions which oppress people. It seeks to free oppressed people for action which will result in a humanized and just social order. Swomley views liberation ethics as social and political engagement which aims to abolish the situation of oppression through non-violent measures. However, he does not identify his position as a uniquely *Christian* liberation ethic. There is no attempt here to posit the Covenant and the biblical God's identification with the oppressed as a primary datum in liberation struggles. A black Christian liberation ethic takes divine liberation as its point of departure. The central starting point for liberation ethics in a black Christian perspective is the emancipatory activity of God which always requires justice for the poor and the oppressed—"the least of these."

"The kind of fasting I want is this: Remove the chains of oppression and the yoke of injustice, and let the oppressed go free. Share your food with the hungry and open your homes to the homeless poor. Give clothes to those who have nothing to wear, and do not refuse to help your own relatives.

"Then my favor will shine on you like the morning sun, and your wounds will be quickly healed. I will always be with you to save you; my presence will protect you on every side. When you call to me, I will respond." (Isa. 58:6-9 TEV)

To "remove the chains of oppression and the yoke of injustice" is inseparable from participation in divine liberation. To participate in divine liberation is more than a social or ethical imperative (i.e., "remove the chains of oppression"), it is the condition of a promise: "Then my favor will shine on you like the morning sun, and your wounds will be quickly healed." Divine liberation is central to a black Christian liberation ethic whereas it is not necessarily central to Swomley's liberation ethics.

2.

The starting point for a Christian ethical analysis in a black liberation perspective is the social and historical context of black oppression and the freedom struggles of black people within the framework of the Christian message. A Christian ethic of black liberation takes the liberating acts of God in Jesus and the experience of black suffering and oppression under the domination of white racism as the starting point for critical reflection and praxis. The task of a black Christian liberation ethic is to expose the system of white injustice and to radically change the systemic character of human exploitation by seeking the transfomation of society and by creating a new and more humane world. This task is at the heart of the gospel of Jesus: "To bring good news to the poor . . . to proclaim liberty to the captives and recovery of sight to the blind, to set free the oppressed and announce that the time has come when the Lord will save his people" (Luke 4:18-19). To state it differently, the task of Christian social ethics from a black liberation perspective is to critically reflect upon the ethos (i.e., the moral outlook, interactions, language and symbols, and convictions of a Christian people) and upon the normative patterns of domination (i.e., the institutionalized social power arrangements) of a society in which that people exists, in light of the gospel of Jesus. Now for some, this may be too narrow a basis for Christian social ethics. But from the perspective of the black church tradition, the gospel of Jesus is pivotal. From this perspective, it is the gospel of Jesus that judges the adequacy of ethical reflection and praxis, and not ethical reflection that judges the adequacy of the gospel. The figure of Jesus as the servant human being who suffers with the least of the disinherited and identifies with the freedom struggles of oppressed peoples is essential to an understanding of the ethical and moral stance of the black church community and its role in liberation struggles.

Ethicist Enoch H. Oglesby argued that black religious ethics expresses the *soul* of the black experience. He defines "black religious ethics as a socio-political ethic of liberation, which aims, objectively, at changing the condition of oppression and sees God's will as congruent with the solidarity of the dispossessed." At the heart of a black Christian liberation ethics is the moral conviction that God cares for the widow and widower, the poor and downtrodden in the land; that God has promised to deliver them and to be their God. Oglesby goes on to say, "For Blacks, this means in part that we must begin to understand and interpret the norms and radical imperatives in the Christian faith from a different theological posture."[10] Black Christian liberation ethics derives its moral mandate from its understanding that God has identified with men, women, and children in their oppression, and that they too must do no less than care about what happens to the poor and oppressed. Their ethical direction and moral vision for today may be informed by critical reflection upon their current political responsibilities and their social and historical roots.

3.

The black Christian community in the United States evolved its ethic in the crucible of brutal slavery and unmerited suffering. From the beginning, Christian ethics in the black slave community was a social or communal ethic—an ethic that emerged from the collective experience of a suffering people. Christian social ethics in the black experience did not develop as an ahistorical, philosophical ethic based upon an abstract individualism. It was an ethic that emerged out of the concrete experience of a suffering people who sought to remain faithful to God as they moved toward the goal of freedom. It has evolved from *three centuries* of systematic effort to deny black Americans their history and humanity. It was an ethic that pointed beyond their captivity to the beloved community. It was a biblical ethic that permitted them to judge the moral life of the nation from the vantage point of God's righteousness and concern for them. Their moral vision enabled them to see with clarity that their enslavement contradicted the divine will. Historian Eugene D. Genovese wrote:

> An old preacher, who had been a slave in South Carolina, remarked, "Brother, you has to have faith in your fellow man befo' you has faith in de lawd." The spirituals vibrated with the message: God will deliver us if we have faith in Him. And they emphasized the idea of collective deliverance of the slaves as a people by their choice of such heroes as Moses, Jonah, and Daniel.[11]

Faith in God and faith and love for one another went together and were inseparable from collective deliverance.

> Oh, walk togedder, children, don't you get weary
> walk togedder, children, don't you get weary,
> Oh, walk togedder, children, don't you get weary,
> Dere's a great camp meetin' in de promised land.[12]

The social and historical context for black Christian ethical reflection is rooted in the awareness that God sees, hears, knows the oppression of black people and that God has freely chosen to act on their behalf. The oppressors were blind to the central message to walk humbly, to do justice, and to love mercy. They failed to practice the righteousness that faith in God requires. The black moral imperative today continues to be what it was then, liberation of the oppressed from physical and spiritual bondage to the false gods of materialism and human arrogance.

In summary, critical ethical reflection in the black community rightly has its starting place with God's claim upon and identification with the liberation interest of the dispossessed. The starting place and hope for black Christian ethical reflection today may continue to be rooted in an awareness of God's active love and concern for the disinherited and known in the Scriptures and community of faith. Reflecting upon the meaning of his own life and work, the murdered civil rights leader, Martin Luther King, Jr., was able to write in his final published statement:

People are often surprised to learn that I am an optimist. They know how often I have been jailed, how frequently the days and nights have been filled with frustration and sorrow, how bitter and dangerous are my adversaries. They expect these experiences to harden me into a grim and desperate man. They fail, however, to perceive the sense of affirmation generated by the challenge of embracing struggle and surmounting obstacles. They have no comprehension of the strength that comes from faith in God and man. It is possible for me to falter, but I am profoundly secure in my knowledge that God loves us. He has not worked out a design for our failure. Man has the capacity to do right as well as wrong, and his history is a path upward, not downward. The past is strewn with the ruins of the empires of tyranny, and each is a monument not merely to man's blunders but to his capacity to overcome them. While it is a bitter fact that in America in 1968, I am denied equality solely because I am black, yet I am not a chattel slave. Millions of people have fought thousands of battles to enlarge my freedom: restricted as it still is, progress has been made. This is why I remain an optimist, though I am also a realist, about the barriers before us.

The biblical God and his active concern to deliver the oppressed of the earth was the central theme that traditionally guided ethical reflection in black Christian communities seeking liberation. From a Christian perspective, the life, death, and resurrection of Jesus is the ground and hope of a suffering, yet struggling black humanity. Christian social ethics, from a black liberation standpoint, is an ethic of involvement and is derived from the activity of God. It is an ethic of involvement that seeks to be faithful to God's emancipatory activity, that is, an ethic that seeks solidarity with the oppressed and their liberation from historical bondage, as well as ultimate salvation.

4.

Black slaves struggled not only to free themselves from bondage, but also to free the soul of America. The sense that liberation is relational has been part and parcel of a black Christian liberation ethics in this country. Black bondage reflects the nation's moral and spiritual captivity to an exploitative system of productive relations.

Today, black Americans and black churches are at a moral crossroad, situated somewhere between their historic past and the elusive goal of full justice and freedom. They proceed toward the twenty-first century more diversified and less unified on their objectives and less certain about a common role in creating a new society.

The active involvement of the black church in issues of social justice has been less visible since the assassination of Martin Luther King, Jr., in 1968. Many ministers perceive a lessening of commitment to issues of social justice on the part of black ministers and churches. Not all ministers and black congregations shared Dr. King's understanding of ministry or his ethical commitment to the oppressed and to victims of racial and economic injustice. Black churches have sometimes understood their mission in very different terms. Many are inwardly oriented and emphasize exclusively the call to personal salvation as the *raison d'etre* of the black church and of all churches that proclaim the lordship of Jesus Christ. In this latter view of the church's mission, social issues that plague the black community, such as crime, economic deprivation and poverty, unemployment, congested housing, poor transportation, inadequate health care, police brutality, inadequate education, unequal justice before the law, and so forth, are often divorced from the biblical understanding of Christian responsibility and freedom as freedom for others. Melvin G. Talbert asked rhetorically:

> What do I see ahead for us in these times? I see apathy, indifference, immorality, and a move to avoid involvement in the issues of social repression. I see a move to escape reality. Even though this move is most prevalent in white churches, there are signs of it in our black churches. Of course, you and I know that many black churches never joined the movement for liberation and justice for blacks. But in some of those who did join, I sense a move toward that kind of spirituality which, in effect, means disengagement from the struggle for human survival.[13]

A black church ethic that actively seeks the interconnection between social structural transformation and the liberating gospel of Jesus Christ is a minority position.

Such an ethic would seek to give meaning to the hope expressed by the late Martin Luther King, Jr., namely, that black Americans would continue to be a transforming presence and that they would someday become "a bridge between white civilization and the nonwhite nations of the world, because we have roots in both. Jesus of Nazareth," he went on to say,

> had no friends in the courts of the powerful. But he changed the course of mankind with only the poor and the despised. Naive and unsophisticated though we may be, the poor and despised of the 20th Century will revolutionize this era. In our "arrogance, lowlessness and ingratitude," we will fight for human justice, brotherhood, secure peace and abundance for all.

The gospel becomes *good news* in desperate circumstances when the poor hear that God is concerned about them now; when broken hearts are healed; when captives are set at liberty and released from oppression (external and internal), and when the blind are able to see. The proclamation of the acceptable year of the Lord must find concrete expression in the present, if the poor and captives of our time are to hear the gospel as "good news."

Many black and white churches do not share this outlook and have adjusted their moral vision to fit within the limited horizon of material capitalism and bourgeois interest, served by class and sex oppression. On one hand, the contemporary black church has tended to reflect the dominant strand within white American Christianity and has been charged with aiding and abetting a system of exploitation. Whether intended or not, many black churches have isolated themselves within the black community. It has often been charged with abandoning its ethical and liberation commitment to the poor and downtrodden. In their turn, the dispossessed have left a church which they perceive has abandoned their hopes. The black church is often assailed for failure to provide leadership and to be a prophetic voice judging a social and economic system that holds its people captive to social oppression, to materialism, and to individualistic values. Joseph Washington asked, "Do black churches have institutional power and authority?"

> If they have, it is by and large squandered without any real serious economic, political, and social impact. It is incumbent upon the black church to discover what its ministry, indeed, its special ministry has to be. When this discovery has been made then it is incumbent upon the black church to see that that ministry takes place wherever black people are. Institutional life needs to be concerned about black people in large urban areas, suburban areas, small towns, and villages. It needs to be concerned about affluent and poverty-stricken Blacks, status-seeking and status-denied Blacks, middle-class and middle-class aspiring Blacks, Blacks who attend church and those who do not. To make any kind of an impact upon Blacks throughout the community at all levels will require institutional power as well as moral discernment, but an institutional power that is efficiently mobilized and directed.[14]

On the other hand, the black church continues to be inseparable from the black community, even when it has isolated itself or limited its ministry within the community. It is still the institution, beyond the black family, where ethical principles are taught and practiced, and a message of emancipation is proclaimed. The central leadership position of the black church in the lives of black people is weakened and compromised as the black intelligentsia, black youth and middle and upper income blacks become marginal to the black church and the struggles of the oppressed. Some of these groups have tended to disassociate themselves from this historic black institution. Others have abandoned the struggle for liberation of the oppressed, as they become more identified with the prevailing ideology of material capitalism. The moral dilemma facing a black Christian social ethics of liberation is one that faces the whole black community and the society. No one segment of the black community can shoulder the entire blame or solve the dilemma alone. The key lies in collective and cooperative action. The Black Theology Project, which met in Atlanta, succinctly states the problem of ethical disengagement.

> We are concerned also about people whose desperation is not abject material poverty but poverty of soul and spirit. We do not believe that better jobs and bigger houses, color televisions and latest model cars prove that people have attained the abundant life of which Jesus spoke. That abundant life cannot be experienced by a people captive to the idolatry of a sensate and materialistic culture.
>
> We abhor the capitulation of some of our people to values based on the assumptions that things make for security and that distance from the distressed masses makes for a trustworthy barricade against the racism that holds us all in contempt. Commitment to physical gratification as the purpose of life and voidance of the gospel's moral, ethical standards provide false foundations for hard choices. Such false values divide and separate a people who would be free.
>
> The identification of black liberation with the material success of a few, physically and mentally severed from the black masses, makes mockery of the unity essential for the salvation of us all. Even the material good fortune of that few is poisoned by emptiness and isolation from the people's struggle without which the mission of Jesus Christ can be neither understood nor undertaken.[15]

In a perceptive analysis of the current crisis facing blacks and American society, Howard Dodson forcefully expressed the view that even if black people are outside or marginal to the American mainstream, they are not immune to the same moral confusion and false consciousness that characterize life in this society. Dodson recognized that the central leadership position of the black church in the black community, the Civil Rights and Black Power Movements of the past three decades which guided an emancipatory interest, is now in complete disarray. He does not attempt to design an agenda for *ultimate* liberation. He is wise to call black Americans to engage in critical reflection upon their current situation in light of their historical past. He is prophetic in continuing the search for a new society, a new subject, and a new collective will. Dodson wrote:

> The task of creating the new society we seek to build in America will require that Blacks be willing to struggle, first, against the enemy within ourselves, our own individualism and our own political irresponsibility, our own victim mentality and our own reluctance to live up to our fullest potential as human beings—allowing us willingly to accept rather than avoid the challenge and the historic necessity to transform American society for the mutual benefit of everyone.

He goes on to pose the questions that ought to be a central ethical question for the black church and community.

> Those who decide to commit themselves to such struggle must then begin raising the question, "What kind of human society do we want here in America?" We must take certain terms that I have used like racism, capitalism and imperialism and try to understand for ourselves what they have actually meant in the development of the structures of American society, and how they have impacted the lives of the people who live in America and around the world. Then, we must begin the process of determining what the alternatives should be.[16]

The questions imply that black Americans, and especially the black church, have a mission consistent with its historic role to transform an exploitative and dehumanizing system of domination and to help create a new and liberating society.

5.

A black Christian liberation ethic is concerned with the central issue of divine liberation and the corresponding questions: What morally ought to be done to effect the liberation of the poor and the oppressed? What virtues, expressions, and attitudes are most commendable to this task? What characterizes

125

the transformed and liberating society? This particular framing of the task of ethics differs from the traditional approach to ethics in that it reflects upon the meaning of black oppression and suffering and the liberation of the oppressed in light of Scripture. Thus it differs from normative ethics which include theoretical reflection on three types of ethical issues: *action* or obligation (what morally ought to be done), *character* or virtue (what qualities or dispositions of a person are commendable or reprehensible), and *values* or goal or ends of human life (what objects or states of affairs are good or bad). A Christian ethic of black liberation has its locus in Scripture, the emancipatory activity of God and the freedom struggles of oppressed peoples. It is an ethic of involvement and searches in hope for a new subject constituted in relationship with others, in freedom and responsibility, and in a new and transformed society.

Doing ethics usually means disciplined reflection. Within a black Christian liberation perspective the doing of ethics includes direct social action designed to transform oppression and then to step back and reflect on that action. The difference between the traditional way of doing ethics and ethics done from a liberation perspective is that the former is understood as disciplined or theoretical reflection while the latter stresses the importance of direct involvement with the oppressed in liberation struggles. The struggle for liberation is the context for reflection. Liberation ethics always involves the language of transformation or praxis. *Praxis* is the Greek term for practice. It sometimes means "action" or "doing." *Praxis is* not the telos of activity, but rather *the act of performing the particular activity.* It means exercising a direct influence on social existence for the purpose of transforming it.[17]

Paulo Freire in *Pedagogy of the Oppressed* emphasizes the importance of keeping together action and reflection. They cannot be separated in liberation struggles. The only true language, he suggests, is transforming language. "Within the word we find two dimensions, reflection and action, in such radical interaction that if one is sacrificed—even in part—the other immediately suffers. There is no true word that is not at the same time a praxis. Thus, to speak a true word is to transform the world." Thought and action must go together if true liberation is to be realized. Action and reflection together and motivated by agape can result in a liberation praxis. When action is separated from reflection or when reflection is unrelated to action then action alone or reflection alone are unable to get a critical hold on the context of oppression and domination. Love, Freire suggests, is the motivating force underlying the unity of action and reflection. Together a true transforming dialogue is possible.

> Love is at the same time the foundation of dialogue and dialogue itself. It is thus necessarily the task of responsible Subjects and cannot exist in a relation of domination. Domination reveals the pathology of love: sadism in the dominator and masochism in the dominated. Because love is an act of courage, not of fear, love is commitment to other men. No matter where the oppressed are found, the act of love is commitment to their cause—the cause of liberation.[18]

Divine love and liberation ought to be the motivating factor for Christians. It underlies a genuine liberation praxis. The black church, as a servant church in-the-world, must be concerned about the poor and the disinherited everywhere who suffer from racism, sexism, classism, and age oppression, and other forms of exploitation.

In light of the above analysis, I briefly describe the praxis of a black Christian liberation ethic as follows. The three important elements that comprise the praxis of a black Christian liberation ethic are: action, reflection, and post-critical reflection. Figure 1 on page 128 characterizes the praxis of a black Christian liberation ethic as a three-legged stool.

This model for doing ethics is derived from the relational paradigm introduced earlier. It has a relevance for the black community, both churched and unchurched. It has been suggested that historically, the ethical question facing the black community takes a communal form, What ought *we* to do and be in response to God's liberating acts in Jesus? The question includes the question of personal responsibility and is guided by an interest in a transformed and liberating community. The "I" question is implied in the communal question. Personal morality is constituted through the web of dynamic relations, and the web is creative of the common moral life of the community. The web here stands for the unity, the interrelatedness and interdependence of human life. The web is the ever-present and inescapable structure within life itself.[19] Personal morality and individual reality are embedded in, and continue to emerge from, the web of dynamic relations which constitute it. In Boesak's proverbial words, "One is only human because of others, with others, for others."[20]

Figure 1

A black Christian liberation ethic
A Relational Approach

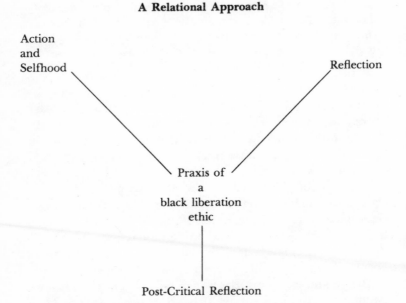

Action
and
Selfhood   Reflection

Praxis of
a
black liberation
ethic

Post-Critical Reflection

Action and Selfhood. The questions to be raised are, What course of action, or strategies, or options should the black community pursue? What ought we to be in American society and in the international community? These questions are ones of survival, but survival for what ends and on whose terms? They imply that what black people think and do is of utmost importance. The survival of the nation is dependent, in part, on the moral vision and leadership of black people and the contribution that they make to the web of life.

Ironically, this very black community is confronted with the question of survival on a daily basis as it faces a society that continues to count it among its chief victims; a society that still regards blacks as a disposable people. Counteraction in response to action that has been initiated against them continues to be a necessary starting point for ethical reflection in the black community. Because of this, the black community is sometimes perceived as *a community on the rebound,* responding to problems that are endemic to a system of economic exploitation and served by race and sex oppression. The social and historical context of black Americans recommends the view of being on the rebound. For example, black Americans have been among the main victims of white American racism, but they are not the only victims. They did not create the problem of race genocide and race hatred in the United States, but major responsibility for confronting and correcting the problem of American racism has fallen to them. It is well known that the influence of black protest and movements for change have often benefited other oppressed groups in United States society. In the eighteenth and nineteenth centuries, black church men and women, boys and girls were in the forefront of the struggle for freedom from the white domination. In the middle decade of the twentieth century, Martin Luther King, Jr.'s, civil rights activities were forged against entrenched racism in the South and against intransigent power in the North, as dramatized in Cicero and Mayor Daley's Chicago.

Moreover, black theologies of "liberation" emerged as a response to white power and black victimization. In a certain sense, the dilemmas and failure of white morality to create justice have served to shape the ethical question with which black Americans have struggled and must help solve. Historian Douglas Henry Daniels contends race prejudice is frequently perceived as the causal agent behind the social activist concerns of black people. But race prejudice is only one among many variables influencing black concern for social justice. When race prejudice is perceived as the primary causal agent, then black people are construed as passive subjects, incapable of initiating creative action of their own. "But when we view discrimination as one variable among many—one that stimulates humanitarian sentiments in a highly individualistic and competitive society, we add a significant dimension to the lives of anonymous

129

urbanites."[21] It is against this background that the question of action is raised for ethical discernment. On one hand, there is *defensive action* as the community of the oppressed responds directly and indirectly to systemic and moral problems that are endemic to "the American way of life." On the other hand, there is the question of *social transformation* and the creation of new and just social structures. It is this later question that poses the real challenge to action for a black Christian liberation ethic from a relational perspective. As the community acts, so it creates its common life and charts its future. Action that is life enhancing, rather than life denying, is the specific challenge to and concern of black Christian liberation ethics and praxis.

Reflection and Praxis. Reflection is a way of bracketing the past; bringing it forward for constructive examination and reinterpretation in light of certain goals or ideals. Reflection provides an opportunity for structuring alternative possibilities. This is something that cannot be accomplished in the heat of action. Action emerges out of previous moments of reflection and novel responses to oppression and pressure. But people usually do not know what the action means until they have had a chance to step aside, so to speak, and critically reflect upon the social act. Reflection provides a distancing, an opportunity to see and know the meaning of what has been done, and provides an opportunity to think about what the community ought to do next.

Reflection upon action taken is an integral part of the ethical task. God's continued activity in society; Scripture, tradition, the situation, and the moral claims of oppressed communities today significantly informs the black Christian community about its task and future direction. Reflection, in the consciousness and activity of oppressed people, will bracket the world of everyday life and will subject to critical reflection the action they have just taken. Reflection is a way of stepping aside to see more clearly what has been done to evaluate it before deciding what to do next.

Post-Critical Reflection. Reflection is itself an activity. In post-critical reflection the community questions the process by which questions and modes of actions arise and become important in the first place. An illustration may help. In systems thinking, the thermostat in a room is set at 72° (the action taken).

Whenever the temperature falls below 72°, the thermostat is activated (through a feedback mechanism) to correct the deviation and to bring the temperature back up to 72°. The feedback loop is like the reflective process. It is necessary to detect what is wrong in the system of action and to bring the system back to its optimal functioning level. The system itself, and the level of 72°, is assumed and not questioned. Action and reflection are both necessary for the realization of certain ideals. But post-critical reflection raises the question, Why 72°?

Post-critical reflection not only examines the given ethos of a society, but it also becomes self-conscious by subjecting its own approach and goals to critical analysis. This is made possible in dialogue with others who occupy a different standpoint from one's own. For example, some black theologians have recognized the importance of establishing dialogue with other victims of oppression within the United States and in the international community. As a result of this more complex level of interaction and exchange of viewpoints, they are able to ask new questions, to enlarge their vision and to discern God's image struggling to be free in oppressed peoples from different backgrounds. They have been able to view the workings of this society from a new and enlarged vantage point, to bring this added dimension to reflection, and to better inform the nature of freedom struggles in this country. Theologian James H. Cone provides the concrete illustration.

> When black theologians and church people have encountered persons born in Asia and who presently live and work on that continent, usually it has been in the context of the World Council of Churches with an ecumenical agenda not related to the unique concerns of Asians and black Americans. Because of our difference in cultural origins and the large geographical distance that separates us, the assumption has been that Asians and blacks do not have much in common with each other.[22]

Cone asked the question, "What has an essentially black, racial struggle for justice in North America to do with an Asian struggle for full humanity in the context of immense poverty and the perpetual dehumanizing effects of European colonialism?" As a result of his experiences in Japan and Korea in May of 1975, Professor Cone was able to write, "The language and other cultural barriers were transcended through a mutual openness to each other's struggles, and through a common recognition that the universalism in the gospel is found in God's will to liberate all oppressed people from the shackles of human bondage." He goes on to say,

> In this small community of Korean Christians, I knew that I had much to learn which would confirm my theological conviction about liberation and also compel me to relate liberation to a larger cultural and political context than my present focus on black Americans. . . . In the context of living, talking, and being with these Korean Christians, Gustavo Gutierrez's reference to theology as the "second step" was reinforced in my theological consciousness. The first step is the political commitment on behalf of the poor and weak in society. The Korean Christians I met in May 1975 had taken the first step, and they have paid a heavy price.[23]

Professor Cone had also taken the "first step." The first step is the act of common recognition. It is the act of seeing one's own struggles in others. Through this experience Professor Cone was able to extend his awareness and gain a stature of mind more adequate to the monumental challenges that confront oppressed people.

The women's movement in this country has played a similar role to black liberation theologies and to a black church not yet sufficiently conscious of the ways in which it has aided in the oppression of women. Black women and feminist theologians have posed questions for black theology and for a black Christian liberation ethic that were not asked before, and which cannot be ignored now, if the black church is to continue to be the custodial institution providing a moral vision for black people. Through mutual recognition of the common thread of oppression, it becomes possible to transcend the determinations of our own standpoint and to consider ethical alternatives which are obscure to us because our reflection is linked with action that functioned in the service of the status quo.

The above statements parallel the dialogue called therapy. Often, the therapist can offer an interpretation that is not seen or considered by the subject, but has the potential for genuine liberation. Interpretations by an outside agent may have a significant impact on the subject and his or her context. The point is that post-critical reflection is *reflection upon the nature of reflection*. Post-critical reflection requires openness and courage to recognize and face what may be painful. It was James Baldwin who said something to the effect that not everything that is faced can be changed, but nothing can be changed until it is faced. Post-critical reflection can provide a radical self-critical dimension necessary for a community to break free from its own tendencies toward self-incarceration.

The question of a Christian liberation ethics from a black perspective centers in how the guiding institutions and leadership within the black community can become self-conscious, self-affirming, and self-critical. Can the black community effect emancipation from within and from without, and become self-surpassing in the interest of creating a just society? Perhaps these questions can never be fully "answered," but they must become directional. The black community may still become a creative force for justice if it can realize the ideal of the "we-relation" in a more generalized international community and as the black North American community continues to evolve the praxis of caring for the oppressed and work for their liberation. The black church may still be the key institution in the black community to provide the moral leadership for the achievement of this ethical ideal.

VI.

Liberation Ethics and Therapy Together:
A Black Perspective

Challenging the internal as well as the external dependency of black people, the change it calls for is a qualitative change. It is our contention that black theologians have not yet taken this aspect seriously.

—*Allan Aubrey Boesak*
in <u>*Farewell to Innocence*</u>

1.

In the last chapter I argued that the gospel of Jesus, the liberator, was central to a black Christian liberation ethic in the context of black oppression. This particular ethical strand has emerged from the lives, convictions, and beliefs of an enslaved people. It is rooted in biblical faith and derived from the freedom struggles of Afro-Americans who continue to exist as a rejected and oppressed group today.

This chapter continues the discussion of a black Christian liberation ethic. It directs attention to the personal and systemic nature of oppression and relates ethics and therapy in a way that will illuminate the meaning of liberation praxis for the ministry of the black church.

Space will not permit an assessment of the critical ethical problems of violent and non-violent strategies for revolutionary change, important as they are. However, it can be acknowledged that the identification of the Christian left's (i.e., liberation and feminist theologians) show of solidarity with the struggles of the poor and oppressed, their resistance to social injustice, and the struggle for liberation, revolutionary change and for social justice has been met with violent measures in such places as the United States, South Africa, Korea, Chile, Manila, and El Salvador. Church people who have used non-violent strategies to bring about social change have themselves become victims of violence. They have been abducted, raped, flogged, tortured, exiled, or killed. Near the end of his own life and ministry, Dr. Martin Luther King, Jr., stated:

> America has not yet changed because so many think it need not change, but this is the illusion of the damned. America must change because 23,000,000 black citizens will no longer live supinely in a wretched past. They have left the valley of despair; they have found strength in struggle; and whether they live or die, they shall never crawl nor retreat again. Joined by white allies, they will shake the prison walls until they fall. America must change.

For King, *love* was the supreme ethical imperative underlying the struggle for non-violent social change because it, along with divine justice, could transform evil and become the authentic foundation for social relationships in the Beloved Community. Perfect love and justice are basic in the reality of God. King affirmed love as an absolute moral principle. The essence of God is love, but the presence of race oppression and segregation is a moral evil which denies the image of God in people, and destroys the possibility of genuine community. Since God is the personal ground of existence and center of value people must struggle against the moral evil of race oppression. This understanding of God was the ethical premise on which King based his redemptive struggle and commitment to non-violent social change.[1]

In a critical comment on traditional Christian ethics, Allan Aubrey Boesak stated:

> The problem with traditional Christian ethics is not only that the black situation has never been taken into account, but that the ethic arrived at was based on a theology that did not in any way recognize the God of the oppressed. As a result, it was, to say the least, inadequately equipped to deal with the realities of oppression and liberation. It is now incumbent upon black people to search for new forms (new wine in new wine skins!) to express the liberation they experience in Christ through his deeds of liberation for them.[2]

Black theologians such as Joseph R. Washington,[3] J. Deotis Roberts,[4] Gayraud Wilmore,[5] Major Jones,[6] and James H. Cone[7] have, in differing ways, taken God's election of the oppressed for freedom as the starting point for critical ethical reflection in the United States. They have employed biblical themes to identify black and oppressed people as a people chosen for deliverance from suffering. Black theologians have understood *freedom* from oppression to be a divine activity. Black people are called to participate in God's redemptive activity of deliverance and by God's grace to reconstitute themselves in a transformed social reality.

In *God of the Oppressed,* James H. Cone asserts, "Christian ethics is meaningless apart from God's election of the oppressed for freedom in this world." According to Cone, God's message of freedom and call-to-community is limited to the victims of oppression. It does not include the oppressors. While there is debate over this last point, there is agreement among black theologians that liberating the oppressed is inseparable from doing the will of God. Black Christian liberation ethics includes direct involvement in liberation struggles and in solidarity with the oppressed. It involves faith in God and in ourselves, a stepping back to reflect critically upon the praxis of liberation in light of Scripture, and engagement in new action. Liberation praxis is ultimately judged, not by liberation praxis itself, but by the Word of God and the liberating gospel of Jesus. Cone was right when he wrote: "For Christians, Jesus is the source for what we do; without his power to make life human, our behavior would count as nothing. We must," he continued, "carve out the answer for every new situation in dialogue with scripture and tradition, as well as with other victims in our social existence."[8] The goal of a black Christian liberation ethic is a transformed and liberating society which seeks to set captives free from systemic injustice and internalized forms of oppression and for self-affirmation and determination as a people in a just and liberating society.

Freedom has been the central theme underlying a black Christian liberation ethic.

In a word, if one wishes to talk about salvation, the only salvation the black church has to offer is through freedom, the only hope of mankind. Freedom is the religion of black people and the responsibility of churchmen to increase it as the appropriate response to the Lord of history and before all mankind.[9]

Freedom as a response to God's love and active concern for the oppressed has been at the heart of a black Christian ethic. Freedom in the black church has been understood in relational terms. Freedom for black Christians has been bound up with freedom for others as a faithful response to the Lord of history.

To anticipate, the problem of freedom addressed in this chapter suggests that the human capacity to unmask the nature of systemic oppression in church and society is crucial to a black Christian ethic of liberation. But in modern technological society, the capacity for critical reflection, upon which genuine freedom depends, appears to be dwindling.

> The technological society requires men to be content with what they are required to like; for those who are not content, it provides distractions—escape into absorption with technically dominated media of popular culture and communication. And the process is a natural one: every part of a technical civilization responds to the social needs generated by technique itself. Progress then consists in progressive dehumanization—a busy, pointless, and in the end, suicidal submission to technique.[10]

Modern social processes and technical forces, which often transform human subjects into objects, limit human freedom to serve bourgeois and materialistic ends and appear to dominate modern consciousness and support conditions that dehumanize the oppressed. Increasingly, men and women feel helpless and unable to mutually create and to reshape their world and themselves in ways that liberate them from oppressive social practices and exploitative relationships. In modern technological society, the loss of the capacity for critical reflection and freedom for self-determination and humanization threatens everyone. Hence, a black Christian liberation ethic requires not only a criticism of modern society, but also its transformation and the emergence of a new subject. This calls for a view of liberation that encompasses outward and inward change.

Boesak has identified a concern which he feels has not yet

been sufficiently addressed by black theologians who are concerned with liberation of the oppressed, namely, the transformation of systemic injustice and emancipation from internal forms of oppression, or psychic liberation. "Challenging the internal as well as the external dependency of black people, the change it calls for is a *qualitative* change. It is our contention that black theologians have not yet taken this aspect seriously."[11] The thesis of this chapter is that *social transformation and psychic liberation can be viewed as interrelated realities responsive to the judgment and grace of God. Their interrelatedness can be joined in awareness and in emancipatory struggles which seek to comprehend and unmask oppressive structures in church and society.*

Social analysis is critical to liberation ethics and therapy if structural transformation and psychic emancipation are to result. A black Christian liberation ethic can help evolve a praxis which is concerned with revolutionary social structural transformation and psychic emancipation when ethics and therapy are joined. This implies a liberation ethic that takes social and psychological analysis seriously and employs a liberating praxis of action and reflection and new action.

Therapy and a black Christian liberation ethic, when kept together and informed by "the dangerous memory of Jesus of Nazareth," can make a contribution toward a radical critique of systemic oppression and deepen our appreciation of the meaning of liberation from without and from within. By inference, both therapy and a black Christian liberation ethic can be viewed as a potentially critical theory and praxis underlying the pastoral care and social action mission of the black church. Both are essential to liberation struggles that seek a fundamental critique of domination and an understanding of social forces and institutional arrangements that affect and are affected by the quality of personal and social life in oppressed communities.

The term "therapy" is used here somewhat arbitrarily. It has as its central reference point psychoanalytically-oriented therapy, but it is not limited to that. Therapy here also includes a systems approach to therapy, family therapy, and group therapy. The important point is that therapy is oriented toward a process of continuing self-critical reflection, change, healing, and growth within a web of social relations. Richard J.

Bernstein's reflection upon the role of psychoanalysis as a form of critique is pertinent.

> Psychoanalysis is a discipline that incorporates methodological self-reflection. It requires a "depth hermeneutics" in which psychoanalytic interpretation is directed to the various ways in which the patient-subject fundamentally and systematically misunderstands himself, and fails to grasp the significance of the symptoms, from which he suffers.[12]

Jerome D. Frank has identified at least three essential features that underlie all forms of therapy:

> 1. A trained, socially sanctioned healer, whose healing powers are accepted by the sufferer and by his social group or an important segment of it.
> 2. A sufferer who seeks relief from the healer.
> 3. A circumscribed, more or less structured series of contacts between the healer and the sufferer, through which the healer, often with the aid of a group, tries to produce certain changes in the sufferer's emotional state, attitudes, and behavior. All concerned believe these changes will help him [and her]. Although physical and chemical adjuncts may be used, the healing influence is primarily exercised by words, acts, and rituals in which sufferer, healer, and—if there is one—group [or family] participate jointly.[13]

The aim of therapy is to help bring to consciousness the individual's, the family's, or the group's self-formative processes. The purpose is to enhance a fuller expression of humanness, interdependence, responsible freedom, and worth, and to deepen the capacity for magnitude and critical reflection.

Can the dialogue called therapy and black Christian liberation ethics be put in a genuinely reciprocal relation for the emancipatory struggle of the poor and the oppressed? Therapy and black liberation ethics together can be viewed as contributing toward a potentially critical theory and praxis underlying the pastoral care and social action mission of the black church. Both therapy and black Christian liberation ethics can help illuminate the freedom struggles of oppressed people who understand domination to be an outer and inner reality. Both therapy and ethics must be grounded in a common theoretical perspective which maintains awareness of the unity of life and provides a basis for enlightened action and social change, as well as a basis for radical social and critical self-reflection.

Because therapy and Christian social ethics are informed by social science perspectives, it will be necessary to examine some select schools of thought that have sought to put in reciprocal relationship the personal and social dimensions of reality. This task does not pretend to be an exhaustive survey. We shall briefly look at how T. W. Adorno, Talcott Parsons, C. W. Mills, and Herbert Marcuse posed the problem of the relationship between the personal and social dimensions of reality, and by inference, we can better see the challenge posed for the linkage between black Christian liberation ethics and therapy.

2.

The Structural Functionalist School in mainline U. S. sociology has been helpful at the point of identifying a relationship between the personal (subjective) side of social reality and the social system. The upshot of this position is that our personal or subjective experiences and outlook are embedded in and derived from a web of social relations, often referred to as the social-cultural system. This web of social relations is autonomous and irreducible. It includes the conferred interests and institutionalized patterns of power relations, as well as informal patterns of interaction.

The importance of this position is that it brings together the contributions of both psychology and sociology within the social sciences. A successful integration or balancing of these two disciplines is not always easy to achieve when explaining human motivation and action, or when analyzing human social reality. A temptation is to reduce explanations of human action to personal constructs such as frustration, guilt, aggression, anxiety, repression, projection, displacement, wish-fulfillment, defense mechanisms, and so on. On the other hand, the temptation in the opposite direction is to attribute human action to class, race, and sex conflict, structural stress and strain, anomie, entrenched power relationships and intransigent power, and so on. These rival approaches have dominated the exploratory landscape of psychology and sociology in the United States.

Often these explanations have functioned in a mutually exclusive conceptual universe. This separation of the sociological and psychological sciences has hindered a fuller understanding of the way the person and the system, objective and psychic realities interpenetrate. Theodor Adorno, in a critical comment on the separation of sociology and psychology, wrote:

> Sociology and psychology, in so far as they function in isolation from one another, often succumb to the temptation to project the intellectual division of labour on to the object of their study. The separation of society and psyche is false consciousness; it perpetuates conceptually, the split between the living subject and the objectivity that governs the subjects and yet derives from them. But the basis of this false consciousness cannot be removed by a mere methodological dictum. People are incapable of recognizing themselves in society and society in themselves because they are alienated from each other and the totality. Their reified social relations necessarily appear to them as an "in itself." What compartmentalized disciplines project on to reality merely reflects back what has taken place in reality.[14]

The separation or compartmentalization of these disciplines reflects the social order. This compartmentalization can be understood as occurring within a complex industrial and modern society that dichotomizes life into public and private, religious, and social spheres. In such a society, with its complex division of labor, individual reality can no longer be comprehended as a simple totality, but rather as a complex phenomenon. In such a society, the complexity of personal reality corresponds to the complexity of the social structure as a whole. "The individual in modern society is typically acting and being acted upon in situations the motor forces of which are incomprehensible to him. The lack of intelligibility of the decisive economic processes is paradigmatic in this connection."[15] The compartmentalization of the disciplines has yielded incomplete approaches to social reality. Through reification of their own approaches to reality they necessarily contribute toward an uncritical view of society that further serves to obscure the real connections between the person and the system.

These compartmentalized and incomplete disciplinary approaches, while remaining separate, have not enabled us to see the real connections between inner and outer reality as dialectically constituted. By remaining compartmentalized, they have contributed to reductionistic theories which preclude a relational and critical analysis of the working of the society as a totality.

> As an inner dimension relatively independent of the outer world, psychology has, in the eyes of a society that ceaselessly calls on its services, become at bottom a form of sickness: hence its successor, psychotherapy. The subject whose psychology was largely unaffected by societal rationality was always looked on as an anomaly, a crank; in the totalitarian era his proper place is in the work or concentration camp where he is "dealt with" and successfully integrated. The psychological left-overs, the people that allegedly count, retire to the top of the totalitarian hierarchies. . . . Even this last intact preserve of psychology which permits or directs dictators to roll on the floor, weep convulsively or uncover imaginary conspiracies is the mere mask of societal madness. . . .
>
> To this extent, certainly, the forms neurosis takes would be derivable from the structure of a society in which they cannot be abolished. Even the successful cure bears the stigma of pathologically exaggerated, self-defeating adjustment. The triumph of the ego is a particularist delusion. This is why all psychotherapy is prompted to become objectively untrue and therapists are frauds. In adjusting to the mad whole the cured patient becomes really sick—which is not to imply that the uncured are any healthier.[16]

This separation of the disciplines contributes to a view of reality that is both true and false. It is a source of correct information in that the disciplines accurately mirror the alienation and split between the person and the system that has occurred in society. It is a source of false information or error in that this split is taken to be the true nature of things. It obscures the real connections that constitute the person and the system and the tension that exists between the two.

The late Talcott Parsons addressed the problem of the relationship between psychology and sociology in "Psychoanalysis and the Social Structure," which appeared in *The Psychoanalytic Quarterly* in 1962. A *theory of action* was his organizing conceptual scheme. Two focuses are in this scheme. One is the irreducible personality system of the individual, and the other is the irreducible social system. Traditionally, the first has been the subject matter of psychology and the other, the subject matter of sociology. Parsons suggested that both of these theoretical approaches can be *integrated* within a broader theoretical system, namely, the system of action. "Nevertheless," Parsons argues, "it is extremely important to differentiate the various levels and ways in which these conceptual components are involved or combined. It is dangerous to shift from the one level to the other without taking adequate account of the systematic differences that are involved."[17] There is a danger inherent in the false assumption that a simple one-to-one correlation exists between personality structure and social structure. Personality structure is not the social structure writ small, e.g., one cannot talk about a schizophrenic social system and assume that such a judgment will make sense to the sociologist or that such a judgment has the same import as it would to a psychotherapist or analyst. Clinical judgments about personality structure are not directly applicable to the social structure. The increasing literature on the sociology of deviance, criminology, delinquency, the human liberation movements, and literature on social-political dissent makes clear the lack of correspondence between personality structure and social structure. Again, *both* the psychological and socological disciplines are essential to an adequate interpretation of social reality. But in general sociologists are not trained in psychoanalytic theory, and psychologists, particularly psychoanalysts, are not competent to apply psychoanalytic theory to an adequate explanation of sociological problems.

Talcott Parsons is but one social scientist who has sought to clarify the relationship between the personal and the social disciplines on a theoretical level. The central thrust of his work has itself been an argument for keeping the two levels of analysis together in social science.

Much criticism has been leveled at Parsons' work by neo-Marxists and such thinkers as the late C. Wright Mills, Alvin Gouldner, Richard J. Bernstein, and others who correctly identify a conservative bias underlying his work. My purpose here is not to defend Parsons or to argue against his critics. My purpose is to argue for a concept of the self that takes its relational character seriously and links the subjective side of human social reality to social structure. Parsons has been a seminal thinker and a principal architect in the U.S. in helping bridge the gap between sociological information and psychoanalysis. His contribution toward a critical analysis of structures of domination and oppression, however, has been tried and found wanting. Parsons' starting point of analysis is the social system itself. The system as a totality is not the object of critical analysis or the object of fundamental change. The real structurally induced antagonism between the person and the system are rationalized as problems of a given state of equilibrium of the system, of conformity or nonconformity, and of maladjustment and malintegration. These tendencies *within* the system are analyzed as problems of social control which the system needs to solve. The system itself is not analyzed as fundamentally problematic. This omission leaves room for the more powerful and subtly transforming irrational forces of oppression and domination to operate virtually unchallenged.[18]

C. W. Mills' understanding of the person in society is useful for stating a central, but often ignored, challenge facing Christian social ethics in contemporary society. According to Mills, the influence of contemporary social structures cannot be adequately understood or analyzed in terms of traditional liberal or socialist-oriented social science. We are now confronted with new kinds of social structures which resist analysis in the liberal and socialist traditions. So, part of the problem confronting social ethical analysis is a search for an adequate theory that can help specify and focus contemporary issues and guide reflection about the nature of contemporary society. The crucial problem centers in reason's relationship to freedom, and freedom's relationship to reason. How can reason be put in the service of human emancipation? And can freedom serve to liberate reason? By "reason" we mean the capacity for critical thinking that permits people to unmask the structural forces that dominate them and to self-consciously envision and create an alternative future. The problem of reason's relationship to freedom cannot be formulated as one grand problem, but neither can it be adequately formulated microscopically as a series of small-scale issues. According to Mills, reason and freedom are structural problems that need to be stated in relational terms, that is to say, the interplay of human biography and epochal history. Both reason and freedom are in obvious yet subtle peril in contemporary society.

> The underlying trends are well known. Great and rational organizations—in brief, bureaucracies—have indeed increased, but the substantive reason of the individual at large has not. Caught in the limited milieu of their everyday lives, ordinary men [and women] often cannot reason about the great structures—rational and irrational—of which their milieu are subordinate parts. Accordingly, they often carry out series of apparently rational actions without any ideas of the ends they serve, and there is the increasing suspicion that those at the top as well—like Tolstoy's generals—only pretend they know. The growth of such organizations, within an increasing division of labor, sets up more and more spheres of life, work, and leisure, in which reasoning is difficult or impossible. The soldier, for example, "carries out an entire series of functionally rational actions accurately without having any idea as to the ultimate end of this action or the function of each act within the whole." Even men of technically supreme intelligence may efficiently perform their assigned work and yet not know that it is to result in the first atom bomb.[19]

Both human reason and human freedom are subtly imperiled, because rational actions in everyday life are subordinated to bureaucratic efficiency obscuring a mature and humane grasp of human limitations and possibilities. "Technique is the totality of method rationally arrived at and having absolute efficiency in every field of human activity."[20] The contemporary crisis in the relationship between human reason and freedom finds expression in bureaucratic rationality. By "bureaucratic rationality" we mean the patterning and control of human activity by powerful cultural forces and organizations to legitimate and achieve definite ends within a particular development of society. Instead of increasing human reason and freedom, it often serves to decrease it. Rarely do human beings understand the structural forces as a whole in which their individual biographies are enmeshed. Their awareness is often limited to the particular context or milieu in which they live, but they do not grasp the structural forces that shape these milieus. The milieus themselves are increasingly rationalized by specific ideologies to fit the prevailing order of things. The interplay of human biography and history-making, of structure and milieu, is obscured. Persons pursuing their everyday affairs seek to adjust their reality within the milieus in which they are enmeshed and tend to be, in their ordinary consciousness, unaware of the rationalizing forces that lie behind them.

> The increasing rationalization of society, the contradiction between such rationality and reason, the collapse of the assumed coincidence of reason and freedom—these developments lie back of the rise into view of the [person] who is "with" rationality but without reason, who is increasingly self-rationalized and also increasingly uneasy. It is in terms of this type of [person] that the contemporary problem of freedom is best stated. Yet such trends and suspicions are often not formulated as problems, and they are certainly not widely acknowledged as issues or felt as a set of troubles. Indeed, it is the fact of its *unrecognized* character, its lack of formulation, that is the most important feature of the contemporary problem of freedom and reason.[21] [Italics my own.]

It is the unrecognized character of structural forces that contributes to uneasy feelings of manipulation and alienation. The idea of "self-rationalization" refers to the way in which the individual actors seek to gain some measure of control and mastery in their situation. But such attempts often serve to adjust the individual's plans of action, reflection, interests, and aspirations *within* the rules and regulations of the prevailing institutional power arrangements.

> It is not too much to say that in the extreme development the chance to reason of most [persons] is destroyed, as rationality increases and its locus, its control, is moved from the individual to the big-scale organization. There is then rationality without reason. Such rationality is not commensurate with freedom but the destroyer of it.

The image of the human person that emerges, then, is that of "the cheerful robot." This image is not commensurate with our ideal image of the role of reason in the interest of human emancipation and responsibility. The cheerful robot is the alienated person who seeks happiness and meaningful existence through self-adjustment and rationalization *within* the prevailing order of things. Even the search for community is a mistaken one in this context, because the elimination of the conceptual and structural conditions that produced the cheerful robot in the first place is ignored. In contemporary society, solutions to the quest for freedom and authenticity are sought rather in piecemeal fashion and in individual terms. Troubles are not seen in relational and structural terms. They are often formulated as private troubles and analyzed as personal problems, not related to or interpreted as problems of social structure. The reason for this lack of linkage, Mills believes, is because the chief capacities and qualities of the human subject (namely reason and freedom in the interest of human emancipation) are threatened and dwindling. C. W. Mills concludes his analysis of the contemporary crisis of human reason and freedom and points to the promise of social science as a possible way to transcend this problem. "The crisis of individuality and the crisis of history-making; the role of reason in the free individual life and in the making of history—in the restatement and clarification of these problems lies the promise of the social sciences."[22]

Herbert Marcuse makes a similar point in *One-Dimensional Man*, namely, that critical appraisals of contemporary industrial society are paralyzed because the technical forces operating in society tend to be totalitarian and preclude an objective-historical analysis of the society as a whole.

> In this society, the productive apparatus tends to become totalitarian to the extent to which it determines not only the socially needed occupations, skills, and attitudes, but also individual needs and aspirations. It thus obliterates the opposition between the private and public existence, between individual and social needs.

Today the capacity of society to stabilize and narrowly channel human possibilities in ways that legitimate the established universe of discourse and action is greater than ever before. The person's attempt critically to challenge society's domination over the individual is suppressed by new and subtle forms of legitimation.

Technology serves to institute new, more effective, and more pleasant forms of social control and social cohesion. The totalitarian tendency of these controls seems to assert itself in still another sense—by spreading to the less developed and even to the pre-industrial areas of the world and by creating similarities in the development of capitalism and communism.[23]

Modern society's capacity to homogenize human self-interest and to repress new and alternative ways for imaging and improving the human condition is absorbed by new techniques and by a prevailing "comfortable, smooth, reasonable, democratic unfreedom" which deprives the person of his or her critical capacity to transcend or overshoot the established universe of discourse and action toward genuine alternatives. This tendency in society to preclude and absorb critical reflection within its own established universe, to preserve the status quo, and to absolutize uncritically the society's *raison d'etre* is itself irrational. Marcuse states the problem of society's irrational tendency this way:

The fact that the vast majority of the population accepts, and is made to accept, this society does not render it less irrational and less reprehensible. The distinction between true and false consciousness, real and immediate interest still is meaningful. But this distinction itself must be validated. Men must come to see it and to find their way from false to true consciousness, from their immediate to their real interest. They can do so only if they live in need of changing their way of life, of denying the positive, of refusing. It is precisely this need which the established society manages to repress to the degree to which it is capable of "delivering the goods" on an increasingly large scale, and using the scientific conquest of nature for the scientific conquest of man.

Marcuse argues for the development of a critical theory and for the critical capacity to "investigate the roots of these developments and examine their historical alternatives"[24] in ways that would enable the transformation of society and the emergence of a new subject.

3.

I have argued that self and society are inextricably interwoven entities and that the relationship between the two is a dialectical, rather than a mechanical one. It has been suggested that society not only defines but also shapes psychological reality in subtle and yet unrecognized ways. Only a limited segment of the total self and social process is ever present to critical reflection. The unconscious represents the underside or hidden dimension of consciousness. It is constituted by forces that are unrecognized by the conscious subject. "The unconscious is the matrix of decisive mental processes. The conscious self is moved out of these unknown depths into actions the true meaning of which it does not understand. Men [and women] are typically ignorant of their own motives and incapable of interpreting their own symbolizations."[25] Hence, a depth interpretation that incorporates methodological self-reflection is needed as part of a critical analysis of contemporary social structures. For this reason I have argued that psychic liberation and social transformation are inextricably interwoven and dialectically related. The interest of both therapy and black liberation ethics, when kept together, can function as a critical methodology guiding an interest in social transformation. Critical theory has a fundamental *practical interest* that guides it—a practical interest in radically improving human existence. The practical interest of a critical theory seeks to foster self-consciousness and illuminate understanding of existing social and political conditions. The objective is to free oppressed groups consciously and meaningfully to shape their own struggle for self-determination.[26] The methodology of psychoanalytically oriented therapy can potentially serve to help lift internal blocks that hinder self-determination.

Psychoanalytic theory remains unfamiliar to many people, and psychoanalytically oriented therapy appears as an anomaly in the social sciences. Its domain is the inner world of the subject. It is there that it seeks to discern and illuminate, through dialogue, the nature of the interconnection between the person and the system. The inner world of the subject is made possible because of dialogue with others. The outer world is made meaningful because it is a shared and mutually constructed world. Therapy is concerned with the inner world of the subject, while a black liberation ethic is concerned with the outer world, its meaning and transformation through emancipatory activity.

The Concept of Action in Therapy. The central purpose in therapy is to engage in a dialogue, which is itself a kind of activity, about past action and its meaning to the subject. It also serves to clarify the present and to empower the individual to help create an open future. In therapy, the subject describes himself or herself in terms of intended, rather than observed, action. The account is subjective and is reported in terms of the meaning things have for the subject as agent. Therapy seeks to affirm the subject and to illumine his or her own self-understanding and to identify the ways in which the subject systematically misunderstands himself or herself. Therapy can help clarify the ways in which the individual participates in self-formation in the course of his or her historical development.

The analyst (interpreter or guide) is interested in the meaning that certain facts or events have assumed in the life of the individual. The reported facts and the way they work are part of the analytic process. The analyst is also interested in what is overlooked or indirectly communicated by the subject's unconscious. What is pertinent in the analytic situation is that meaning unfolds for the subject when his or her experiences come to light through another language dissociated from the common language of daily speech.[27] The other language is supplied by the subject himself or herself in the form of symptoms, dreams, slips of tongue, forgetting, resistances, transference, and so forth. This language is nonreflective, that is, its meaning remains unrecognized until it is deciphered and integrated into a meaningful context with new efficiency for the subject.[28]

Hence, there is a concept of action in therapy. The task is to reflect upon action that has already been taken by the subject as agent and to review such action in light of the subject's past intentions and purposes and life experiences. The reasons for engaging in this kind of reflective activity is to free the subject to act with increased self-awareness and with responsibility toward the future. Therapy may serve to heighten awareness of the subject's social location, values and communities of reference. It may give the person greater objectivity in directing future actions.

The Concept of Action in Black Liberation Ethics. Liberation ethics is concerned with action and character,[29] i.e., the kind of persons we *ought* to be, and with the question, What kind of communities

150

ought we to create? "The black church is called to be not only a reflective and action-initiated community of those whose will and purpose is to glorify God and uplift man in thought and deed, but also to be the community which puts to work its institutional power in support of its moral thought and action."[30] The focus of black liberation ethics is the larger social context in which personal reality is constituted. It is concerned with direct involvement in liberation struggles and with reflection upon the kind of activities that contribute toward a just and liberating society. Ethical reflection is concerned with examining alternative theories of vision and action and criticizing social processes and social structures in church and society in light of the kind of persons and future they produce.

Ethics assumes that human beings, although conditioned by society and culture, are yet in some measure free to construct alternative futures. Human beings are not wholly or rigidly determined by the past. Humans are free to reflect upon the past, to evaluate the present, and to act within their situation, as moral agents, to effect a new future.

> Ethics introduces a radical kind of doubt into the everyday world: it questions the adequacy with which social forms embody the moral intentionality of the culture; moreover, it questions the goodness of those cultural intentions, setting the cultural horizon of meaning within a more universal and ultimate context.[31]

Ethics and Therapy Together. In the ideal situation to be achieved, both ethics and therapy would share a common concern—namely, the *assumptive world* of the reflecting subject. The assumptive world is the interior world of the individual, derived from his or her continuous interactions with others. Jerome D. Frank employs this term to refer to the implicit and unquestioned conditions that lie behind our actions, guide our responses, and influence our thinking. The totality of such implicit assumptions is what he called "the assumptive world."

> This is a short-hand expression for a highly structured, complex, interacting set of values, expectations, and images of oneself and others, which guide and in turn are guided by a person's

perceptions and behavior and which are closely related to his emotional states and his feelings of well-being.

The assumptive world is a complex system permeating different levels of consciousness. We never experience it as a totality. "Only a minute part of it is in awareness at any one time, and the relative accessibility to awareness of different aspects of it may differ greatly."[32]

The assumptive world of the individual is a part of a wider normative framework within which persons and collectives make moral choices. The social ethicist clarifies that normative framework. He or she attempts to provide a critical basis for evaluating what is morally right and what is morally wrong in human actions. The social ethicist is thus interested in opening up new possibilities for human action. According to Gibson Winter, "Religious social ethics is . . . the disciplined inquiry of a community of those who are committed to the struggle for justice and peace. The critique of ideology is the central task of such a community. It can only be advanced by communication within these specialized disciplines where true nature is defined by this common task."[33]

From the perspective of therapy, the aim is to bring to conscious reflection the internalized, yet unrecognized, sources of oppression and to enable the subject to make appropriate changes in his or her assumptive world. The discipline of psychology heightens awareness that assumptive worlds, rooted in our cognitive and affective system, tend to resist change. They do not automatically yield to rational or moral persuasion. As a psychological fact, our assumptive world is internalized at levels that escape our awareness. The analogy of the iceberg is useful here. A part of the assumptive world is hidden from awareness and exists as the residue of internalized past experiences, which play a significant yet unrecognized role in current activity. In this light, Howard Clinebell has identified pastoral psychology and counseling as an invaluable therapeutic resource whereby the church can stay relevant to human need and translate the transforming and healing news of the gospel into the language of relationships. Hence, "The ministering church aims at becoming a supportive community of faith in which people will find the motivation, insight, and strength to be powerful therapeutic agents to others in need, both within and without its fellowship. Counseling is an instrument in achieving this goal. Second Corinthians gives the theological basis for this: 'Blessed be the God and Father of our Lord Jesus Christ, the Father of mercies and God of all comfort, who comforts us in all our afflictions, so that we may be able to comfort those who are in any affliction' (II Cor. 1:3-4)."[34]

Admittedly, there are problems with arguments for keeping social ethics and therapy together. The social milieu, the conceptual incarceration of the human disciplines and institutional boundaries do not easily support their linkage or their potentially emancipatory interest in a new and transformed social order. Yet the concern of the ethicist for social transformation is crucial for the practice of therapy. The practice of therapy is also crucial for the practice of ethics in that it is concerned with emancipation from unrecognized and distorted self-understandings which may accompany ethical reflection and action.[35]

It has been argued that therapy takes the inner world of the subject as its starting point and seeks to effect changes in the subject and within the existing order of things. Within this context, therapy serves to perpetuate an uncritical view of social reality by supporting the idea of the individual's autonomous subjectivity, separate from the objective social conditions that lie behind his or her suffering. Under the conditions of advanced modern capitalism, the fate of all therapies that derive from the Cartesian model of autonomous individualism may be to reproduce in the individual the distortions of the social system itself. In this way, therapy may serve to adjust the individual within the limited horizon of the dominant ideology. Therapy, in this case, may be seen as a delusional system, perpetuating the split between the person and the system. Therapy is then itself in need of emancipation. In order for therapy to serve its own implicit emancipatory interest, it needs to function in a different context and under social conditions that are more supportive of this interest. But such an ideal situation does not yet exist. In this light, it may be argued that the interest of liberation ethics in social transformation takes priority over an interest that takes for granted the assumptive world of individuals. Liberation ethics is concerned with transforming the everyday-life world from which our assumptive systems derive. Liberation ethics can be a resource for bringing about awareness of the transformations required for therapy to realize its liberating potential. Because of its own interest in social transformation and a corresponding interest in the assumptive world of the subject, liberation ethics can be put into a genuinely reciprocal relationship with the dialogue of therapy. Human beings will continue to experience difficulties of a personal nature which require some form of therapeutic intervention and psychic healing, even in a changed and transformed social order. People, even ethicists, may still need therapy. In this light, the purpose of ministry is to help form the character of a people to empower them to collectively transform structures of oppression and to sustain those in the struggle for justice and liberation.

Transformation in both social and personal life will require the courageous, creative, and liberating responses of human agents to bring or call forth new possibilities through revolutionary struggle. This requires a desire to construct an alternative and liberating future. The social process itself is imbued with possibility and with the potential for meaningful change as well as the potential for further fragmentation and destructiveness. For the Christian, faith is at work when the struggle toward social and personal emancipation, guided by the "dangerous memory of Jesus of Nazareth," continues even when the prospect for its achievement face formidable challenges and appear bleak under the circumstances. That this faith in freedom and in an alternative future was operative in black communities is indicated in the accounts and records of black slaves and freed persons themselves.

> Oh, Freedom! Oh, Freedom!
> Oh, Freedom, over me!
> And before I'd be a slave,
> I'll be buried in my grave,
> And go home to my Lord and be free.[36]

There, under different historical circumstances, personal freedom and responsibility were inseparably linked in the community of the oppressed. Now, under new historical and social developments, the need for awareness of the linkage between outer and inner emancipation is even more urgent because of unrecognized totalitarian tendencies in modern societies. A critical approach to black liberation ethics and therapy can help highlight the need for this linkage when the insights and contributions of these disciplines are kept together in efforts that seek to be faithful to God's liberating activity, instructed by the "dangerous memory of Jesus, the Liberator," and guided by an interest in social *and* personal transformation.

What black liberation ethics and therapy have in common, then, is concern for the kind of persons we are becoming and the future we can help create and shape. The mutual concern is in freedom from domination and internalized oppression, informed by a tradition that leads to a radically new kind of life, announced in Jesus of Nazareth. The common concern is in the creation of a new and just society and a responsible subject free to be self-conscious and self-critical and free to help shape an open future.

The future, although conditioned by the past, need not be a repetition of the past, nor need it necessarily be limited by it. Black Christian liberation ethics and therapy are properly concerned with the past, to learn from it and to discern the alternatives within which human reason and human freedom can become responsive to God's judgment and liberating action and responsibly serve the emancipatory interest in an open future.

Black liberation ethics and therapy have a practical interest in emancipation. Both employ a critical methodology which can, when kept together, contribute toward a critical theory and prophetic faith that maintain awareness of the interconnection and dialectical relationship between inner emancipation and outer social transformation.

VII.

The Person and the System: the Role of Ideology

Society confronts the individual as mysterious power, or, in other words, the individual is unconscious of the fundamental forces that shape his life.

—Peter L. Berger
in Facing Up to Modernity

Don't let the world around you squeeze you into its own mould, but let God re-mould your minds from within, so that you may prove in practice that the Plan of God for you is good, meets all His demands and moves towards the goal of true maturity. (Rom. 12:2 Phillips)

This chapter directs attention to the fundamental conditioning force of society itself, highlighting the authority of society in the connection between the individual and the social system. On the one hand, society is not reducible to people. People are not simply a mirror reflection or mechanical reproduction of society. People are self-conscious, reflective agents, and social beings who are complex and changing. On the other hand, society is an open system of relatively enduring and unfolding relations which underly various forms of social life; and its workings may be opaque to the agent's spontaneous under-standing.[1] It is the web or totality of the relations within which individual and group reality is constituted. *People* and *society* refer to radically different, yet mutually interdependent kinds of realities.

The reality of self is in relations. Society is derived from relatively autonomous and enduring relations between people, rather than derived entirely from the conscious and intentional activity of individuals. Society is also open to the transforming activity of human subjects. Societal liberation and transformation must seek to comprehend and address the enduring or systemic nature of social relations and their mode of production and reproduction. Society can become an object of knowledge and critical reflection through experience and rational investigation, and it can be reproduced, modified, or transformed through human activity or praxis. Praxis is a way of doing and knowing which arises from self-conscious and self-critical activity in concrete situations. Praxis is action that is reflectively done.

1.

The person and the system conjures up many different images including self and personality systems, family systems, institutions as systems, and bureaucratic and social systems. The person is intimately identified with and shaped from infancy by the dynamic interplay between all of these systems. Viewed individually, these systems play a subordinate role to the even more powerful and larger sociocultural and political systems in which they are embedded.

The phrase "the person and the system," refers here to the interconnection between the wider sociocultural system and the individual. The family and other institutions (religious and secular) are among the concrete socializing agents and systems of action that determine the person's place in the wider society. Institutions and their collective arrangements make up the wider economic, sociocultural, and political power systems. The mode of productive relations, institutional practices, and accompanying technologies and ideologies together comprise the structural elements of this objective complex system. Sometimes referred to as the *prevailing reality* or as the objective social order, this complex system cannot be readily divorced from either the psychological-emotional roots that underlie it or from the social historical context which constitutes it. The family, the media, the church, the school, and government (or the state) are among the key institutions that mediate the dominant ideology that underlies this sociocultural system.

This complex system is the underlying structure and context common to all institutions. It also underlies the many, often separate, struggles for freedom within the United States. In order to have an adequate understanding of various ideologies and forms of domination and oppression, such as race, sex, and class exploitation, we must comprehend their interconnection and the common structure (the real relation) that lies behind them. To ignore the objective social order and its working does not put an end to its existence. It is still there, although its working is largely unrecognized. The objective social order, constituted and maintained or changed by human activity, is the context in which experience is organized and from which modes of thought and plans of action arise. Individual thought only gradually emerges from and differentiates between specific dimensions of existence and operates within the wider and particular social and historical context. For example, family life is the primary context for mediating to the young the basic values and role expectations of the society. In the family, the young person learns from various family members what it means to be a male or female in this society. If he is a black male, he may get the message early that this society will not honor his presence; that he is not expected to go very far; or that trouble will be his lot in life. He may internalize the belief that he was not born to succeed. The girl undergoes a different socialization, but one that will adjust her innate abilities and aspirations to fit the requirements of a male-dominated society. If she is black, she may come to believe that her life will be hard and that she will need to make sacrifices that are not typical for her white counterpart. The socialization process will vary from family to family and from group to group. But the dominant values and role expectations are learned. In many and contrasting ways the dominant values of the system are reproduced symbolically in the individual and through the typical channels of socialization.

Human activity is dependent on a specific context and social forms of interaction for its meaning. The particular ways in which we arrive at, diagnose, and guide our personal, social, and political destiny are construed within a specific mode of thought, or ideological categories. Ideological categories may be thought of as unquestioned assumptions which underlie specific contexts and ways of thinking. They in turn guide our everyday activity.

The underlying assumptions are taken for granted by the society and remain largely unrecognized and unchallenged in the exigencies of daily living.[2]

2.

Roy Bhaskar has suggested a model for thinking about *the connection between the person and the system* or society. His model is shown in the figure below.

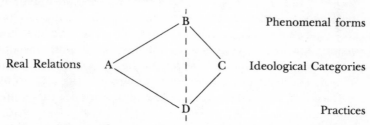

Real relations refer to the underlying structure of material subsistence in society, for example, the capitalist mode of production. This mode of production necessitates a class society which includes a ruling class, working class, and the poor. Albeit, the structure of modern capitalism is a highly complex system of productive relations. The underlying structure or the real relations give rise to phenomenal forms. *Phenomenal forms* refer to specific manifestations of social reality which are conceptualized in human experience. They are the institutionalized and taken-for-granted social arrangements in society, such as the wage-labor relations under capitalism, a complex occupational hierarchy, and a complex class structure. Phenomenal forms appear as "the prevailing reality," "objective truth," or "the way it is." Phenomenal forms appear as truth as long as one does not go behind the social forms to reflect critically upon the underlying structures that created them. Phenomenal forms in their turn are reflected in certain ideological categories. *Ideological categories* refer to explanations or justifications that legitimate the status quo of society or attempt to radically change existing social realities. Ideologies function to connect the subjectively held beliefs to the objective social structure. Examples of ideologies that serve to legitimate the status quo of capitalist production are: "any one who has it in him can get ahead," "success is a matter of individual merit," "poverty is God's way of punishing those who do not want to work." Ideological categories in their turn undergird and are reflected in specific social practices, such as the ethic of "hard work leads to success." Social practices refer to activities (e.g., buying and selling, wage negotiating) that the phenomenal forms produce. Social practices in their turn sustain the phenomenal forms and are necessary for the reproduction of the real relations. The dotted line through BD in Bhaskar's model denotes the world of everyday life. The workings of this everyday life-world tend to mask the real relations that lie behind the phenomenal forms, ideological categories, and underly specific social practices. The major point is that society exists as a reality, a profound source of authority independent of the preceiving subject, but one also causally connected to the subject through practice.

Bhaskar's model can be restated and summarized in the following way:

The Person and the System Connection

The remainder of this chapter will elaborate a specific dimension of this model, namely the role of ideology in the connection between the person and the system, or society. We shall be concerned with the following themes: the legitimation of structural contradictions; individualism, social practice and reproduction; ideology and the subject; the human person as subject; and ideology and the unconscious.

3.

We look first at *the legitimation of structural contradictions.* By "structural contradictions" I mean crises or incompatible relationships that arise between social groups and classes as a result of the way society is organized. The competitive relations between capitalists, which result in high rates of unemployment among the laboring masses and deprive them of their means of livelihood, is an example of a structural contradiction that emerges from the economic organization of a capitalist society.

The structural contradictions of the system are perceived by most of its members as being a normal part of the workings of society. A further example of a structural contradiction is the existence of poverty in the midst of plenty. It may be assumed that some will naturally fair better than others. It may further be assumed by many that contradictions such as poverty amidst plenty can be remedied through changes in social policy, legislation, or social reform. The contradiction, then, is viewed as a problem of system maintenance rather than as a fundamental structural problem.

Structural or objective contradictions stem from material life, i.e., the relationship between the natural environment and modes of production under modern capitalism. The contradictions in the system of production are *objective* social conditions. Objective contradictions stem, in part, from the human species relationship to the physical environment which includes natural resources such as plants, animals, minerals, water, and air. These natural resources are needed for human survival. Contradictions stem from the mode of productive activity, which converts such natural resources into commodities for profit and transforms work relations into wages for labor. The objective contradiction can be stated in the following way. Human subjects, who may know themselves to be of intrinsic value, engage in activity that transforms them into means to serve the ends of the system of production. Capitalists themselves are constrained by the contradiction of the system. Ruling classes, in capitalists' economies, perceive the contradictions of the system and seek through adjustive reforms to correct them. For example, they may give workers more benefits and leisure time. Eventually this humanitarian gesture breaks down because it becomes too costly and diverts resources away from the real aim of production which is *to make* profit, not to give it away. The contradictions are inherent in the system of production itself, because the individual worker is made subordinate to the system. In other words, the system does not function to serve the interest of workers. Workers exist to serve the interest of the system of production.

Human subjects suffer the imposed limitations of the natural *and* social order. For instance, humans may be hungry, but hunger must be satisfied within the constraints of available and edible resources. Furthermore, persons need to be loved and accepted and understood and valued as intrinsic human beings. But the quality of life that supports the fulfillment of such human needs are objectively conditioned by the prevailing liberal ideology and mode of productive activity. The derived social relations that constitute family life and the social order are legitimized by the encompassing ideology. Social relations refers to the way people use the objects in the natural world and construct their cooperative relations to achieve social objectives.[3] The needs of individuals are constricted by their concrete situation, the mode of productive relations in society, and by the quality of life. For instance, workers develop health problems such as cancer and heart disease. Health problems may be related to the competitive life-style in a bourgeois culture and to the way in which this culture relates to the natural environment, i.e., the pollution of water and air. Workers develop health care needs as a result of poor environmental conditions. But access to the quality of health care is regulated by a number of objective factors, including health, receptivity of medical practice to the client population, the existing state of knowledge to treat certain forms of disease, and the availability of medical resources. In these ways human subjects suffer the imposed limitations of the natural and social order. Structural contradictions may also be seen in the American ideal.

There is an *American ideal* of equality which emphasizes social position and achievement based on personal qualities. The ideal can be stated in summary form:

1. This is a society of equality of opportunity and free, competitive placement. ("Anyone who has it in him can get ahead.")
2. Hence, success is solely a matter of individual merit.
3. Hence, those who are at the top deserve to be there; those at the bottom are there because of lack of talent or effort: it is "their own fault."
   Thus, the placement of individuals could not be otherwise without violating the value of individual achievement.[4]

While there exists an American ideal of equality of all persons, there is also a built-in contradiction concerning who gets what and when. The question of equality is rationalized by the prevailing ideology and conditioned by specific social practices and the social relations that derive from them. For a great many people, actual equality does not exist, especially for minorities such as Native Americans and blacks as a group. The structural contradictions are mediated by the religious, political, cultural, and social arrangements that are binding in bourgeois society. These institutions and their interstructuring are guided by a particular, yet encompassing ideology, which channels social activity and thinking in specific ways. Social activity and individual thought, in turn, take for granted the structural contradictions of the system. Contradictions and transformations within the megaenvironment of industrial capitalism reverberate throughout the system and are mediated by the varying institutions, including the family, the church, the school, and the media that comprise this larger system. The effects of these contradictions and transformations are absorbed within the deep structure of the individual unconscious. As we shall see, church religion sometimes plays a significant role in adjusting the individual to the status quo, e.g., "keep religion out of politics" or "God helps those who help themselves." Through private withdrawal into "religion," the church sometimes encourages support of the system of sex, race, and class domination when it serves to adjust the individual within the existing order of things. Sometimes it challenges some forms of oppression and domination, such as racism, as it did in the nineteenth- and twentieth-century Civil Rights and Black Liberation Movements. At other times certain aspects of religion serve to legitimate the status quo. It is the working of this larger complex phenomenon and its legitimation that I refer to in this chapter as the *person and the system and the role of ideology*. The individual does not create this complex system *de novo*, but rather establishes a relationship with it and derives an identity through continuous activity. The individual is an integral part of a complex system of domination, including the family, the media, the school, the church, and government. These institutions are central influences which help shape individual consciousness and convey the dominant ideology that underlies the objective social order.

4.

Individualism, Social Practice, and Reproduction. In what sense is the individual free in a society where race, sex, and class oppression function in the service of an exploitative social and economic system? I maintain that a person's freedom and consciousness are shaped in multiple, yet subtle and unrecognized, ways by certain ideologies and self-understandings and specific social practices. These social forces support race and sex oppression and contribute to the definition of the individual. To assume that one is somehow unaffected by race, class, and sex oppresion while remaining a member of society is to ignore the extent to which we are all socialized and influenced by the workings of a dynamic social system of exploitative economic relations. To remain ignorant of the working of this complex system of oppression and its interstructuring is to side with our impotence and therefore to accept a lack of freedom to diagnose and formulate relevant challenges to it. The question, In what sense is the person free from domination? leads to a discussion of social practices, ideology, and the relationship between ideology and the unconscious under capitalist domination. This question is an important one for the church and its ministry in society.

The church is a mediating institution and a potentially

powerful structure, standing between the individual and the wider society. If the church is to better understand its prophetic and liberating role in contemporary society, it must also comprehend the deep and complex structure of domination that not only shapes the lives and priorities of its members, but also hinders or enhances the church's practice of ministry as well.

Cartesian individualism, as a specific mode of thought, emerges from a particular social and historical period and intellectual tradition in which the original connection between the individual and the group has been lost sight of. In actuality, human subjects unfold in a cooperative process and within a common structure of life. Their reality emerges from inter-action, through struggle and within a particular social structure, history, and pattern of thought. Unwittingly, Cartesian individ-ualism helps establish, in the modern period, assumptions that the individual thinker is detached from a social and historical matrix in which the thinking subject is embedded. This is a false assumption. As we shall see, the arguments of both Marx and Freud implied a challenge to the Cartesian foundation of certainty, "Cogito, ergo sum" (I think, therefore, I am).

Descartes suggested that the conscious subject was the basis of certainty. He argued that the existence of things could be doubted. The one entity that could be certain of its own existence was the doubting (i.e., thinking) solitary subject. This was Descartes' discovery which he interpreted as the basis of certainty for all people. According to this Cartesian assertion, certainty comes through individual mental processes. One knows one's self through conscious awareness that one is a thinking subject.

This didactic relationship between subject and object, knower and known was proposed as the fundamental construct for arriving at true knowledge of the subject and of the world. Philosopher William Ernest Hocking critically observed, "Through three hundred years this formula has had a stream of critics; but the definitive escape is the deed, I am inclined to say the necessary deed, of the present century."[5]

It was this Cartesian foundation of certainty that was implicitly challenged in the arguments of both Marx and Freud. Neither of them directly addressed Descartes' argument. The

Cartesian foundation of certainty is a particularist delusion by implication because it ignores the "real relations" and the social historical conditions that underlie human thinking and activity. It was both Marx and Freud who, by contrast, helped illuminate the deep structures of the social and historical process in the origins of the thinking subject. But their social contributions, especially their emphasis on the social character of knowing, continue to play a marginal role in the thinking and activity of most citizens in industrial society. Individualism continues to be a guiding framework for the formulation and articulation of problems and their resolution.

Although Marx and Freud held very different outlooks, their social theories were complementary. In different ways each of them acknowledge that one does not know one's self directly. Rather, self-knowledge is produced through discourse and in specific social and historical contexts and in struggle. An individual only comes to consciousness through another individual and within a particular social history. Both Marx's and Freud's arguments implied that the Cartesian foundation of certainty was indeed *uncertain*. To assume that self-knowledge is an autonomous and private mental achievement alone is delusional because it ignores the far more powerful determining influences of the real relations that lie behind the objective social order. The opacity of the objective social order itself embodies the social relations and dominant interest that mold, to a large degree, the monadic consciousness of individuals. "Social tendencies assert themselves behind the backs of individuals and that they do not know these tendencies to be their own—this is the ideological smokescreen with which society surrounds itself."[6]

Yet unrecognized instinctual, social, and historical forces are conditioning the subject and his or her relationship to reality. Relations of productive activity contribute toward the delusive or false quality of consciousness. For example, we implied earlier that religious institutions, such as the church and school, convey certain values and beliefs that are internalized at the individual level and then expressed in the lives of individuals. In this way, real reproduction is *internalized reproduction*. The subject reproduces in himself or herself the values of an objective institutional order. For instance, certain values and beliefs, conveyed by religious institutions, may become the significant ordering principles in personal life.

Certain aspects of religion in the United States, within mainline denominations, illustrate this point of internal reproduction. During the 1960s a large movement toward racial and social justice was epitomized in the Civil Rights and Stop-the-Vietnam War Movements. There was involvement of religion and politics as churched and non-churched people participated together in such events as the 1963 March on Washington, The Poor Peoples' Campaign, the 1965 March on Selma, and the many demonstrations and draft-card burnings in opposition to the undeclared and racially signaled war in Southeast Asia. For example, the Berrigan brothers were among the many church people who believed that the church should be actively engaged in the struggle against social injustice and the activism of the 1960s emerged from the black church's struggle against segregation and racism and was supported by the political left in the United States.

By contrast, the decade of the 1970s was marked by a retreat from the political activism of the 1960s. The political mood of the country was shifting to the right, away from the social gospel and toward private religion. The 1970s witnessed the proliferation of a variety of cults, sects, new religions, and the human potential movement. Conservativism was growing within certain mainline denominations. In certain religious circles a renewed emphasis was on private withdrawal and a conservative return to traditional values, including a return to traditional women's roles, "the dutiful or productive worker," militarism, loyalty, and defense of the "American way of life," private individualism and personal salvation, such as "religion is a private matter," "it must not interfere with politics," "religion and politics don't mix," or "each person should decide his or her own conscience." In the 1970s certain aspects of religion, whether deliberate or not, supported the liberal bourgeois ideology that governs modern personal life, namely that it is entirely an individual affair.[7] It has helped to strengthen an uncritical commitment to the structural arrangements and social relations that underlie an expanding and exploitative economic system, namely profit-centered capitalism. Within the purview of this orientation to religion, the major problems of the society tend to be explained away in individualistic terms, i.e., the breakdown of the family, pornography, loneliness, poverty and selfishness, corruption of individual politicians, ingratitude, and so forth. The major solutions also tend toward narrowly individualistic and personal interpretations, i.e., "they should get off welfare," "anyone who really wants to work can," and "it is their own laziness that is the problem."

When religion moves in this vein, it obscures the contradiction and the connection between personal life and the social structure. Whether intended or not, it serves to reproduce and to strengthen the separation of the personal from the social in consciousness and fosters the idea that personal life can be transformed apart from a transformation of relational patterns, the system of production and its sustaining ideology.[8] In this sense certain aspects of religion serve to reproduce specific values, beliefs, and self-understandings that strengthen the individual's tie to the status quo of society.

As we move into the 1980s a new kind of turning outward appears in the emergence of the new religious-political right and the connection between biblical morality and defense of the free enterprise system. Religion and politics have been publically linked in a Christian-capitalist alliance from the right, e.g., "America must be saved before it is too late," "elect godly men to public office," "America is the last logical base for world evangelization." Conservative religious groups that may have argued for keeping religion out of politics in the sixties and seventies are now actively espousing political involvement in defense of "the American way" and a version of individualism based on a literal interpretation of the Bible and a belief in biblical inerrancy. What is new in this conservative form of religion is its aggressive involvement in electoral politics. The new religious-political right illustrates a version of religion that identified Christian American Fundamentalism with traditional values and established social power arrangements.

For many decades the vast majority of conservative Christians have been in a political slumber; now these new groups are sounding the alarm. Concerned that the United States has fallen from a position of world power into decadence and that our society is collapsing under the weight of its own immorality, they call for a return to

168

America's God-inspired foundation of morality, free enterprise, and patriotism. At the ideological heart of many of these organizations are traditional conservative beliefs in individual freedom, limited government and personal diligence.[9]

The main intent of the new religious-political right organizations is to "save America before it is too late." Its most visible figure today is T.V. evangelist Jerry Falwell, founder of Moral Majority, Inc.

The new religious-political right emerged in response to a widespread sense of loss of conviction and confidence in elected officials, and in response to a perceived moral crisis that threatens to destroy the fundamental values and institutions of American society, such as the patriarchical authority of the family and America's military superiority among world powers. As historian Edwin Harrell, Jr., observes, "In the twentieth century, American conservative evangelicals have entered politics only when it seemed to them that the very structure of society was seriously threatened by modernism and liberalism."[10] From this perspective, groups and movements such as feminist, gay rights, and Marxist oriented-liberation movements (i.e., Christians toward socialism and theologies in the Americas) are perceived to be subversive elements destroying the very fabric of "the American way." In this view, the moral crisis threatening "the American way" is attributed to perverts, radicals, leftists, secular or godless humanists, communists, welfarism, and liberal government officials. "From the perspective of the Religious Right, the nostalgic return of American Society 'to the ways things were' must be predicated on the election of 'Godly men' and 'Christian statesmen' who will work for the legislation of moral absolutes by the state." The underlying assumption is "that American institutions and social structures are essentially Christian. All that is needed is the moral strengthening of individual citizens."[11] The orientation in this perspective remains essentially individualistic. The underlying structure of bourgeois society itself is not deemed problematic. "When enough souls are saved and begin living righteous lives, so the argument goes, then the Christian nature of society automatically will be enhanced."[12]

Ignored in this orientation to religion is a self-critical and historical consciousness that would provide a fundamental and comprehensive analysis of "the American way of life" and the various contexts of oppression in which it is implicated the world over. Ultimate salvation and historical liberation tend not to be linked in consciousness and in ways that would engage a fundamental criticism of liberal ideology or the mode of productive activity that underlies it. Certain aspects of religion have tended to support imperialism and capitalism, racism and sexism, and in turn, they have been fostered by these forms of domination. Certain forms of religion are big business, influencing the values of the primary socializing institutions of society. Its entrepreneurial interest is the message. The interest in the family, the school, and the mass media work together with the prevailing liberal ideology to reproduce a quality of consciousness that is uncritical and unprophetic and consistent with the historical interest of capitalist domination. In this way, the already structured information is internalized and reproduced at the individual level and acquires a *truth value* distinct from the particular institutions that embody it.

Human thought is said to be false consciousness when thinking and human activity are narrowly construed in individualistic terms, without reference to the broader social context from which it is derived. Ideologies are first and foremost *social,* not private creations. The private or assumptive worlds of individuals are constituted by the dynamic interplay of objective conditions and subjective appropriations. Objective and subjective dialectical processes together constitute human reality. Human thought is false consciousness when it excludes from awareness the objective social conditions in which thinking takes place. False consciousness, then, is incapable of corrrectly diagnosing reality because it precludes from awareness the possibility of critical reflection upon the underlying causes of social conditions in which subjectivity is constituted. False consciousness thereby serves to legitimate the very conditions that determine its contents. It functions to conceal, rather than to reveal, the objective social context in which the thinking subject is enmeshed. Reality, then, appears as the resultant of abstracted personal or individual achievements, thereby obfuscating the working of the wider social context which conditions human activity and produces concrete individual projects and modes of thought.

The subject may assume that he or she is an autonomous and free agent in contemporary society; free to determine his or her own fate; free to transform problematic situations. The hypothetical free and autonomous subject may be an ideal situation in a non-repressive social order, but such a social order has to be achieved. It does not exist in actuality. The so-called free and independent individual remains obscurely dependent on the social order, but unable to recognize that society is the essence and antithesis of the self. Yet more powerful material and dynamic forces are determining both the subject and the content of consciousness in modern society. People are not free from the domination of bourgeois ideology and material interest. They are not free to transform the social process that reduces them to non-persons as long as they remain captive to a materialistic, profit-oriented system of production. The free and unrepressed subject who determines his or her own consciousness is still a myth. The ideal social order that embodies freedom from domination is not being realized under the conditions of advanced, modern capitalism.

Under modern conditions, individual consciousness represents and reflects the contradictions of the social and moral order from which it is derived. It, therefore, is a delusional or false consciousness that ignores the system of domination which channels social relations, religious orientations, and consciousness in particular directions. From this perspective, all varieties of psychology that take the individual as the point of departure and ignore the social structure and institutional power arrangements in which they are embedded are delusional, because they are conceptually removed from a social context from which they can never be empirically separated.

The theme running through the preceding two sections has been that the model of the atomized individual is a part of a pervasive thought pattern in Western society. It has contributed to a reductionistic outlook that underlies much of social and psychological analysis. It has also supported a narrow and individualistic conception of religion. In turn, an individualistic outlook has obscured critical awareness of the inherently problematic and contradictory nature of existing social struc-

171

tures. The contradictions are not uniform and do not appear as contradictions in the system of production. Rather, they appear as contradictions in personal life, i.e., "I should have stayed in school. Had I stayed, I would not be unemployed today." Within this individualistic outlook the relationship between the person and the system and the true meanings of structural contradictions have become imperceptible. The preponderance of information and interpretive schemes tend to be focused on an individualistic level. This contributes to a distorted view of reality. It obscures a critical and comprehensive analysis of the dialectical relationship between objective and subjective dimensions of reality. It is the function of ideology to distort reality by fixing the individual within a limited cognitive horizon and by rendering established social arrangements as natural and unproblematic. This latter problem can be more clearly seen in the relationship between ideology and the subject.

5.

Ideology and the Subject. Karl Mannheim identified two distinct and separable meanings of the term ideology, the *particular* and the *total.*[13] The particular refers to the distortions of reality at the individual level, such as "I should have stayed in school," where the person either consciously or unconsciously distorts the truth about his or her situation or that of his or her opponent, such as "they should pull themselves up by the bootstraps like the rest of us." Total ideology refers to specific thought patterns characteristic of the general outlook of a group, social class, or an entire social historical epoch.

The ideas on self-understandings expressed by the subject are thus regarded as functions of his existence. This means that opinions, statements, propositions, and systems of ideas are not taken at their face value but are interpreted in the light of the life situation of the one who expresses them. It signifies further that the specific character and life situation of the subject influence his opinions, perceptions, and interpretations. Two strands of the concept ideology can be recognized here. One is that self-understandings reflect the subjective outlook of the individual in his or her concrete situation. The second is that his or her concrete situation (i.e., work place or family) or milieu (i.e., neighborhood or school environment) is an outgrowth of the collective life of the social and historical epoch in which it participates. The *particular* (subjective) concept of ideology refers to the former (self-understandings) and the *total* (the social) concepts refer to the latter (the general outlook of a group). The two levels are not interchangeable. For example, a person may blame herself for not "making it" in the business world and agree that she should not be promoted (i.e., "I'm not smart enough"). While the company itself may have a fair practice employment policy, the limited upper-level managerial jobs are, in reality, "for men only," and those are all filled. At one level she blames herself and agrees with her fate. On the other level, real constraints outside herself exist, i.e., sexism in the labor force, plus no room to move in the company. They require different levels of analysis. The subjective side of ideology requires a psychological approach, while the objective social order requires a more general or sociological approach. Both, however, must be kept together if we are to arrive at an adequate understanding of the social context and of the dialectical relationship between the person and the system within a specific social and historical development.

The concept *ideology* is crucial for our discussion of the agency and emancipation of the human person. Louis Althusser's theory of ideology is expressed in the following definition: ideology is "the system of the ideas and representations which dominate the mind of a man or a social group."[14] By "system of ideas," he means a particular pattern of thought and social practices produced to legitimate a particular social structure and power arrangements which are deemed necessary for the continuance of society by ruling groups. For example, traditional ideological supports serve to "explain" poverty as an individual defect, or support racial discrimination by pointing to the alleged inferiority of black people. Both explanations work together as a part of a general thought pattern for diagnosing and "curing" social ills. The following quote from Edward C. Banfield illustrates this point.

That racial prejudice has long been declining and may be expected to continue to decline at an accelerating rate counts for little if the Negro *thinks* that white racism is as pervasive as ever; that his opportunities to improve his position by acquiring skills are at last fairly good counts for little if he *thinks* that "massive" government welfare, housing, and other programs—and *only* these—can help him. If he misperceives the situation in these ways, he is likely to do things that are counterproductive (for example, to cut himself off from "white" schools, jobs, and politics and to enter the fantasy world of black separatism). Such a course, if carried far enough, may validate his original (false) hypothesis—that is, he may become in fact as dependent upon government programs as he (wrongly) supposed himself to be and may revive the fact of white prejudice by giving it some objective grounds to feed upon.[15]

This particular thought pattern, or system of ideas, blames the victim while it legitimates certain power arrangements and supports specific relational patterns of discrimination. It serves to entrench both the oppressed and their oppressors within particular forms of domination, false self-understandings, and patterns of exploitation.

The "system of ideas" and its supporting technology elevates a limited aspect of reality to the level of truth and does so in such a way that the resulting reality appears as "natural," "the way things are," or as "common sense." It appears inherently unproblematic. "Representations" are specific and reified patterns of behavior, ritual interactions, ideas and mental images. They are produced and reproduced through social practices that mirror the interest of dominant groups. This is more complex than it may appear, in that oppressed people may positively support their own oppression by "agreeing" with the ruling ideology. Hence, not only the dominant group, but also the oppressed groups reproduce in their own minds the ideas that keep them captive. Representations refer to the limited and rather fixed ways in which men and women adjust to and locate themselves *within* the existing order of things. They serve to reinforce the status quo and govern the way people normally act and feel about themselves as individuals by saying such things as, "My vote doesn't count, so why bother?" or "You can't fight city hall, so don't even try!" "Systems of ideas" and "representations" can dominate the outlook and consciousness of individuals or entire groups. Representations do not appear as redundancies and do not reveal, but conceal, the true situation or social location of subjects. "Representations" and "systems of ideas" appear as results of individual and private strivings and as natural outcomes of human activity. Representations thereby mask awareness of the historical development of the objective social order and the underlying interest it serves.

Representations are necessary features of any social order. For institutions to endure, it becomes necessary for members of society to carry in their heads images of the kind of society that "it's supposed to be." This is one way in which chaos is forestalled, and it provides a means for achieving concensus, so that members of a society can live cooperatively. Representations, therefore, become necessary features of social systems reproducing or presenting again the dominant value concensus and institutional power arrangements of a society. The representations of existing power arrangements not only stabilize the social order and make it predictable, they also enable dominant groups to find in the individual habitual obedience to the social arrangements that support their way of life.

Ideologies come about as a result of class, race, and sex antagonism and struggle. Ideologies are manifest in concrete social forms and in established institutional and power arrangements within society.

> It will then be clear that a theory of ideologies depends in the last resort on the history of social formations, and thus of the modes of production combined in social formations, and of the class struggles which develop in them. In this sense it is clear that there can be no question of a theory of ideologies in general, since ideologies . . . have a history, whose determination in the last instance is clearly situated outside ideologies alone, although it involves them.[16]

What is important to note is that it is impossible for the human subject to exist outside of ideological formulations or reformulations of social existence. "The critique of ideology involves a hermeneutic of suspicion, an attempt to deconstruct a prevailing ideology in order to trace the interests that sustain it and the societal realities which it conceals." We only have proximate truths, not the whole truth. Ideology is perennial, a shortened map of reality that we all have and which helps us make sense of the world. Hence, there can be no adequate moral critique of ideology apart from some broader vision and encompassing symbolization of justice.[17] The Latin American liberation theologian Juan Luis Segundo explained, "Any attempt to put through a radical change in the existing structures must present itself as an ideology."[18] While any attempt to support uncritically the status quo reflects an ideology as well. One can only denounce one ideological formulation in the name of another. As long as one does not call into question his or her own position, but regards it as an absolute, fully adequate proposition which is unquestionable or unproblematic (i.e., "my country, right or wrong!"), then one is arguing from an ideological position without recognizing it, or at least without admitting to it. The human subject is a product of social practices which are sustained through established institutional arrangements in which ideological formulations exist.

> But ideology is not a slogan under which political and economic interest of a class presents itself. It is the way in which the individual actively lives his or her role within the social totality; it therefore participates in the construction of that individual so that he or she can act. Ideology is a practice of representation; a practice to produce a specific articulation, that is, producing certain meanings necessitating certain subjects as their supports.[19]

The human subject is mediated through established institutional arrangements by necessity of the fact that he or she is a social being, and has his or her origin within some ideological formulation of reality and specific social practices. I have already suggested that the family and religious institutions are among the most important institutions at the community level which convey the ideologies of the culture to the infant and his or her position within society. Ideology functions not only to legitimate and reproduce existing social arrangements, but it also functions to narrow the range of alternatives. The system of domination and oppression reproduces itself in the lives of its subjects by incorporating the identity of the individual within existing practices and social arrangements.

Ideology is thus a material practice in both senses of the term: first, because it is produced and reproduced in concrete institutions; second, because it produces fixed relations and positions in which the individual represents himself, relations and positions which are a material force in the process of the social formation. Ideology produces the individual in a relation to representation within the social process in which he or she is situated, as an identity (a point of self-reference) rather than a process. The practice of ideology then expresses a will, a purpose, a fixed position or tendency.[20]

The human subject, through practice and ideology, represents to self and others the dominant, yet veiled interest of ruling groups in society. Their interests are taken as representing "the common good" and comprehended as the culmination of history, and hence intrinsic to the intent of history. Ideology, while it exists to guarantee existing social practices and institutional and power arrangements, is false consciousness when it proposes its own conception of reality as the only valid interpretation of events. False consciousness is another way of saying that ideology is idolatrous faith. It is idolatrous faith or false consciousness because human subjects represent to themselves the distorted and limited view that existing social arrangements are necessary and natural, rather than a specific construction of reality. It is this deluded view of reality that is at the center of every ideological representation of social reality.

There is another important sense in which ideology, as false consciousness, is also a true consciousness. As a true consciousness, the mental ideas and images people reproduce in themselves are true or become true for them. What is true is that the ideas they represent to themselves depict true domination. An example would be, "I guess they had to lay me off to stay in business," or "Black people will never make it in this society." This is true consciousness because it correctly reflects how people identify themselves—as less than subjects. Hence, they reflect true domination. Ideology is a true consciousness in that it is an accurate reflection of a particular appropriation of a specific social and historical development. Ideology as a reflection of a specific social and historical development points to the subjective or intersubjective side of ideology. This

177

intersubjective dimension is significant in that concrete human subjects, themselves, are the bearers of ideology and constantly practice the ritual of ideological recognition, a ritual deemed meaningful even to them. "To gain access to the subjective outlook of individuals, therefore, is to gain access to an accurate portrait of their experiences of their society as mirrored in their thought forms." Edward Sampson, in pointing to this true-false, objective-subjective quality of ideology writes:

> [Theodore W.] Adorno asks us what sense we would make out of the data from an extensive public opinion survey that showed that people no longer describe themselves as workers. He first rejects the simple truth of this assertion, noting that simply because people no longer define themselves as workers does not mean that they are, in fact, no longer workers. Thus, if they occupy particular roles within the societal productive process, objectively they can be said to be workers. Their subjective belief that they are not represents the false-side of ideology, their false-consciousness. Our question here would inquire about the particular interests that were served by this ideological veil.[21]

In this last quote we can see that what is ideological (i.e., false consciousness) is also a true consciousness and one serving social interests that may be injurious to the welfare of oppressed people. On one hand, ideology obscures to the workers a true grasp of their objective position in the social structure. On the other hand, it accurately reflects a constitutent element of their social reality. This dual quality of ideology necessitates awareness of the linkage between the objective side of ideology (and hence the sociological dimension), and the subjective side of ideology (and hence a psychoanalytic understanding of social processes).

In summary, ideologies are linked in two fundamental ways. First, ideology is a necessarily and a historically developed characteristic of institutional arrangements, reflecting the interest of dominant groups, sustained in and through social practice, and mediated through the activities of individuals who occupy specific positions within the social totality. Second, ideology may be seen as intersubjectivity and as a practice of representation. Ideology as an objectified, institutionalized reality is a basic component of human consciousness. From this second perspective, human subjects, as individuals, do not create history; history creates human subjects. The dialectical relationship between the objective and subjective side of ideology can be stated as follows: specific social practices give rise to particular ideologies, and particular ideologies sustain specific social practices.[22]

6.

The Human Person as Subject. To be a subject means to act and to be acted upon; to single out as well as to be singled out as an object. The term subject further implies a prior material—i.e., a historical condition that is responsible for its emergence in the first place. The problem of the subject in dialectical materialism is how to account for the emergence and constitution of the subject, who is an acting being whose agency is determined by material forces, such as *relations of production,* which he or she cannot completely control or manipulate. By "relations of production" I mean specific contexts of interaction that support the dominant ideology. Contexts, such as the family, the work place, the school, the church, often serve to produce and to reinforce a specific social outlook that underlies a particular social order. The subject, in time, becomes a primary source in the social process for the support of ideologies. Subjects reproduce in themselves the ideas and thought patterns that serve to adjust them within the prevailing ideology and systems of control. Hence, the subject can now supply his or her own reasons as to why he or she should not have a raise at this time: "The boss has just given himself one and the company cannot afford my raise at this point. Besides, money isn't everything," or "I just work here; I'm not important."

The human is born into a world already lived in and organized by predecessors. The world into which the person is born and socializes has already achieved a certain oganization, structure, and cultural identity. Before the infant develops the capacity for language, or is able to question or critically evaluate his or her position in society, he or she is already socialized, without conscious awareness, into a particular stratification of society through the very context into which he or she is born.

179

What determines the formative relationships and the social processes that produce them are the material conditions of life, the established relations of productions built upon them and their supporting ideologies. Althusser writes:

> You and I are *always already* subjects, and as such constantly practice the rituals of ideological recognition, which guarantee for us that we are indeed concrete, individual, distinguishable and (naturally) irreplaceable subjects.
>
> But to recognize that we are subjects and that we function in the practical rituals of the most elementary everyday life . . . this recognition only gives us the "consciousness" of our incessant (eternal) practice of ideological recognition—its consciousness, i.e., its recognition—but in no sense does it give us the (scientific) knowledge of the mechanism of this recognition.[23]

Through representations and legitimations the human subject comes to hold as his or her own, the distorted view that the existing order of things is the natural and necessary order. Ideological representations are internalized distortions that become unnoticed, yet are constitutive elements in the subjective outlook of individuals. The objective realities of society, then, are not provisional conditions of the mind which disappear over time. But from the outset objective social realities condition individual consciousness and transform the subject into an agent of the system of domination. This system then limits and conditions the freedom of the individual in ways that remain partially unnoticed. Hence, it is in the problem of the constitution of the subject that the problem of ideology and freedom becomes an even more complex issue. The complexity of the issue is that ideology, which is both an objective and subjective phenomenon, works to channel individual freedom in certain predetermined ways. The subject is not simply an autonomous individual, but is simultaneously the agent of the social determinations that condition him or her. We are faced not only with a "system of ideas" external to the individual, but also with the more complex interplay between the subjective and unconscious determinants in the social formation of the subject.

> What is produced in ideology is the very basis of the subject's activity, the conditions of its positions as subject, and the coherency

of that subject in the face of contradictions which make up society. Ideology produces the subject as the place where a specific meaning is realized in signification. It is thus an active part of social relations since it creates their intelligibility, and intelligibility which in a capitalist society tends to serve the interest of one class.[24]

The meaning of the person as a subject originates in language, the signifier. Language, as a symbol system, predates the individual and is "imposed on the human subject in its construction in history and ideological formulations."[25] Althusser gives an illustration of the mechanism through which the subject comes to be what he or she is through language. The concrete subject is called forth (interpellated) in a speaking (ideological) situation that enables the subject to act within the social totality. Althusser writes:

> To take a highly "concrete" example, we all have friends who, when they knock on our door and we ask, through the door, the question "Who's there?" answer (since "it's obvious") "It's me." And we recognize that "it is him," or "her." We open the door, and "it's true, it really was she who was there." To take another example, when we recognize somebody of our (previous) acquaintance ((re)-connaissance) in the street, we show him that we have recognized him (and have recognized that he has recognized us) by saying to him "Hello, my friend," and shaking his hand (a material ritual practice of ideological recognition in everyday life).[26]

It is through language (the call and response) that particular expressions of the self are impelled and become known in a vivid social process. The individual comes to recognition of himself or herself as having a particular meaning to others through language. A concrete self emerges in relationship to other concrete selves and in specific context of interaction. Whenever we hail someone through handshaking or verbally as in, "Hey, you there," we undergo a ritual of mutual recognition and represent to ourselves and to the other the fact that we already exist in a world of highly structured and commonly shared symbols. Both parties, the one who hails and the hailed one, know how to act and what is expected in this mutual exchange without thinking about it. Language makes this possible.

We can summarize the main role of language in the emergence of the subject and ideology as follows:

1. From the beginning of our existence we are called out in discourse and limited by the use of language and through specific social practices that fix our reality within a particular mental horizon.

2. We come to recognize the other and ourselves (and vice versa) as being a certain kind of subject (i.e., a friend, an employee, or an enemy) and as occupying a certain position within a social process and structure of relationships.

3. The cultural symbols we use (i.e., language) determine to a certain degree how we represent reality to ourselves and to others and how they represent reality to us. It is through sociality and symbolic interchange that we come to exist as concrete subjects, with specific identities and within a social and historical context.

The subject who comes into being evolves from specific social processes that are themselves determined by the material conditions of life, the forces of production, the relationships that arise from them, and the ideologies that support them. Language and ideology within society and history are significant determiners in the social processes that account for the social formation of the conscious subject. But the subject that emerges is not identical, i.e., not a simple mirror reflection of the symbolic relations or of the ideological processes that formed it. The human as subject is capable of differentiating himself or herself within the social process. Coward and Ellis argue that human beings, as subjects

> are different from and not reducible to specific ideological relations. At the same time, they are not to be separated from ideology, as somehow "coming before it." The symbolic relations, a subject in position of predication, are always manifested within ideological formulations.[27]

Coward and Ellis, building on the work of Althusser, point to the important, yet often ignored dialectical and dynamic relationship between objective, material reality, and the subjective or inner world of the subject. They have argued for the importance of keeping sociological theory and psychoanalysis together for an adequate understanding of the human subject in emancipatory struggles. Psychoanalysis and the idea of the unconscious can facilitate a deeper appreciation of the human subject by distinguishing between the function of language and ideology in the formation of the subject.

7.

Ideology and the Unconscious. I have argued that it is the function of ideology to fix the individual within a specific and limited mental horizon. This function of ideology is never wholly successful for all members of society. Some people, especially victims and minority group members, while a product of prevailing social practices, also resist conforming to the dominant ideology, and some even manage to challenge it radically. Others pay the price of challenge and struggle with their lives. Modern social reality is itself composed of multiple contradictions. It is extremely complex, evolving through processes that are inconsistent, disruptive, and differentiating. It is important to recognize that the subject's conscious and unconscious life is shaped by multiple inconsistencies in modern society. While ideology functions to conceal or rationalize the contradictions within society and to adjust the individual within the existing order of things, the real effects of societal contradictions are nonetheless constitutive of the unconscious life of the subject. From the perspective of psychoanalysis, the human subject is not an undifferentiated, unified whole. The unconscious is not a mirror reflection of the subject's conscious life. Rather, the unconscious is itself a source of alternative possibilities and information, unrecognized by the subject acting within the routine and common sense world of everyday life.

Because the individual is never totally socialized into the larger social structure, there will always be an *outside*, or unsocialized and unpredictable, dimension to human activity which is resistant to the prevailing norms, roles, relationships, and ideologies imposed by society. This unpredictable outside contains the seeds of alternative possibilities to the status quo of society. In other words, the whole of the social process never fully gets into the limelight of consciousness. Repressed or forgotten and unnoticed aspects of social processes will always assert themselves behind the smoke screen of conscious activity, but nevertheless will shape and determine social relations. The fundamental and ideal purpose of Freudian psychoanalytically oriented therapy, and pastoral therapies informed by this practice, is to make conscious that which is unconscious. The ideal is to bring into the open what has been shut off from conscious reflection. The task is to restore to the subject the capacity for critical reflection, responsible and ethical decisions, and emancipatory activity. But these ideals will be impossible to achieve as long as therapy functions to adjust the subject's mental horizon within the constraints of an ideology consistent with capitalist domination. If the latter interest prevails, then therapies serve, perhaps unwittingly, to support the reproduction in consciousness of the domination of bourgeois ideology.

Marx emphasized the objective and consciously determined side of social and historical processes. Freud saw and emphasized the subjective side. These two complementary levels, the social and historical and the subjective or intersubjective, are continually interrelated and dialectically constituted. According to Freud, the human subject is not only a social structure—i.e., socially constituted, but the human subject is also a biological and instinctual structure as well. Freud distinguished between the *pleasure principle,* which he identified with the subject's unconscious and presocialized, instinctual structure, and the *reality principle,* which governs the conscious and socialized life of the subject. The latter subordinates, suppresses, and channels individual freedom to fit the requirements of society. Suppression and control, in turn, are legitimated by ideology. According to Herbert Marcuse:

> The individual exists, as it were, in two different dimensions, characterized by different mental processes and principles. The difference between these two dimensions is a genetic-historical as well as a structural one; the unconscious, ruled by the pleasure principle, comprises "the older, primary processes, the residues of a phase of development in which they are the only kind of mental processes." . . . The reality principle supercedes the pleasure principle; man learns to give up momentary, uncertain, and descriptive pleasure for delayed, restrained, but "assured" pleasure. Because of this lasting gain through renunciation and

restraint, according to Freud, the reality principle "safeguards" rather than "dethrones," "modifies" rather than denies, the pleasure principle.

These two dynamic principles are eternally antagonistic and exist in tension. According to Marcuse these dynamic and antagonistic principles are far from unique. They recur throughout the history of both humankind and every individual.

> The fact that the reality principle has to be re-established continually in the development of man indicates that its triumph over the pleasure principle is never complete and never secure. . . . The claim of the pleasure principle continues to exist in civilization itself. The unconscious *retains* the objective of the defeated pleasure principle.[28] (Emphasis my own.)

Again, there is an irreconcilable tension, an *eternal antagonism* between the instinctual needs of the individual organism and the requirements of society. This antagonism, however, is more than an individual phenomenon; it is also an objective, historical reality as well.

Marcuse saw the emancipatory potential of psychoanalysis precisely because its methods were geared toward the unconscious, "the deepest and oldest layer of the mental personality." In psychoanalysis and through recall or memory, fantasy, daydreaming, and dream analysis, the tabooed contents of the unconscious can yield their hidden truths.

> If memory moves into the center of psychoanalysis as a decisive mode of cognition, this is far more than a therapeutic device; the therapeutic role of memory derives from the *truth value* of memory. Its truth value lies in the specific function of memory to preserve promises and potentialities which are betrayed and even outlawed by the mature, civilized individual, but which had once been fulfilled in his dim past and which are never entirely forgotten. . . .
>
> The psychoanalytic liberation of memory explodes the rationality of the repressed individual. As cognition gives way to re-cognition, the forbidden images and impulses of childhood begin to tell the truth that reason denies. Regression assumes a progressive function. . . .

Psychoanalytic theory removes these mental faculties from the noncommittal sphere of daydreaming and fiction and recaptures their strict truths.[29]

Freud, however, in *Civilization and Its Discontents,* was pessimistic concerning the success of emancipatory struggles for the majority of human subjects, especially the oppressed and dispossessed who had internalized the mechanisms of control which sustained the system of domination and its accompanying ideologies. Marx was more hopeful that history was now on the side of the oppressed and that emancipation from domination would eventuate through the self-conscious and revolutionary struggle of the downtrodden, a collective struggle. In this light, the liberal bourgeois idea of the triumph of the detached, and unmediated, solitary individual ego, capable of self-emancipation alone is a particularist delusion. It is a delusion because it obscures the dynamic interconnection between the person and the system which constitutes it and from which it is never separated. "Individualism in the American tradition has, to be sure, exaggerated the social significance of personal transformation, assuming that societal improvement comes about primarily through change in the attitudes of individuals."[30]

This chapter has emphasized the fundamental conditioning influence of society itself in the constitution of the subject. The subject while conditioned by society is not a mere puppet or solely a reflection of the social system. Rather, the human subject is a self-conscious, creative agent as well as a recipient of symbolized orders of experience.[31] Human subjects have the capacity to step back and to critically reflect upon and to transform the very social practices and relations that formed them. The ideal of the human subject as a co-architect of a new and liberating social order, free from totalitarian domination is a challenge where masses of people are alienated and continuously rendered superfluous in a modern technological society. Critical reflection and ethical inquiry are essential to liberation praxis. Critical reflection, however, is not in itself an ultimate criteria or a final truth. It can function as a guide in a liberating praxis which is itself self-critical and which seeks divine justice and mercy and continuously struggles to free poor and oppressed people from new forms of human and systemic bondage.

VIII.

An Interpretation of the Peoples' Temple and Jonestown: Implications for the Black Church

"The mana of the mana-personality is in the eyes of the beholder; the fascination is in the one who experiences it. This is the very thing that has to be explained: if all people are more or less alike, why do we burn with such all-consuming passions for some of them?" . . . *"What is creative projection? What is life-enhancing illusion?"*
—Ernest Becker
in *The Denial of Death*

"The great source of evil in life is the absolutizing of the relative, which in Christianity takes the form of substituting religion, revelation, church or Christian Morality for God."
—H. Richard Niebuhr
in *The Meaning of Revelation*

This final chapter will pull together the themes of the earlier chapters in an interpretation of Peoples' Temple and the Jonestown holocaust. The themes to be emphasized are: the relational self and its construction in group relations; the fate of the self under ideological and structural domination; and the role of the church when personal and social transformation are kept together in Christian ministry with an emancipatory interest.

1.

Prior to the events of November 18, 1978, the San Francisco-based Peoples' Temple was relatively unknown to the

187

American public, to many church leaders outside the Bay Area, and to the social scientists who studied the new religious movements in the United States. The mass murders and suicides in Jonestown, Guyana, forcefully brought the Peoples' Temple to national and world attention and provoked widespread indignation, condemnation, and reflection.

Most of the interpretations of the Jonestown tragedy analyzed this event from a journalistic perspective,[1] or from a sociological perspective,[2] or from the perspective of psychiatry[3] or psychology. A number of books have appeared including an eyewitness report,[4] a former member of the Peoples' Temple,[5] and by those who had close contact with the Temple and its activities.[6] With one exception,[7] these accounts have not interpreted the Peoples' Temple or the Jonestown, Guyana, tragedy from a black church perspective, or assessed the implications of this event for the ministry of the black church.

The pupose of this chapter is to identify some implications of the Peoples' Temple and the Jonestown, Guyana, tragedy for the pastoral care ministry of the black church. My task is an interpretive one. I am convinced that there are serious implications for the pastoral care ministry of black churches, and I am equally concerned that this event be remembered and not become a victim of social amnesia.

I shall give a brief sketch of Jim Jones' origin and the emergence of Peoples' Temple and: (1) identify several theories which emerged to "explain" Jonestown; (2) identify secularism as a central theme; (3) relate this theme to a plausibility crisis in black church religion today; (4) assess the appeal of the Peoples' Temple in light of that crisis; and (5) draw some implications for the black church and its ministry from a particular relational standpoint. This is an expanded reflection about an area that was neglected in the media and that appeared to escape the attention of most social scientists who were called on to interpret the tragedy.

2.

Little is known about James Warren Jones' origins—family background, childhood, and adolescent years. Briefly, he was born in 1931, the only child of James T. and Lynetta Jones. His father was gassed in World War I and suffered severe respiratory problems. He drew a disability check most of the time and worked little. His father was a member of the local Ku Klux Klan, a group which the younger James would publicly denounce. His mother was an anthropologist and worked in Africa prior to her marriage to the severely disabled and older James T. Jones. Lynette Jones was viewed by neighbors as an odd woman who always wore dark clothes and stayed to herself. As a youngster, Jim Jones came under the influence of a neighbor, a Mrs. Kennedy who introduced him to Fundamentalist religion. Jim Jones regarded her as his second mother. The younger Jones was also a loner. In grade school and high school he was seen by neighbors and peers as having an unusual interest in religion. By his junior year in high school he was giving serious thought to entering the ministry which he eventually did. He turned to religion not as a follower, but as a leader. As a child he would often organize funeral services for dead pets, an early indication of his identification with the powerless and lowly ones. At age fourteen his parents separated and then divorced. It was shortly after this that Jones had his first opportunity to preach from a pulpit in a nearby black church. Six years later his father died alone in a hotel. Jim Jones attended Indiana University after graduation from high school, dropped out to work at a hospital where he met a nurse named Marcelline. She was four years his senior and became his wife in the same year of their meeting. Jones' mother died in 1977, approximately one year before his own death.[8]

It is common knowledge that the Peoples' Temple did not originate in the San Francisco Bay Area. James Warren Jones founded it in Indianapolis in 1956. The temple brought together Jones' longtime interest in religion, politics, and his ideal of racial justice. He held to and persisted in his ideal of racial equality in the early 1950s, in a time and place where these views were not popular. Indianapolis was a tough blue-collar industrial city which had been the home of the national office of the Ku Klux Klan. Jones' dream was to establish a relatively independent power base for a racially integrated congregation, a dream that he realized in his family of creation. "Jones' adopted children were black, white, and Asian, and he presented them as a strong example of his pro-integration

189

beliefs. His notions about assembling families and arranging relationships within the church circle took shape during this time."[9]

By 1963, the Peoples' Temple was called the *Peoples' Temple Full Gospel Church*. It had a strong and impressive civil rights and social outreach program which included free meals to the city's destitute, and it appeared to be at the forefront of struggles to combat race prejudice. Jones promised economic security, a sense of belonging and purpose in life, and freedom from a hostile, fascist world. All of this was in return for property and other financial assets and an unwavering commitment to the leader and "the cause."

During his time in Indiana, Jones was constantly threatened and assailed by racists who made known their anti-black sentiments. He was also held in suspicion by authorities who questioned his business and profit-raising ventures and his acclaimed method of exorcising tumorous cancers.[10] The embattled leader and his congregation grew closer and more secretive as they drew a protective line between themselves and *outsiders*.

Jones and his followers numbering less than two hundred left the Midwest in 1965 and settled in Redwood Valley, California, a rustic farming community near Ukiah and approximately one hundred twenty-five miles north of San Francisco. In the move from Indianapolis, Jones held tent revivals along the way and recruited more members who joined him in his move West. Many who joined were members of black churches. Black churches in San Francisco later proved to be a prime target for recruitment of membership into the Peoples' Temple. Many congregations lost members to Jim Jones.

Redwood Valley became the second home of the Peoples' Temple. In its new location, the temple continued its active and responsible involvement in social justice issues. Looking back, the city manager of Ukiah was reported as saying, "Jones was a different thing because he was around town. . . . When his people got in trouble, he saw they made restitution. They gave to community groups. They had pretty good public relations. So there was shock and surprise when they went off the deep end."[11] This may have been the way they were perceived and remembered by some leading officials in Ukiah, but things did not start off easily for Jones and his predominantly black, but racially mixed congregation. Jones and his followers experienced some of the same racism and hostility in Ukiah that they had known in Indianapolis.

Jones was influenced by Father Divine, the Philadelphia-based black religious leader. He was fascinated by the complete control Father Divine exercised over his racially mixed congregation. He modeled himself and his organization after Father Divine, emulating his flamboyant style, approach to faith healing, and organizational structure. Although Jones was greatly influenced by Father Divine, he was a charismatic figure in his own right and capable of calling out an unusual degree of commitment from his followers. They became committed to *him* and not primarily to his ideology. The late Jeannie Mills, who joined the Temple in 1969 and defected in 1975, wrote of her experience:

> This minister, Pastor Jim Jones, has a strange power over his members. The power is fear, guilt, and extreme fatigue. While we were in it we did many strange things. We each had to admit that we were homosexual or lesbians. We were forced to stop all sexual activities with our marriage partners. Pastor Jim Jones claimed that he was the only person who knew how to love, and frequently had the women and men he had had sexual relations with stand up and testify to what an excellent lover he was. We had to participate in humiliating and often painful punishments for various things that Pastor Jones felt were "bad." . . . These disciplines were for such minor things as forgetting to call Jim Jones "Father" or for talking about the church to an "outsider" or for losing secret church papers, for forgetting to pay a bill, for giving a piece of candy to one child and not to another, and other trivial things. These are only a very few of the thousands of inconsequential things that could cause cruel or sadistic punishments to be meted out by Pastor Jim Jones.[12]

Jones used blackmail to keep his followers in line. He ruled with strong lines of control and delegated authority to only an inner circle of followers who were fiercely loyal to him.

The Peoples' Temple remained in Redwood Valley for approximately seven years. But Jones became restless soon after moving to Redwood Valley and decided to branch out. As one observer put it, "Jim Jones started leaving about a year after he got here."[13]

The predominantly black Filmore and Bayview districts of San Francisco became the place where he made contact and developed his political religion[14] and established his integrated congregation as his base of power. On weekend trips from Redwood Valley to San Francisco he was billed by followers who had prepared the way as: "PASTOR JIM JONES . . . Incredible! . . . Miraculous! . . . Amazing! The Most Unique Prophet Healing Service You've Ever Witnessed! Behold the Word Incarnate in Your Midst!"[15] Jones' reputation as a healer, a benevolent father who cares and provides for his own, a visionary, a champion of the oppressed, and prophet of God spread before him. He was also perceived to be "one of the most politically potent religious leaders in the history of the state."[16] By 1970 he was ready to make the move to San Francisco. In 1972 he purchased an empty auditorium on Geary Boulevard in the Filmore district of San Francisco and made it his new headquarters and the third home of the Peoples' Temple.[17] In 1974 he founded the agricultural community in Guyana, now remembered as *Jonestown*.

In San Francisco, Jones' political influence grew, along with his wealth and congregation. In time he founded another congregation in Los Angeles, although his headquarters remained in San Francisco. He founded a newspaper, The *Peoples' Forum: Brotherhood Records,* "a church subsidiary that produced and sold music by the Temples' large interracial youth choir and orchestra"; and purchased thirty minutes of broadcast time each Saturday morning on a religious radio station.[18] He made large financial contributions to charity and organizations in need, humanitarian causes, and political groups in the city. The late major of San Francisco, George Moscone, was reported as praising Jim Jones:

> Your contributions to the spiritual health and well-being of our community have been truly inestimable . . . you have demonstrated that the unique powers of spiritual energy and civic commitment are virtually boundless, and that our lives would be sadly diminished without your continuing contributions.[19]

The Peoples' Temple was also one of the largest contributors to their affiliate denomination, the Christian Churches of the Disciples of Christ. Jones was both highly esteemed and feared as a powerful community organizer. To some he was an asset to their political ambitions. To others he was a Christlike figure, a man of God doing good for the disinherited. To still others he was an insane and dangerous man, and a master manipulator.

Jim Jones had come a long way from his humble beginning in the small, obscure farming town of Lynn, Indiana. In the words of John P. Nugent, "As a child he played minister; at the end of his life he played God."[20] Although some were suspicious of Jones' motives from the beginning, few would envision the magnitude of the destruction wrought in Jonestown, Guyana, on November 18, 1978. In retrospect, it becomes possible to see more clearly that the end of the Jonestown colony results from the common thread of tyrannical power. The strategies Jones and his faithful inner circle employed throughout were focused around one central and overriding concern, namely, the maintenance of the authority and power of the leader and the support of fledgling power relationships within the groups—at any cost.[21]

3.

When the news of the mass murders and suicides first broke, from across the nation social scientists of various orientation were called on to interpret or "explain" the tragedy of Jonestown. One group of nationally known scholars met in New York on January 22 and 23, 1979, to reflect upon Jonestown and assess its meaning. These scholars directed their attention to "the dangers inherent in unconventional religion, especially its potential for authoritarianism and exploitation"; and to "the great diversity that characterizes unconventional religion today."[22] Particular concern with the implications of racism and sexism, the role and fate of the seven hundred or more black people victimized at Jonestown was not on the agenda for systematic attention.

The leading and most widely read magazines, *Time* and *Newsweek,* interviewed and recorded the responses of prominent authorities on the new religious movements in the United States.

The responses from black church leaders and black scholars were conspicuously absent, despite the fact that approximately 70 percent of those who perished at Jonestown were black. The majority were women; many were poor and elderly and from mainline black churches. The December 4, 1978 issue of *Newsweek* reported:

> Jones sought out the oppressed—especially poor Black prostitutes and other outcasts—who would welcome his message of egalitarianism and his offer to a communal home. But religious groups such as the Moonies, the Children of God and the Hare Krishnas prefer college students of above-average intelligence and idealism who will be a credit to the cult.[23]

The problem of racism in both the nature of the reporting on the events and in the movement itself never surfaced as a central feature in the explanations of what went wrong. I shall return to discuss racism as a structural and ideological problem which was not only manifested in the larger society they left behind but was also reflected in the movement itself.

A number of theories emerged to "explain" the events of November 18, 1978. Among these explanations were:

1. Peoples' Temple members were drawn from the disillusioned, malcontents, and outcasts of society.

2. The deprivation theory of religion as an illusion source of false consciousness, or opiate of the masses.

3. The "only in California" explanation.

4. Jonestown was an apocalyptic movement which manifested itself as a protest against persecution and a yearning for deliverance out of it into a new transformed social order.

5. Group-think and trance behavior explanations.

6. Jim Jones was planted by the Ku Klux Klan, a part of a general conspiracy to reestablish white supremacy.

I do not attempt to address all these explanations here. I shall only address the first three.

4.

Members of the Peoples' Temple were drawn from the sick, disillusioned, malcontent, and outcast of society. Margaret Thaler Singer, who has studied the cult phenomenon and worked with those who are "coming out of the cults" reported that "about one-third are very psychologically distressed people. The other two-thirds are relatively average people, but in a period of depression, gloom, being at loose ends."[24] Many of the statements that emerged to explain Jonestown cast much of the membership in the sick role. They were perceived as people with "problems": problems of adjustment, emotional problems, problems of dependency, problems of loneliness, depression, and low self-esteem.

There have been few attempts to search out the social motives *and* historical forces that made the appeal of Peoples' Temple and Jonestown, Guyana, so attractive to so many. The folk who joined the Peoples' Temple ranged widely in their motives, life-styles, and values orientation. Some joined for personal reasons; some joined for religious and political reasons; most joined for validation of some sort; many joined for humanitarian reasons. They believed in the vision of a new social order, a sense of kinship and family that was projected by Peoples' Temple.

Fauset offers some important social and psychological reasons for joining cults in black America.

> Negroes are attracted to the cults for the obvious reason that with few normal outlets of expression for Negroes in America due to the prevailing custom of racial dichotomy the cults offer on the one hand the boon of religion with all its attendant promises of heaven either here or above or both; and on the other hand they provide for certain Negroes with imagination and other dynamic qualities, in an atmosphere free from embarrassment or apology, a place where they may experiment in activities such as business, politics, social reform, and social expression; thereby these American Negroes satisfy the normal urge of any member of our culture who wishes to contribute positively to the advancement of the group.[25]

Cults, then, are neither the beginning nor the ending of black folk religion. Cults, as Joseph Washington observes, may well

195

"represent the middle through which Blacks must pass in the process of creating and finding their special role in religion and society." According to Washington, cults are power communities in which black selfhood, history, and culture come to expression, enabling many blacks to participate more effectively in a society that denies them their full humanity. Black cults, then, may be perceived as the "initial stages of a religion prior to its later development into diverse communities and institutions."[26]

It would not be accurate to say that the Peoples' Temple movement was socially regressive, or that only the socially maladjusted or down and out went to Jonestown. Jonestown was a commune of people—young and old, black and white, from wealthy as well as poor backgrounds, the well-educated and the illiterate, widows and widowers, single parents as well as husbands and wives, the religiously committed as well as those who were indifferent to religion.[27] Reports from the news media, pastors, relatives, and survivors reveal that a cross section of the black community was present in Jonestown—although the majority were from low-income neighborhoods, and many were welfare dependents. Some were persons of means; some were in good standing with their local black church. One black pastor reported that a beloved member of long-standing and deep involvement in her own church was a Jonestown victim. In a conversation with her pastor, she reported that she was attracted to Peoples' Temple because "they did things together, ate and took trips together." They were able to provide a family-like atmosphere, a sense of belonging on a daily basis in ways that she could not find in her own church. For her, the church still functioned as the central community institution which strengthened her participation in a larger social and political process. It was not that her home church failed her, but that she found in the Peoples' Temple *more* opportunities for involvement. It is not unusual for blacks to claim membership in more than one or two churches. This particular woman never gave up membership in her home church, even though she claimed membership in the Peoples' Temple. She was not alone in her desire to see the church more involved in issues of social protest and reform. Participation in her home church may well have been a motivating factor for involvement in the more socially active orientation of the Peoples' Temple.[28] Therefore, it would betray the facts to conclude that the people who joined the temple, and those who moved to Jonestown, were sick, less rational, or more deviant than the rest of us. Most of the membership was aware of loneliness, depression, exploitation, racism, alienation, sexism, and a general sense of despair that affects many in our society. They were people of hope in that they, at least, were actively seeking an alternative to the status quo.

They thought they saw an alternative in Jones and his movement—a mechanism and an opportunity to change their condition. In many ways the initial motivation that led many people to the Peoples' Temple and then on to Jonestown was admirable. They were seekers after a new communal and egalitarian society. They did not seek refuge in a privatized faith, but in a renewed and transformed social order. One person reportedly told a relative that in Jonestown she found something she had never found in the United States. For the first time, she believed she had found a society free of sexism and racism and one in which she experienced full acceptance as a black woman. She had a cause to live for. American society had never given her that. Her vision, however, was not broad or critical enough to perceive the barriers of class, sex, age, and race in the social structure of the organization itself. The top echelon and key decision-makers were white, educated, and professionals, calling the shots which determined and sealed the fate of the 70 percent black membership, mostly women, many elderly, who had given up everything to follow Jones. According to Jeannie Mills' account, "There were attorneys, college professors, a man who had graduated with honors from MIT, social workers, nurses, businessmen, and lots of other professional people on that council."[29] I use the term *racism* to call attention to the perpetuation of an established relational pattern of superior-inferior power relationships in the Peoples' Temple Movement that has been characteristic of race relations in the West since the sixteenth and seventeenth centuries.

Intragroup domination in the form of race, sex, and class exploitation was prominent. The key decision-makers were primarily white and educated, with a few token blacks. The followers were the masses of predominantly black and minority group members. The dominant group was a "group for itself," in that the maintenance of the status quo in power relations was a primary goal. The vulnerable position of blacks and women in the Peoples' Temple reflected their position of vulnerability in the wider society. The ruling elite and their power to shape the social outlook functioned to perpetuate inequality within the group and to control the flow of communication. The ruling ideas of race, sex, and class domination in the wider society were reflected in the organizational structure of the Peoples' Temple and ultimately at Jonestown.

The belief in freedom and equality that some assumed was there was a false consciousness. This belief misrepresented the true subordinate position of blacks within the group. The opportunity for black self-determination within the Peoples' Temple, i.e., the freedom and opportunity for black people to develop their own group consciousness and to become reflective and critical of the wider social process that carried them was obviously nonexistent. A false consciousness was a partial obstacle to black self-determination. A more social critical analysis of their situation was impossible to achieve under the circumstances. In this sense, the position of blacks within the Peoples' Temple was reflective of their vulnerability and was consistent with their position within the wider society. Had there been the freedom and opportunity to reflect upon and critically analyze their situation, then revolutionary activity within the group may have been a possibility. By revolutionary activity, I mean a critical questioning of the social process and an opportunity to radically change it. The people themselves were the real victims of a system of oppression and brutality which they supported or rationalized and were powerless to change. The interest of the ruling group in their own position of control and ideological domination functioned effectively to maintain the center of political power within the group. The white-controlled leadership of blacks was deeply rooted in the conventions of white supremacy.

Interviews with Temple defectors reveal that:

Racism, sexism and ageism—in fact, an utter disregard for the respect due any group or person—were systematically practiced

198

within the group itself. Our respondents report that it was Black people who bore the heaviest burden of PT "discipline" (physical abuse) within the group; that women were systematically used by Jones as objects of sexual gratification; and that senior citizens were, by some reports at least, systematically made marginal to the life of the community.[30]

This negative picture must be balanced by other factors. There were those who hated Jones and defected. They saw mainly negative things in the movement. But there were also the true believers who saw no wrong. There were survivors who saw good in Jonestown, affirmed its ideals, and believed in what Jim Jones had attempted to do relative to social change and social justice. And there were those who saw in Jones a sadomasochistic madman, a Charles Manson, Idi Amin, or an Adolph Hitler, but not a reformer or champion of the oppressed. One Temple participant may have come closest to the truth when she said, "There were two Jim Joneses."

5.

One of the major thought models that emerged to explain Jonestown was the psychoanalytically oriented view. This explanatory thought model cannot be considered exhaustive by any means. It is a highly condensed version for this presentation, and it reflects what I take to be the essence of the explanations put forward by many of those responding to Jonestown.

What is of particular importance here is the implied understanding of black religion and cultic experience. The bottom line in this explanatory world view is that religious cults are based upon an illusion—perhaps the oldest, strongest, and most persistent illusion of humankind. Within this thought model, religion is perceived as an inadequate attempt to channel the infantile and sadistic impulses of humankind. Religious cults, formed around a charismatic leader, have their origins in the sociopathic makeup of the leader. Persons who are drawn to religious cults and are members in them tend to be passive-dependent types in search of a surrogate parent or authority figure. The prime targets for recruitment into such movements as the Peoples' Temple were the oppressed, especially poor blacks, the lonely, dependent, and insecure, who welcomed the message of egalitarianism. In Jones' movement many sought a communal, family-like environment and an authority figure who could bestow an identity and give them the direction and help they needed to bear their emotional burdens. According to this thought model, such persons had little or no sense of inner value and sought direction from a paranoid and narcissistic charismatic leader, and in the process took on his developing psychosis and messianic hopes. A fusion or total and fatal identification was made with the charismatic leader in the isolated jungles of Guyana. He and the group had become one. When the leader made the decision to commit suicide, he took the entire group with him. Death by suicide and murder, then, was the end result of a long process of self-surrender of personal responsibility in exchange for spiritual and physical security.

Religious cults prosper in a time of profound social dislocation and cultural crises. Cults are perceived as an answer—capable of protecting the adherents from the reality demands of civilization. According to this thought model, religious cults are based on a *defect*—because it is a search for a perfect world beyond this one. It is a defense against the childish helplessness of the members, preventing them from facing and coping with reality as it really is. Hence, Sigmund Freud,[31] for example, referred to religion as an "illusion," a wish-fulfillment incompatible with reality. Religion, in this thought model, arises from profound feelings of helplessness. Under such conditions, the uneducated, disillusioned, and oppressed are particularly vulnerable to the egomania and sadomasochistic wishes of a paranoid charismatic leader.

This general thought model was one of the more widely accepted explanations that emerged to give meaning to the mass murders-suicides at Jonestown. This particular view sought to locate the origins of the holocaust of Jonestown within the psychological framework—i.e., the narcissistic personality and thinking processes of Jim Jones and the borderline personalities of many of his followers.

Audience corruption is a term used to identify the interaction between the leader and his followers. Followers learn to give the responses the leader wants them to learn; they feed it back to the leader on cue. He in turn believes even more in the power of the rightness of his leadership. When he announces that he is God, the followers feed back the supporting behavior, and then the leader believes unquestionably in his own deification. In turn, his unquestioned assent to divinity is believed by his followers. Absorbed in the immediate crisis, the present is the only reality, and the sole authority within that closed cosmos is the leader, who is deemed beyond challenge.[32] Isolated from the real world and pressured by their peers, converts wholly accept the leader's power—and his paranoia—and they put their welfare and their will totally in his hands. This world view is often utilized to "explain" that cults, and religious phenomena in general, have their origins in the narcissistic personality of their leaders and are sustained through the infantile dependency needs of members.

This, in brief form, is the essence of the psychoanalytically oriented view of religion. Religious cults, from this perspective, are a form of psychosis, a break with reality. In Marxism, religion is a source of error, a false consciousness incapable of correctly diagnosing reality as it actually exists. From a liberation perspective the psychoanalytic view may be useful in pointing to some of the inner forces—family origins and the need for validation and belonging—that motivate people. But it has tended to ignore the underlying sociological and historical forces that move people to join a group like the Peoples' Temple. Psychoanalytic explanations can become more useful when they are linked with a critical sociological and historical perspective which promotes an interest in emancipation.

With few exceptions the explanation underlying the actions of the victims was sought within the life history of the individuals who comprised the commune. However, the commune itself, as a social system, was not the fundamental object of critical reflection, nor was the society from which it derived. The traditional psychoanalytic view has often served to divert attention away from the social order by focusing on the individual's psychodynamics. This approach often serves to legitimate, not challenge, the status quo, when the individual is taken as the sole object of analysis.[33] This thought model has not been decisive for understanding the social context or relational character of our existence.

The larger social and political questions center in asking why Jonestown was necessary in the first place. What does the Jonestown event reveal about the nature of social structures and communicative processes that obsure awareness of the linking between social justice, personal and political impotence.

The concept *audience corruption* is worth underscoring. In essence, the followers learn to give the responses the leader wants them to learn, and they feed it back on cue to the leader, who in turn believes even more in what he or she is doing. "The cult preached absolute faith and dependence on Mr. Jones, and he apparently wielded complete control over the will of his adherents."[34] But the knife cuts both ways. The followers in turn feed back the delusions of the leader. The circle of deception was complete when both Jones and his followers took him to be the deity.

The narrowing of the individual's mental horizon and personal freedom did not originate at Jonestown. It was a central, yet unrecognized, part of a social dynamic in becoming a true believer and loyal member of the Temple and its cause in the first place. One Temple defector stated:

> I am faced with an unanswerable question: "If the church was so bad, why did you and your family stay in for so long?" . . .
> Only months after we defected from the Temple, did we realize the full extent of the cocoon in which we'd lived. And only then did we understand and deplore the fraud, sadism, and emotional blackmail of the master manipulator.[35]

The dynamics of interpersonal deceit, the toleration of sadism, and emotional blackmail was maintained by a false consciousness—i.e., the unwillingness or inability to perceive and critically question the social "cocoon" in which they lived and the lack of power to change it. Interpersonal deceit served to bolster the center of power within the group and to prevent a critical social analysis within the context of a wider reference of values.

The derived scenario goes something like this: in the isolated laboratory-like environment of Jonestown there was no ultimate authority or reality beyond the leader himself. Jones knew that he had led his people, most of them black and elderly, to the paradise of Jonestown. He was well aware of the pressure on him to prove his experiment was a viable one; that the trust invested in him was justified. But there was no place in Jonestown for critical and independent thought to question the paranoid fears of the leader. Conflict of opinion or alternative perspectives were not tolerated, and anyone expressing a different view was severely punished. Over a period of time, through techniques of thought control, fear, shame, induced guilt, the use of informers and widespread mistrust, and the use of tranquilizing drugs, many members of the Jonestown colony were reduced to passive cogs in a machine. Having no genuine freedom of choice, they became footnotes in some larger drama orchestrated through the megalomania of Jim Jones.

Such experiences as I've described in *audience corruption* go on all the time, and such a process may be quite unconscious, subtly developed over a long period of time. This process is difficult to resist, since it proceeds largely without the participant's conscious awareness. This idea of *audience corruption*, whereby both cultic leader and followers together construct social reality, will not permit us to attribute all the blame to Jim Jones for what happened.

> The leader is as much a creature of the group as they of him and that he loses his "individual distinctiveness" by being a leader, as they do by being followers. He has no more freedom to be himself than any other members of the group, precisely because he has to be a reflex of their assumptions in order to qualify for leadership in the first place.[36]

Jones could not have orchestrated the idea of his deification without the support of his followers. Jones, too, was a victim of his ego deification process.

R. D. Laing used the term "collusion" to further identify a social process whereby two or more people deceive themselves. The process is one of mutual self-deception.

> Two (or more) people in relation may confirm each other or genuinely complement each other. Still, to disclose oneself to the other is hard without confidence in oneself and trust in the other. Desire for confirmation from each is present in both, but each is

caught between trust and mistrust, confidence and despair, and both settle for counterfeit acts of confirmation on the basis of pretence. To do so *both* must play the game of collusion.

Collusion is always clinched when self finds in other that other who will "confirm" self in the false self that is trying to make real, and vice versa. The ground is then set for prolonged mutual evasion of truth and true fulfillment. Each has found an other to endorse his own false notion of himself and to give this appearance a semblance of reality.[37]

This concern around *audience corruption* and collusion serves as a possible window into some of the dynamics that may have transpired between Jones and his followers once they moved to the isolated jungles of Guyana. However, it is important to underscore that this dynamic was working before the move to Jonestown. In the isolated jungles of Guyana, the dynamic of *audience corruption* was intensified and became a central feature in the arsenal of control wielded by the leader and his inner circle. The Jonestown colony became engulfed in a closed cosmos where *audience corruption* and collusion may have been the paramount social process permeating everyday life. Lincoln and Mamiya suggested that the creation and maintenance of an isolated and private cosmos was Jones' ultimate goal and single achievement. In Jonestown, he achieved communicative, social, and physical isolation.

In a completely private cosmos reality is reconstructed in terms of the vision of the leader as they are reinforced by the affirmation of the faithful. This may well set the stage for a sustained corporate relationship at variance with the real world outside as to encourage, if not in fact to ensure and produce, an extreme paranoia for all concerned.[38]

If we cast a critical eye on Jim Jones, then we must also raise some hard questions about the social process itself, about the structure of authority, and about his followers, especially the well-educated and the religiously committed ones who surrendered personal responsibility, abandoned critical thinking, took him for God, and then expected from him almost everything one expects from the Divinity.

6.

Many concluded that Jonestown could only have come out of California. California is perceived as both receptacle and propagator of the bizarre. California gave the nation Richard M. Nixon. It was where Robert Kennedy was assassinated. It has been the home of Charles Manson, Aimee Semple McPherson and her Four Square Gospel Church, Father William Riker's Church of the Perfect Christian Divine Way, the Zebra Murders, the Symbionese Liberation Front, Synanon, the Free Speech Movement, EST, Bakke, and Proposition 13, to name a few wide-ranging examples. In California "Black Panthers become born again Christians; Ronald Reagan switches from being a liberal democrat to becoming Mr. Conservative."[39]

A black New York playwright was reported to have said many blacks on the East Coast were

> appalled not just that so many California Blacks were gullible enough to join Peoples' Temple, but that they accepted doom so willingly once they found themselves in the Guyana jungle. "It could never happen in New York or the deep South. . . . It's California. In Harlem, there's always someone who will help you. There's neither of that in California."[40]

The November 26, 1978, issue of the *New York Sunday Times* quoted a prominent social scientist from Columbia University.

> It is no accident that California is the World Center of all of these doctrines as well as the home of dozens of cults like the Peoples' Temple. . . .
>
> It is no accident because California has led the way in the creation of a natural and human wasteland peopled by bewildered souls roaming the freeways in search of clean air, the American dream, and some explanation—any kind of explanation—for what went wrong.[41]

Is California unique? Can anything sound or stable come out of California? Is it a bewildered wasteland?

I am not prepared to conclude that Jonestown could only have come out of kookie, eccentric California, not out of Harlem, South Philadelphia, Southside Chicago, and so forth, as some have reasoned. We recall that the Peoples' Temple originated in Indianapolis and that Jim Jones derived his inspiration from

Father Divine, a Philadelphia-based cult leader. An explanation such as "only in California" precludes a relational understanding of social reality. I will concede that the chances of a Jim Jones movement starting in large urban centers in the Northeast, where there tends to be a stronger identification with blackness than in the San Francisco Bay Area as a whole, is, perhaps, less likely. Nevertheless, no urban center is immune.

The idea behind "only in California" is the notion that California represents individualistic hedonism, a retreat from reality, a playland; that, perhaps, it is the insane ward; that out West a peculiar ethos of normlessness has emerged which puts certain groups and kinds of folk at high risk for all kinds of exploitative adventures. California, as someone said, is on the edge, facing out toward the Pacific Basin and its rim. If your dreams don't come true here, then they won't come true. It is, perhaps, then, not by accident that San Francisco has the highest suicide and alcoholism rate than any other city in the nation. There *is* a special ethos in San Francisco, an international city, which tends to attract the eccentrics, drifters, the lonely, and those in search of something new. There is also a sense of greater freedom. Sydney S. Ahlstrom, a New Englander, wrote,

> California has come to have the largest and most heterogeneous population in the Union. More important still, this rapid growth prevented the development of powerful traditions and restraints. It would thus be senseless to deny the frequently made claim that quantitatively speaking, California leads the nation in the proliferation of diverse religious movements. Perhaps one could say that just as the United States is an extreme form of Western civilization, so California is an extreme form of American civilization.[42]

San Francisco, as Howard Thurman once observed, is the most secular of cities in the United States. But given this, I cannot accept the idea that Jonestown, Guyana, could have emerged *only* from the soil and social ethos of the San Francisco Bay Area and nowhere else, and that Jonestown is solely a product of California culture. Jonestown was a product of U.S. society and Western culture. To put it succinctly, Jonestown was not an anomaly. It was a product of the evolving ethos of our time.

Explanations of Jonestown, as event, cannot be reduced to the personality of one man, or the uniqueness of California. We are much the wiser to understand Jonestown *as a product of a culture which tends to repress and trivialize the essentially religious impulse.* In our time, the dominant cultural themes are science, secularization, secular*ism*, global industrialism, and social revolutions.[43] The theme I want to identify is secular*ism*. By this I mean a preoccupation with the immediate rather than the ultimate questions, with natural or practical morality. Secular*ism* may be defined as the attempt to establish an autonomous sphere of knowledge free of supernatural presuppositions. Its modern roots may be traced to the later Middle Ages of Western Europe.

Secular*ism* is a product of the historical process of secularization. Secularization is the historical and cultural process by which science freed itself from theological constraints and society freed itself from domination by the church. Secularization means the *erosion* of traditional religious symbols of orientation and meaning centered around a compelling belief in one ultimate reality, and the increasing openness to a plurality of competing beliefs—all of which claim to be equally ultimate and meaningful.[44] American church historian Eldon G. Ernst makes the point:

> In its technical historical definition secularization is the process whereby Christian institutions and symbols cease to participate in sectors of society and culture. By this definition secularity implies that certain dimensions of human life fall outside the proper activities of churches.
>
> It is when the Christendom outlook combines with the acceptance of secularization that a common kind of religious isolation occurs. Churches do not become involved in social problems because they assume that the religious and the secular are two distinct spheres of life which ought to be kept separate. Yet these same churches may also assume that American institutions and social structures are essentially Christian. All that is needed is the moral strengthening of individual citizens, which is where the church comes in.[45]

7.

In the remainder of this chapter I will briefly sketch this central theme of secularism; relate it to the Peoples' Temple movement and the Jonestown holocaust; and identify some implications of this for the ministry of the black church in the black community.[46] Secularism, as a molding power of modern consciousness, is easily underestimated. It does not stand alone but is supported by individualism and privatism. Each of these forces creates problems for the black church and a challenge to its ministry. In other words, we are facing a plausibility crisis in the black church which cannot be fully appreciated apart from an adequate grasp of the meaning of secularism and the historical process of secularization.

The origins of modern secularism can be traced back to the later Middle Ages of Western Europe. There will be no attempt made here to account for the whole of that long and complex history. The starting point for an analysis is a matter of choice. I take the seventeenth century as a point of departure, marking a break in the continuity of ideas in the history of Western civilization when secularization emerged as the dominant historical process. Secularism is a by-product of this historical process and may be interpreted as a revolt against theological and metaphysical absolutes, indicating a break with the past and its presuppositions.

The extent of the break with the past can be illustrated by Niccolò Machiavelli, in *The Prince,* who took the final cause concept out of politics; René Descartes, who took God out of nature and declared God and nature to be two independent entities and submitted everything to the scrutiny of reason; and Francis Bacon, who opposed the ancient authorities and emphasized experimentation and observation of facts as the new basis for inquiry. The significance of the break with the past by these thinkers is that the modern period became preoccupied with an enlightened mind, a rational epistemology—and a subordination of other ways of knowing.[47] The works of such men as Galileo, Copernicus, Kepler, and Newton in the seventeenth and eighteenth centuries gave scientific support to the philosophers' attempt to break with the past.[48]

The works of these men and others, such as Locke, Leibnitz, Hume, Kant, and Hegel, mark the rise of the modern way of thinking, as well as the rise of the physical sciences. It is from these formative figures that our concepts and perceptions of the nature of reality are derived. The largely unquestioned assumption or idea that Western society is a fundamentally rational one can be traced back to the above mentioned figures, although its roots lie in the Constantinian wedding of church and society.

With the emancipation of reason came the triumph of a new ideology, namely secularism. Secularism assumes the autonomy of the human person and places him or her and this world at the center of speculation where God or the supernatural once stood. Secularism further assumes that the world is subject to rational control by the scientific method and can, in time, usher forth in utopia. The notion that the world is under rational control by the scientific method is reflected in all current thought and life. Secularism assumes, in Machiavellian fashion, that the human being makes his or her own rules on the basis of an enlightened humanism. Under the impact of secularization and with the emergence of a secular society black church religion is only one among many contesting centers of orientation. Understandably, a plausibility crisis is the result. A secular society implies the recognition of multiple realities, or pluralism as a central feature of modernity. A multiplicity of competing interest and ways of thinking emerge as a central feature of a secular milieu and result in a central problem of authority and identity.

The process of secularization paved the way for a natural, rationalistic view of reality to triumph. Every religious movement in the West since the seventeenth century can be seen as an attempt to reestablish the West and its institutions upon theological foundations, or at least upon religious values, but such attempts have often yielded to other social (non-religious) faiths and to secularism—a preoccupation with immediate rather than with ultimate questions. A secular milieu implies the recognition of multiple realities, each with its own autonomous center, cognitive style, boundaries, and values. Reality, then, is defined in pluralistic terms. In a secular world our reality awaits the confirmation of other historical beings. There is no central authority beyond the human community itself to which it can appeal.

What I am suggesting is that secularization is and has been a long-term social and historical process resulting in a secular social order. It has given rise to a social outlook essentially concerned with this world rather than a world beyond, with immediate rather than with ultimate questions, and with natural or practical morality. This social outlook or attitude has permeated the established institutions of our society, including the black church.

> The process of secularization has a subjective side as well. As there is a secularization of society and culture, so is there a secularization of consciousness. Put simply, this means that the modern West has produced an increasing number of individuals who look upon the world and their own lives without the benefit of religious interpretations.[49]

The end result is a secularized conscience, closed to the claims of religious truths. The cunning feature of this subjective process of internalization is that it happens without our conscious recognition of it. In short, we are deeply embedded in a culture and historical process that tends to deny the presence of a transcendent and immanent God who is the ultimate source of all new possibility and moves in and through all living things. We live in a period that stresses the autonomy of the individual, to the point that individualism, autonomously held, contributes to a false understanding of the human self. It has tended to veil the real interdependence of humanity. Perhaps one of the most dangerous and fastest growing myths in the black community is that we are more individualized, autonomous, and independent than we are related and interdependent. A relational under- standing of the black community as a whole has implications for the aftermath of Jonestown, the ministry of the black church and the praxis of pastoral care in the black community.

An implication of living in a secular milieu is that the black churches' claim—that Jesus Christ is Lord—faces a plausibility crisis. A plausibility crisis occurs when the social milieu itself has undercut the basis for belief and when an increasing number of people intellectually attack and attempt to destroy the founda- tions upon which the faith rests. For the black church, God's liberating, healing, and reconciling activity manifested in Jesus was once the center of orientation. The black church must recognize, however, that secularization has pulled the rug of absolutism from under Christian feet, and the choice to stand with Jesus is an alternative decision amidst the possible contesting centers of orientation. The choice to stand with Jesus as the suffering and triumphant Lord has again become a radical and daring choice amidst competing claims for loyalty. Not everyone in the black community will choose to stand with Jesus. Indeed, an increasing number of young people and intellectuals have chosen not to. But this fact does not mean that such persons stand outside the scope of God's grace and concern for a black and suffering, and often co-opted humanity. The black church must stand with the whole black community, because God's struggling, liberating, and reconciling presence is to be discerned there.

8.

As an alternative, I suggest a conceptual basis for ministry that is consistent with the historic role of black church religion, and one that can see the connection between political impotence and personal disintegration; a concept that seeks to strengthen awareness of the connection between self-affirmation and community empowerment in light of the biblical covenant and liberating gospel of Jesus Christ. The key concept here is *relationality*. The central theme is the unity, interrelatedness and interdependence of human life, even the unity of all life. This is not only an ancient theme, but a perennial topic, and a recurring insight which asserts our common and universal interdependence. Relationality is grounded in the insight that one's life is constituted in relations with others; that one's life belongs to others just as much as it belongs to one's self. The relational self is solidly embedded in community. Relationality expresses the biblical idea that God is alone God, the underlying, unitive presence and power, and comprehensive ground of all reality—personal and social—struggling in and through the efforts of human beings. Bernard M. Loomer expresses the idea of relationality in his concept, "the web of life."

> The fact of the web means that we are members one of another. In this relational mode of life we belong and participate in the web because we exist. Through our activities we help create the web. The web in turn gives birth to us. The influences flowing from any point within this field reverberate throughout the web in varying

degrees of intensity. The increase in relational value for one individual is the enrichment of all. The lessening of one is the diminution of all. The faithlessness of one adds to the impoverishment of each. As individuals we are fulfilled through, with, and in others. . . .

This web is the primordial covenantal relationship, a covenant in which all peoples have membership as their birthright, and for whose enrichment all peoples are chosen. Special historical covenants, religious or secular, of less generality are finally justifiable in terms of their contribution to this more inclusive community. The evolution of the human spirit consists in the emergence of a deeper understanding and exemplification of this elemental covenant.[50]

Charles Hartshorne also expresses the idea that relationality is not simply a human achievement, but has its basis in a fundamental primordial unity. Relationality is more than the sum total of social relations in a society. It points to an ultimate and underlying reality in the world.

The conception of God which our argument leads to is that of a social being, dominant or ruling over the world society, yet not merely from outside, in a tyrannical or non-social way; but rather as that member of the society which exerts the supreme conserving and coordinating influence. . . . For religion as a concrete practical matter, as a way of life, has generally viewed God as having social relations with man, as sympathizing with him and gaining something through his achievements. God was interested in man, therefore could be "pleased" or "displeased," made more or less happy, by man's success or failure, and could thus be "served" by human efforts.[51]

According to Hartshorne, God is inconceivable apart from social reality. God is the most comprehensive personal guarantor of society struggling in and through the efforts of all humans. In other words, relationality is a primordial fact of black social life. The basic notion is that of an underlying unity, a primordial unity in which all human activity is constituted. Relationality expresses the idea that personal faith, responsibility, and accountability are derived from a collective context and from a sense of belonging to a common culture and to an oppressed and yet struggling black community. In this context no one is free until everyone is free. Some scholars have argued that a collective sense of belonging and elements of Africanisms survived the middle passage and acculturative process in the United States and somehow live on in the religions, culture, and psyche of black people today.[52] In this connection the family can be viewed as the primary unit for the reproduction of a relational sense of peoplehood. Henry Mitchell has argued that despite the Western trek to secularization . . . "The pull of African world view is still evident even in Blackamerican street culture, among those who have made a break with formal Black religion and the organized Black church."[53] "We-consciousness" is the more authentic ground for ethical reflection in black communities, rather than reflection based upon an isolated individualism. The theme of relationality in the family can enable blacks to apprehend the biblical way more truly than enlightenment individualism permits the establishment culture to apprehend it. Whether or not a sense of relatedness and common destiny can continue is an open question. Bongenjalo Goba, a Black South African, makes the point.

We have lost so much of our sense of corporate personality. Influenced by capitalism we have become materialistically self-centered, and the emphasis seems to be on individual enterprise and material acquisition for the individual. . . .

I am afraid that in our stress on personal autonomy and freedom of the individual which has undermined the traditional authority of the community, weakened indigenous forms of social control and raised doubts about formerly accepted traditional norms, we have lost, or perhaps we are losing, our kinship ties and thus our sense of corporateness. In our struggle to create a unified black front, somehow we must remind ourselves of the significance of our living as a related people, our blackness suffering disinheritance must be a force which shall make us a community with a united loyalty, purpose and commitment.[54]

A diminished or lost sense of corporate identity, however, can be attributed, in large measure, to the disruptive influences of urbanization, modernization, and the impact of secularizing influences on traditional institutions such as the church and the family. While such influences tend to dismantle identities and obscure or repress awareness of the relational character of life, they do not obliterate it.

Relationality suggests that the black family and community and the black church, though interdependent, are related in a common enterprise. The black church cannot realize its historic role of liberation and empowerment in the present situation apart from black culture, the family, and the black community as a whole; and the black community and culture cannot exist as a viable community and culture in a racist society by denying or destroying the key institutions that have enabled it to survive, namely the black family, black church, and black religion.

From this perspective, black selfhood is constituted in its relations with others. The age-old African proverb makes the point: "One is only human because of others, with others, for others."[55] The relational self becomes a whole self by virtue of its relationship to other selves. The self, then, is more than an autonomous center of consciousness and decision-making.

> What is uniquely characteristic and constitutive of the human world is something that takes place between one person and another. It is in meeting, in bi-subjective communication, that [human persons are or become] truly [human]. The essence of human life is what happens betwen man and man in community. For human existence is essentially dialogue, claim and counter-claim, demand and response.[56]

The relational self not only gains self-conscious selfhood in its relations, but it also becomes aware of the structures of life in which it exists. C. W. Mills was correct to argue the importance of grasping the interplay of person and society, of biography and history, of self and world. "Neither the life of an individual nor the history of a society can be understood without understanding both. Yet men do not usually define the troubles they endure in terms of historical change and institutional contradiction."[57] Without awareness of the interconnection and interdependence of social reality, the community of persons cannot hope to transform the societies in which they live, move, and have their being. James Cone's expression of the relational perspective moves in the right direction.

I think that the time has come for Black theologians and church people to move beyond a mere reaction to White racism in America and begin to extend our vision of a new socially constructed humanity in the whole inhabited world. We must be concerned wtih the quality of human life not only in the ghettos of American cities but also in Africa, Asia and Latin America. For humanity is whole, and cannot be isolated into racial and national groups. Indeed there will be no freedom for anyone until there is freedom for all.[58]

Reflexivity is the key for understanding the capacity of the self to bring a critical perspective to bear in the present in light of the whole. Here selfhood, in the context of family and community, can be understood as a source of consciousness, imagination, and novelty in social life. The self in relation and through critical discernment can gain awareness of the underlying social forces that move people and the institutional arrangements that contribute to their social isolation, apathy, and personal disintegration.

Only in this way [through reflective thought and critical analysis] can we avoid binding ourselves to some myth of the past and begin to understand that our social relations are subject to our collective intervention. . . . What we face are our own antecedents and the causes for our own development—not some universal dilemma.[59]

Relationality is a way of speaking about the interdependent, yet dialectical and constitutent character of black communal life as a whole. The challenge that faces the black family and community is the same challenge that faces the black church and personal existence. The challenge is to grasp the unity of life as a primordial condition of our existence in spite of and because of the presence of persistent (and destructive) conditions that appear to negate life's unity. The challenge is one of affirming solidarity amidst an ethos that pushes it toward fragmentation. The black church, family, and personal existence are challenged to confront the principalities and powers that would obscure their interconnection and fundamental relational and communal character. Some nineteenth- and early twentieth-century black church leaders in California, such as Jeremiah B.

Sanderson, Philip A. Bell, F. W. Cassey, and George Washington Woodbey, had a relational vision which enabled them to link personal faith and responsibility with social justice issues. Their vision embraced the liberation struggles of the whole black community, religious and secular. They made the social and political advancement of black people the burden of their life commitment.[60] Their sense of mission courageously confronted conditions of segregation as they sought to humanize the social order.

> It is that though the Black church was effective in the nineteenth century partially because of the circumstance of history, it was effective mainly because it never was free to separate its interior institutional life from its mission in and on behalf of the world. From the perspective of seventy years later, if the Black church has had a diminishing impact it is because it has turned more and more in upon itself, and faced less and less outwards the world.[61]

Many black people originally responded positively to Peoples' Temple because it was a movement that provided psychic support and linked it with a program of social/communal outreach. Black people's involvement in the Peoples' Temple Movement can be seen as an attempt to make black religion relevant to their social, political, and economic condition. By breaking with the insularity and seemingly irrelevant style of some recent black church worship, many thought they had found in the Peoples' Temple a form of church involvement that spoke more directly to the issues of spiritual uplift, justice, social empowerment, and change. Their vision of a new social order was not wrong. It was expressive of the relational paradigm. It was a vision broader than that found in many of the black churches they left. But their vision was not enough. It lacked a relational and self-critical dimension that would have enabled them to discern the false claims of Jim Jones toward ego deification.

9.

What happened at Jonestown is wide open to the persistent charge that Christianity is a white man's religion and that religion is an opiate of the masses. C. Eric Lincoln characterized this basic sentiment:

> Some contemporary black scholars in the positivistic tradition see religion as a false issue, the worse aspect of it being the preemption of too many good minds which might otherwise be turned to more pragmatic pursuits. Religion, they argue, whatever its source, and whatever its uses in the past is irrelevant today because black people have outgrown it. We do not need religion to define our problems or to prescribe a means of coping with them. We do need the total intellectual energies of the black community directed toward the alleviation of empirical conditions we can see and account for.
>
> The black positivists are not alone in their desire to dismiss religion and get on with social change. Their impatience with religion is shared by black youth.[62]

The Jonestown tragedy lends credence to a further interpretation that the white man's bag of tricks (personified in the Reverend Jim Jones) was used on black people to carry out the ultimate ritual of depersonalization—by getting them (black people) to defect not only from their own institutions (family and church), but also to destroy their babies and take their own lives as well. This could only happen in an ethos where black cultural identity and religion had already been seriously compromised.

Black peoples' involvement in Peoples' Temple and Jonestown is difficult to explain in light of the black power and black theology liberation movements and the developing of black nationalism of the 1960s and the African roots phenomenon of the 1970s. These movements did have an impact on San Francisco Bay Area black churches. Many of them see the need for social uplift and political liberation, but their individual capacity to provide such leadership is limited. Jim Jones and his Peoples' Temple were able to speak to the issues of marginal participation in the economy, poverty and isolation, loneliness, unemployment, and political impotence with much more force and drama and on a larger scale. They had the peoples' money, their commitment, and their property. What the Peoples' Temple was able to offer black people was a social-political-economic program linked wih a tangible cause and an authoritative, charismatic leader who espoused a vision of a new social order.

The Western Addition of San Francisco had one of the most comprehensive mental health and social service networks to be found anywhere. Although the Peoples' Temple was not formally identified as a part of this network, it did have a strong working relationship with it. This network and the Peoples' Temple developed a kind of ideal working relationship that many activists and socially concerned church people (who work with poor and elderly people) desired and were drawn to. The appeal of Peoples' Temple was not only its charismatic leader but its interpretation of religion and social outreach programs. The Peoples' Temple appeared to be concerned with black unemployment, problems of poverty, juvenile delinquency, criminal justice, welfare dependency, alcoholism, drug addiction, and related problems. The Peoples' Temple's ability to influence structures of power gave folk a sense of being somebody, a sense of belonging to a great cause of social reform and uplift. In order to appreciate its appeal, we must see it amidst the comparatively weaker social and political influence of black churches. Many San Francisco Bay Area black churches have a strong inward religious orientation, but the majority are without the outward thrust of significant social action programs or political involvement. There are exceptions to this, such as Glide Memorial, the Third Baptist Church, and Bethel A.M.E., to mention a few. However, most find cooperative effort difficult to achieve or sustain. There is little agreement among the black churches as to how far or how deeply involved the black church should be in issues of social and political protest. In some instances, the church is not at all involved or concerned about people beyond their membership. There are a few exceptions.

After the Jonestown tragedy, one embittered person who was a participant in Peoples' Temple put it to me this way:

Most Black churches do not even want to be bothered with understanding or framing a response to Guyana. Peoples' Temple emerged out of a need and filled a vacuum in the Black community; a need that was missed by the Black churches. Peoples' Temple ministered to the unchurched, the Black elderly, the addicted and alcoholic, welfare dependents, juvenile delinquents, the lonely and alienated of all sorts.[63]

It is small wonder, then, that many found in the Peoples' Temple Movement a place to belong, an outlet for their religious and political aspirations, a social program and a cause to which they could give themselves.

On the surface at least, the Peoples' Temple Movement appeared to connect a concern for social justice with personal empowerment. Those who deeply felt the need for this kind of structural connection saw in Peoples' Temple the power potential for achieving it. Indeed, Jones and his movement were a power to be reckoned with, and the educated, wealthy whites were the power elite within the movement. It was reported that Jones could deliver jobs and sway an election. He proved to be an influential political force in the electoral politics of San Francisco. It was reported that his influence was decisive in such places as the NAACP, the district attorney's housing department office, the San Francisco Police Department, and the mayor's office and that his influence proved to be decisive in the city's 1975 election. It was further reported that Jones was a synthesizer able to hear the ideas of a broad spectrum of viewpoints and blend them together into a world view that appealed to Marxist and social revolutionaries, humanitarian idealists, and black religionists. Disillusioned young people, singles, the down and out, and many others who saw themselves as victims of social dislocation and injustices were drawn to Jones' charisma and promise to deliver and transform their conditions. In many ways, Jones' appeal was responded to by many who were committed ideologically to the struggles of the 1960s. John Moore, a white minister formerly of the First United Methodist Church in Reno, lost two daughters and a grandson at Jonestown. In a sermon delivered the Sunday following their murder, he said,

In our family you can see the relationship between the events of the sixties and this tragedy. . . .

Our children took seriously what we believed about commitment, caring about a better, more humane and just society. They saw in Peoples' Temple the same kind of caring people and commitment to social justice that they had lived with. They (the Peoples' Temple) found people no one else ever cared about. . . . They cared for the least and the last of the human family.[64]

"Jim Jones" (with his more than two-thousand-member congregation) "was the only political leader in San Francisco who could completely control the way his followers would vote." The December 18, 1978 issue of *New West* magazine reported:

The Reverend Jones could turn out a crowd for any politician's speech and did it so often that Peoples' Temple members became known among the mayor's and district attorney's staff as "the Troops." If you gave Jim Jones six hours' notice, he could deliver 2,000 people. "They were made to order," one Democratic county chairman's staff member raved, "You should have seen it—old ladies on crutches, whole families, little kids, blacks, whites."[65]

If *New West* and other news reports can be trusted, then we must raise the following question, Was there not a force or a power strong enough in the black community itself to counter the influence and fraudulent claims of Jim Jones (or anybody else for that matter)? He moved into the heart of the Fillmore District and took over the lives of young black men, older women, mothers, and babies. According to news reports, he infiltrated black organizations, diluted their effective counter moves, took hundreds of poor and black people with him to the isolated jungles of Guyana, and murdered them by inducing them to take their own lives. In the interim, he did much to give people hope and a vision of a new society. There were unbought critical voices in the black religious community, but these few voices alone were not enough to counter the effects of Jones and his movement. Can this happen again in San Francisco or in other American cities? And, if so, then what kind of questions ought black churches raise for critical ethical reflection and analysis? What kind of leadership and resources ought black churches provide in a time of deep religious quest and potential exploitation of religious freedom? Such questions need to be raised and faced before new and unfamiliar religious movements take hold and escalate into strong politically and financially backed movements on the scale of the Peoples'

Temple. Would such a movement have gotten as far as it did if the chief victims were not the disposable people—black youth (some of whom were wards of the state and juvenile delinquents), elderly black women on Social Security, drug addicts, and left-wing social activists?

10.

In the wake of Jonestown, Guyana, the temptation will be strong for black church leaders not only to denounce Jim Jones and the Peoples' Temple, writing it off as the work of a madman or the devil, but also to avoid appropriate criticism. In a society as interdependent as ours, no one can walk away clean, not even the white Christian church. Such denial is unfortunate if it is used to justify no change in the way the church sees its ministry. If this is the case, then Jonestown was a message that fell on deaf ears.

It will be important to remember the positive and heroic things done by the Peoples' Temple which somewhere, somehow, need to be continued. The official closing of the temple on December 31, 1978, created a vacuum that other groups may not be able to fill as successfully or quickly enough. The Peoples' Temple has already demonstrated the need for a ministry that will reach those for whom no one else seems to care. Black churches are challenged to consider the possibilities of a multifaceted, cooperative outreach and social change ministry, shared by a number of black ministers and laypeople, and to combine such efforts with other community resources. No one church or pastor should try to fill this vacuum alone. To go it alone tilts in the direction of messianism and egomania.

The idea of relationality suggests a cooperative enterprise, a shared ministry. This is a challenge because it is often difficult for the pastor to share authority and leadership roles or acknowledge one's own limitations. Ego problems, apathy, and limited resources often get in the way of fashioning creative and cooperative responses to broad social issues. On the other hand, the community and church members sometimes expect miracles from their pastor—things that they do not expect from other professionals. The potential for *audience corruption*, self-deception, or collusion is always present. The seduction is that church members often look to the pastor to provide answers to problems that are too great for any one person to solve. Only on rare occasions can one person possibly answer or fill the void in someone else's life: no one person (or church) can transform the social order. To attempt such creates false hopes and false dependency, and it thwarts the necessary development of communal efforts to fashion responses for creative social change. The tendency toward messianism is just as real for the rest of us as it was for Jim Jones. We all participate in the same structure of finitude that Jim Jones failed to recognize.

Here, in brief, are some further implications for the black church's ministry derived from this presentation:

1. *Interpretive*. This chapter can be viewed as an attempt to play a critical interpretive role. The black church as a witness to the presence of the living God has a critical interpretive role to play, as well as being a gathering place for worship and fellowship. The interpretive role includes: an understanding of black history and cultural traditions in such a way as to inspire self-esteem, faith, and action; to link faith with responsible involvement in the events that mark and circumscribe the lives of black people; to interpret the biblical Word and foster relational and therapeutic patterns which mediate the active care of God's presence to the oppressed in our time.

The interpretive task is one of illuminating the social and historical context in which the community of faith lives, works, and makes moral or ethical decisions. Historically, the black church understood itself to be a servant church. And it has been a faithful church wherever it has brought good tidings to the afflicted, proclaimed liberty to captives, and helped break the yoke of oppression. Today it has the same task as it did from its inception, namely to work for the moral social transformation of an exploitative system of social relations. The real relations produced by a system of profit-centered capitalism do not appear as inherently exploitative and demonic, nor do the social structure of competitive and hierarchical power relations and the ideologies which support and legitimate it. The contradictions and oppression that emanates from such a system tend to confront the individual as a potentially mysterious or sinister power, shaping the lives of oppressed people. For example, poverty and high infant mortality, high unemployment, substandard and congested housing conditions may appear as "the will of God," or as "the way things naturally work." Such conditions are neither the will of God nor the natural state for black, poor, and disenfranchised people. Rather, these conditions are the products of a special organization of life, a particular history and social structure and system of economic exploitation. They are created and maintained by the ruling class and their particular system of domination. The black theologian Cornel West has been especially helpful in identifying the idea of "the ruling class."

> Within the complexities of post-industrial capitalist America, the capitalist class—or ruling class, since its primary aim of profit-maximization is the most dominant and successful one in American society—consists essentially of trans-national corporations which own large segments of the means of production and employ a disproportionate number of the citizenry. Of course, elected and appointed government officials also rule. But, since their rule is undeniably sedimented, permeated by and usually subordinated to the primary aim of the capitalist class, it is appropriate to designate the latter, the ruling class. The most glaring example of this relationship between the capitalist class and government is the historic refusal of the latter to ever even raise the issue of redistribution of the wealth by calling into question the primary aim of the former.[66]

The black church is challenged to help illuminate the generally unrecognized workings of the capitalist class and the supporting system of exploitative social relations it engenders. The black church is challenged to interpret and to help change the workings of this system in similar ways it has helped to interpret the history and meaning of slavery, to empower victims toward self-determination, and to become agents in nurturing relational patterns.

It is not enough for the black church to promote equality and integration of the oppressed into the mainstream of society. The black church is challenged, by its own history, to move beyond an interest in integrating the disinherited into a higher status within an unchanged structure of oppression and exploitation. The task is to transform the social order and to work to humanize social relations. The black church, in faithful obedience to its Lord, calls persons to become therapeutic agents in the process of transformation, to proclaim liberty to captives, and to work for their physical and spiritual release from material and ideological bondage to ruling groups. The spirit of truth, which interpretation seeks, is concealed by ideologies which present the status quo as the true and ideal way. The black church is challenged to seek the truth that sets prisoners free to create a liberating and just social order.

In this interpretive mode, the human person's chief danger lies in the unruly forces of contemporary society itself, with its alienating methods of reproductive relations, its enveloping techniques of political domination, its international anarchy, in a word, its pervasive transformations of the very "nature" of the human self into a tool or agent in the system of domination.[67] The church's interpretive role ought to enable us to identify the forces that move us, our social location, and give insight concerning the nature of the social structures under which we labor, as well as preparing us to fashion creative responses as persons of faith and agents of change.

Perhaps one of the lessons to come out of Jonestown and the Peoples' Temple Movement for the black church is that we need to understand better the history of our faith and possibilities for action in light of the biblical Word. An inmate at Vacaville Correctional Facility recently told me that he wasn't sure where it was to be found in the Bible, but that "the law of self-preservation" was the first law of the Bible. How wrong he was! Although he grew up in a San Francisco Bay Area black church, he was still in the fog on the Bible and its message. Yet he thought he was quoting from the Bible. He could not distinguish the biblical message from other messages or social philosophies he had acquired. This brother and inmate does not stand alone. He represents many in our churches who profess the faith, but know very little about what the Scripture really has to say to us when we enter into serious dialogue with it and critically reflect upon our praxis in its light. In this case a little bit of knowledge can be dangerous. The black church as a servant and therapeutic community may interpret as clearly as it can the central proclamation of the gospel in ways that liberate black Christians to link critical reflection upon praxis with their faith and with a responsible and daring commitment to the living God who struggles with us, in and through every case of oppression.

2. *Communal Empowerment and Interdependence.* The black

church is challenged to assert itself as a communal church, seeking to heal, empower and undergird black families, support the alienated, psychically distraught, and socially abandoned, and to feed the spiritually hungry. One church cannot do this alone, but must see itself as our extended family form and as a part of the community effort. The church may give vision and leadership to this effort.

The black church has a continuing supportive and empowering function to play in black family life. Historically, the black church has been the backbone of the black family.[68] The black church has functioned for many as an extended family fostering nurturing relational patterns which reinforce and strengthen a sense of inner worth, respect, and value of each for the other. Eugene Genovese referred to these values as "weapons of defense." The black church in the past has nurtured a religious faith ". . . that taught [slaves] to love and value each other, to take a critical view of their masters, and to reject the ideological rationale for their enslavement."[69]

We are still challenged to reject the ideological rationale and debilitating relational patterns that support our enslavement. Again, Genovese writes: "And the slaves, drawing on a religion that was supposed to assure their compliance and docility, rejected the essence of slavery by projecting their own rights and values as human beings."[70] The black church is challenged to play a similar role in the lives of black families and single persons today who face new forms of alienation and spiritual bondage to materialistic values.

The black church is still challenged to enable black families and singles to break the bonds of enslaving action and to develop therapeutic relational patterns which contribute to change and growth and enhance the capacity to care. "Liberation of the oppressed" will become a vacuous euphemism if the intended audience is itself too emotionally crippled to respond. The black church must link liberation with healing, salvation, and critical reflection within a therapeutic community which is concerned with spiritual uplift and reconciliation and salvation. These motifs come together in Wimberly's understanding of pastoral care.

The fact that social oppression existed did not mean that healing did not take place in the black church. Although the black person's personality was damaged by racism and oppression, wholeness did come for many through the experience of God's love toward them. When the caring resources were brought to bear upon persons suffering from low self-esteem and self-hatred, they experienced themselves as accepted and as "somebody" in the eyes of God and their black brothers and sisters.

Racism and oppression have produced wounds in the black community that can be healed only to the extent that healing takes place in the structure of the total society. Therefore, the black church has had to find means to sustain and guide black persons in the midst of oppression. In this effort, much attention has been focused upon reducing the impact of racism upon the black personality, but it has been difficult to restore the wholeness of the person caused by the impact of oppression. People need guidance and hope in the present while making the most of their situation; at the same time they look forward to a future time of ultimate healing.[71]

3. *Social Action.* Interpretation, healing, sustaining, guidance, and confrontation must incorporate social action. Interpretation must be linked to praxis. Social action must seek to comprehend and transform the processes and social arrangements that maintain and legitimate structures of oppression. In the words of the August 6, 1977, National Conference of the Black Theology Project in Atlanta, the black church "must come from behind its stained-glass walls and dwell where mothers are crying, children are hungry, and fathers are jobless."[72] Social action ministries must be open to the critical perspectives of others as the church and community continue to evolve the praxis of caring, emancipation, and social transformation.

4. *Prophetic, Critical, and Self-Critical Reflection.* The black church in the United States has often played a prophetic role when it has proclaimed the power of the gospel in judgment upon an exploitative economic and social system which ensures structural inequality and insidious forms of racism. That role was expressed in the witness of Harriet Tubman, Richard Allen, Jeremiah B. Sanderson, Martin Luther King, Jr., and a host of other witnesses. The prophetic role must be reflexive and ask, What is the black church doing now in light of Scripture and the oppressed? This role is consistent with the interpretive task and social action ministry of the church.

11.

This chapter has attempted an interpretation of the Peoples' Temple and the Jonestown tragedy. It identifies the historical process of secularization and secularism as important themes and relates them to a plausibility crisis in black church religion and to the appeal of Peoples' Temple. Finally, I have identified some implications for the black church and its ministry in light of the Jonestown tragedy in Guyana. Secularism found expression in the dominant theoretical explanation that emerged from social science about the Peoples' Temple and Jonestown. Yet this theory, which I called the psychoanalytically oriented world view, was incapable of diagnosing the larger social world that produced Jonestown, and it failed to enable a critical analysis of the social structure, even if it did help explain the mind-set of Jim Jones, the social dynamics of the Jones' cult, and some of the inner forces that may have moved individuals to join the Peoples' Temple and move to Jonestown.

The plausibility crisis in the black church referred to a posture of withdrawal from involvement in liberation struggles and a retreat into privatized religion. In part, this retreat has been occasioned by objective factors of secularization, conditions of rapid social change, new complex patterns of urban life, and dwindling financial resources in some cases. As a partial response, the church has protected the individual from overwhelming impersonal forces but at the same time has tended to limit the range of personal religious commitment. The black church faces a plausibility crisis wherever its prophetic voice has been effectively silenced or relegated to the margin of society without a critical social vision to help discern or interpret what is going on. The black church, then, may be seen by fewer and fewer people as an institution capable of moving us toward liberation or responsible involvement, hope in a more open future, or a resource for critical discernment of the social order. In this case, it is more likely to be seen as a source of false consciousness and as an opiate to militancy, rather than as a stimulant to therapeutic and relational patterns of liberation, social responsibility, and empowerment. This may be the case wherever the black church has lost sight of its historical mission, emphasized personal faith, and separated it from critical reflection, liberation struggles of oppressed people, social transformation and healing in the social world. Decreased involvement of the black church in the struggle for liberation necessarily contributes toward a plausibility crisis.

The chapter then attempted to frame an adequate response from a broadened perspective of the church's mission based on the relational character of reality. From a relational perspective, psychic liberation and social transformation are dialectically related and interwoven. They are rightfully the concerns of the dialogue called therapy and of a black Christian liberation ethic. In this context, ideology and false consciousness emerge as central themes for the church to address. The black church can effectively address these themes by becoming aware of its own historical context and the forces that gave it rise and through continued critical and ethical reflection upon the faith that gives it hope. To fail to confess its faith and its sins of omission and commission, to leave unquestioned its own *raison d'etre* and that of society, is to contribute to the problem of false consciousness and idolatrous faith. I have tried to point out that emancipatory struggle must seek to strengthen awareness of the interrelatedness and interdependence of human life; this includes the life of the psyche as well as social life.

I have tried to show in the earlier chapters of this book how therapy and social ethics, when kept together, can strengthen awareness of the necessary tension between the person and the social system and the dialectical nature of personal and social transformation. Emancipatory struggle must continually involve a social and self-critical dimension enjoined with faith in the One who underlies and struggles through the efforts of black and oppressed people to be free and struggles through conditions of oppression and tragedy everywhere. Genuine social emancipation is inseparable from the emancipation of the human self and mind.

Emancipation of the oppressed is inseparable from love and justice. They are the hallmarks of a liberating society. These themes are central to the gospel. They were central in the historical consciousness of the black church. And, they are the operative concerns at work in the community of the oppressed, on this side of Jonestown.

Figure 1

Jonestown Victims by Sex and Race

	Black	White	American Indian	Latino	Asian	Mexican American	Total
Female	49% (438)	13% (121)	(4)	1% (12)	(2)	1% (10)	66% (587)
Male	22% (200)	10% (88)	(3)	(3)	(1)	1% (8)	34% (303)
Total	71% (638)	23% (209)	1% (7)	2% (15)	(3)	2% (18)	100% (890)

This information was tabulated from a list of victims of the Jonestown mass suicides and murders released by the State Department. The list of victims was obtained from the San Francisco Ecumenical Council, May, 1979.

Figure 2

Jonestown Victims by Age, Sex, and Race

	Black		White		Latino		Mexican		Asian		Indian		Total
	F	M	F	M	F	M	F	M	F	M	F	M	
11 years & younger	6% (55)	5% (44)	1% (9)	2% (16)	- (4)	- -	- (2)	- (4)	- -	- -	- (2)	- (1)	15% (137)
12-16 years	4% (37)	4% (36)	2% (16)	2% (16)	- (1)	- (1)	- -	- (3)	- -	- -	- -	- -	12% (110)
17-21 years	5% (49)	4% (30)	2% (19)	1% (9)	- (1)	- -	- (2)	- -	- (1)	- -	- -	- -	13% (120)
22-29 years	4% (34)	3% (29)	3% (27)	1% (10)	- (3)	- (1)	- (3)	- -	- (1)	- (1)	- (1)	- (1)	12% (111)
30-40 years	4% (37)	1% (10)	2% (20)	2% (14)	- (1)	- (1)	- (1)	- -	- -	- -	- -	- (1)	10% (85)

												Total
41-50 years	3% (30)	- (4)	1% (11)	1% (10)	- -	- -	- (1)	- -	- -	- -	- -	- (1)	6% (56)
51-65 years	8% (70)	2% (18)	1% (9)	1% (9)	- (1)	- -	- -	- -	- -	- -	- -	- (1)	12% (108)
66 years & older	14% (121)	2% (18)	1% (6)	- (2)	- (1)	- -	- (1)	- -	- -	- -	- -	- -	17% (149)
age unknown	1% (5)	- (2)	- (4)	- (2)	- -	- -	- -	(1)	- -	- -	- -	- -	2% (14)
TOTAL	49% (438)	22% (200)	14% (121)	10% (88)	1% (12)	1% (3)	1% (10)	1% (8)	- (2)	- (1)	- (4)	- (3)	100% (890)

This information was tabulated from a list of victims of the Jonestown mass suicides and murders released by the State Department. The list of victims was obtained from the San Francisco Ecumenical Council, May, 1979.

NOTES

Introduction

1. Allan Aubrey Boesak, *Farewell to Innocence* (Maryknoll, N.Y.: Orbis Books, 1977), p. 150.
2. In this book the black church will be treated as a microcosm of the Christian church. There will not be a separate chapter to treat the black church presence in the United States. Instead, the author points the reader to some select literature and history of the black church. Carter G. Woodson, *The History of the Negro Church* (Washington D.C.: The Associated Publishers, 1921); Benjamin E. Mays and Joseph W. Nicholson, *The Negro's Church* (New York: Institute of Social and Religious Research, 1933); Arthur H. Fauset, *Black Gods of the Metropolis* (Philadelphia: University of Pennsylvania Press, 1944); C. Eric Lincoln, *The Black Muslims in America* (Boston: Beacon Press, 1961); Donald G. Mathews, *Slavery and Methodism* (Princeton: Princeton University Press, 1965); H. M. Nelsen et al., *The Black Church in America* (New York: Basic Books, 1971); Joseph R. Washington, Jr., *Black Sects and Cults* (Garden City N.Y.: Doubleday & Co., 1972); E. Franklin Frazier, *The Negro Church in America* and C. Eric Lincoln, *The Black Church Since Frazier* (New York: Schocken Books, 1974); Melvin D. Williams, *Community in a Black Pentecostal Church: An Anthropological Study* (Pittsburgh: University of Pittsburgh Press, 1974); Hart M. Nelsen and Anne Nelsen, *Black Church in the Sixties* (Lexington: University Press of Kentucky, 1975); Olin P. Moyd, *Redemption in Black Theology* (Valley Forge, Pa.: Judson Press, 1979); Randall K. Burkett, *Black Redemption* (Philadelphia: Temple University Press, 1978); James Deotis Roberts, *Roots of a Black Future: Family and Church* (Philadelphia: The Westminster Press, 1980).

3. Paulo Freire, *Pedagogy of the Oppressed* (New York: The Seabury Press, 1970), p. 28.
4. Russell Jacoby, *Social Amnesis* (Boston: Beacon Press, 1975).
5. Eldon G. Ernst, *Without Help or Hinderance* (Philadelphia: The Westminster Press, 1977), pp. 72-78.
6. James H. Cone, *Black Theology and Black Power* (New York: The Seabury Press, 1969), p. 92.
7. W. E. Burghardt DuBois, *The Souls of Black Folk* (New York: Fawcett Publications, 1961), p. 148.
8. Eugene D. Genovese, *Roll, Jordan Roll: The World the Slaves Made* (New York: Vintage Books, 1976), p. 74.
9. Henry H. Mitchell, *Black Belief* (New York: Harper & Row, 1975), p. 12.
10. James H. Cone, *God of the Oppressed* (New York: The Seabury Press, 1975), p. 234.
11. H. Richard Niebuhr, *The Meaning of Revelation* (New York: The Macmillan Co., 1941), p. 117.
12. Rudolf J. Siebert, *From Critical Theory of Society to Theology of Communicative Praxis* (Washington, D.C.: University Press of America, 1979), p. 137.
13. H. R. Niebuhr, *The Meaning of Revelation*, p. 110.
14. Ronald L. Johnstone, "Negro Preachers Take Sides," in Hart M. Nelsen et al., *Black Church in the Sixties*, pp. 274-86. Also see Peter J. Paris, *Black Leaders in Conflict* (New York: The Pilgrim Press, 1978).
15. Moyd, *Redemption in Black Theology*, chapter 3.
16. Roberts, *Roots of a Black Future*, chapter 4.
17. Martin L. Gross, *The Psychological Society* (New York: Simon & Schuster, 1979), p. 17.

Chapter I.

1. Gordon M. Torgerson, "Peace Activity in a Local Congregation and How It Affects a Ministry," *Foundations, a Baptist Journal of History and Theology*, Vol. XV, No. 4 (October-November, 1972).
2. The city itself, with a large predominantly Irish-Catholic population, was nonetheless controlled by a Protestant Industrialist elite. Although Worcester tends to be a working class community, its local political style was non-partisan and embodied the ideals of the Anglo-Saxon middle class. While ethnicity was a significant factor in local politics during the 1960s, the presence of non-white ethnics (i.e., blacks and hispanics, approximately 2-3 percent) remained on the periphery of local government (as would be expected by their

small percentage). During the turbulent 1960s, especially during the anti-poverty, model cities programs, participatory democracy, and Revenue Sharing program of the early 1970s federal funds were targeted to address ethnic minority concerns. But this fact, in itself (beyond token gestures) did little to encourage or include non-white ethnics into the power structure of local politics. My ministry had its origins in this context. Looking back, such a ministry can be seen as an attempt on the part of a local congregation to nurture and lend a voice to the voiceless of that city. See Morris H. Cohen, "Worcester Ethnics," *The Holy Cross Quarterly*, Vol. 5, Nos. 3-4, Worcester, Massachusetts, pp. 42-47, for a brief history of the ethnic or immigrant groups in this community. Although blacks have been in Worcester for at least two centuries, their numbers remain small, about 2 percent of the population, and they continue to be marginal to the city's political life.

3. C. Wright Mills, *The Sociological Imagination* (New York: Oxford University Press, 1959), p. 8.

4. Roland Warren, "The Sociology of Knowledge and the Problems of the Inner Cities," *Social Science Quarterly* (December 1971), p. 472.

5. *Ibid.*, p. 477.

6. *Ibid.*, p. 474.

7. *Ibid.*, p. 489.

8. *Ibid.*, p. 491.

9. Thomas M. Gannon, "Religious Tradition and Urban Community," *Sociological Analysis: A Journal in the Sociology of Religion*, Vol. 39, No. 4 (Winter 1978), pp. 283-302.

10. Peter L. Berger and Richard J. Neuhaus, *To Empower People: The Role of Mediating Structures and Public Policy* (Washington, D.C.: American Enterprise Institute for Public Policy, 1977), p. 2.

11. *Ibid.*

12. *Ibid.*, p. 3.

13. Gannon, "Religious Tradition and Urban Community," p. 285.

14. Berger and Neuhaus, *To Empower People*.

15. *Ibid.*, p. 26.

16. Hugh Dalziel Duncan, *Symbols in Society* (New York: The Macmillan Co., 1966,) p. 169.

17. Gibson Winter, *Elements for a Social Ethic* (New York: The Macmillan Co., 1966), p. 159.

18. Rosemary Radford Reuther, *New Women/New Earth: Sexist Ideologies and Human Liberation* (New York: The Seabury Press, 1975), p. 8.

19. See Eldon G. Ernst, "A Concept of Christian Evangelism in a

Secular Society," *Foundations, A Baptist Journal of History and Theology,* Vol. VXI, No. 2 (April-June, 1973) (Rochester, N.Y.: The American Baptist Historical Society).

20. Pauli Murray, "Black, Feminist Theologies: Links, Parallels and Tensions," *Christianity and Crisis,* Vol. 40, No. 6 (April 14, 1980), p. 90.

Chapter II.

1. Also see Clifford Geertz, "From the Natives Point of View: On the Nature of Anthropological Understanding" in Paul Rabinow and William M. Sullivan, eds. *Interpretive Social Science* (Berkeley: University of California Press, 1979), pp. 225-41; and James Ogilvy, *Many Dimensional Man* (New York: Harper & Row, 1979). Both, Geertz and Ogilvy arguing from an anthropological, and a social psychological view, respectively, move away from a western conception of selfhood as singular, bounded, centralized and hierarchical toward a conception of selfhood as contextualized, processual, decentralized, relational, and plural in character.

2. See, Bernard M. Loomer, "The Free and Relational Self," *Belief and Ethics,* eds. Gibson Winter and W. W. Schroeder (Chicago: University of Chicago Press, 1976).

3. "Marxism and Monastic Perspectives," *The Asian Journal of Thomas Merton* (New York: New Directions Publishing Corporation, 1968), p. 341.

4. Martin Luther King, Jr., *Strength to Love* (New York: Harper & Row, 1963), p. 341.

5. Anselm Strauss, ed. *George Herbert Mead on Social Psychology* (Chicago: University of Chicago Press, 1956), pp. 207, 199.

6. Herbert Blumer, *Symbolic Interactionism* (Englewood Cliffs, N.J.: Prentice-Hall, 1969), p. 62.

7. *Ibid.*

8. George Herbert Mead, "The Genesis of the Self," in Chad Gordon and Kenneth J. Gergen, eds. *The Self in Social Interaction,* Vol. 1 (New York: John Wiley and Sons, Inc., 1968), p. 57.

9. Blumer, *Symbolic Interactionism,* pp. 63, 64.

10. Strauss, *George Herbert Mead on Social Psychology,* p. 227.

11. *Ibid.,* p. 208 (footnote).

12. Arthur W. Munk, "The Self as Agent and Spectator," *The Monist,* Vol. 49, No. 2 (April, 1965).

13. John MacMurray, *The Self as Agent* (London: Faber & Faber Limited, 1957).

14. Munk, *The Self as Agent and Spectator,* p. 269.
15. Edward E. Sampson, *Ego at the Threshold* (New York: A Dell Publication, 1975).
16. Robert K. Merton, foreword. Jacques Ellul, *The Technological Society* (New York: Alfred A. Knopf, 1965), p. viii.
17. Jai P. Ryu, "Self, Society and Human Nature." An unpublished paper presented at the consultation on religion and human development. *Institute for Ecumenical Studies and Cultural Research,* Collegeville, Minnesota, June 27, 1981, p. 30.
18. Loomer, "The Free and Relational Self," p. 23.
19. Mead, "The Genesis of the Self," pp. 54-55.
20. Edward E. Sampson, "Scientific Paradigms and Social Values: Wanted—A Scientific Revolution," *Journal of Personality and Social Psychology,* Vol. 36, No. 11 (Washington, D.C.: The American Psychological Association, 1978), p. 1334f.
21. Verne Paul Alexander, *The Theological Significance of the Thought of George Herbert Mead.* Unpublished Th.D. dissertation. Graduate Theological Union, 1971, p. 17.
22. Alfred Schutz, *Collected Papers I: The Problem of Social Reality* (The Hague: Martinus Nijhoff, 1971).
23. Gibson Winter, *Elements for a Social Ethics* (New York: The Macmillan Co., 1966).
24. Schutz, *Collected Papers I,* p. xxxii.
25. *Ibid.,* pp. xxxii-xxxiii.
26. Alfred Schutz, *Collected Papers II: Studies in Social Theory* (The Hague: Martinus Nijhoff, 1977), p. 177.
27. Winter, *Elements for a Social Ethics,* p. 106.
28. *Ibid.,* p. 197f.
29. *Ibid.,* p. 219.
30. *Ibid.*
31. *Ibid.,* p. 218.
32. *Ibid.,* p. 262.
33. *Ibid.,* p. 234.
34. Gibson Winters, *Liberating Creation: Foundations of Religious Social Ethics* (New York: Crossroads, 1981), pp. 49-50.
35. Bernard Nachbahr, "The Embodied Self and Religion." An unpublished paper presented at the consultation on religion and human development. *Institute for Ecumenical and Cultural Research,* Collegeville, Minnesota, 27 June 1981, p. 5.
36. Jerome D. Frank, M.D., "Psychotherapy: The Restoration of Morale." *American Journal of Psychiatry,* Vol. 131, No. 3 (March, 1974).
37. See Barbara Lerner, *Therapy in the Ghetto: Political Impotence and*

Personal Disintegration (Baltimore: John Hopkins University Press, 1972). Lerner's research heightens awareness of the interconnection between political impotence and a sense of personal or psychic disintegration. Her finding is that psychotherapy, when linked with strategies of social change can strengthen self-affirmation and build self-esteem. "From the perspective detailed here, the conflict over individual versus group methods in community mental health rests on a false dichotomy because the essential nature of constructive psychotherapy and social action is the same. So too are the goals of both: to promote effective action in one's own behalf, in the former case by removing internal psychological obstacles to such action, and in the latter, by removing external social obstacles to it." (11)

38. W. E. Burghardt DuBois, *The Souls of Black Folk* (New York: Fawcett Publications, 1961), pp. 140, 141, 143.

39. For an explication of the administrative function of the black church as "therapeutic," see: Floyd Massey, Jr., and Samuel Berry McKinney, *Church Administration in the Black Perspective* (Valley Forge, Pa.: Judson Press, 1976); also, Henry H. Mitchell, *Black Preaching* (Philadelphia: J. B. Lippincott Co., 1970); and H. Beecher Hicks, Jr., *Images of the Black Preacher* (Valley Forge, Pa.: Judson Press, 1977).

40. See Speed Leas and Paul Kittlaus, *The Pastoral Counselor in Social Action* (Philadelphia: Fortress Press, 1981).

41. H. Richard Niebuhr, *The Responsible Self* (New York: Harper & Row, 1963), p. 126.

42. Thomas R. Bennett, "Project Laity: Groups and Social Action," in John L. Casteel, ed. *The Creative Role of Interpersonal Groups in the Church Today* (New York: Associated Press, 1968), pp. 53-72.

43. Robert C. Leslie, "The Uniqueness of Small Groups in the Church," in *Pastoral Psychology* (June 1964), pp. 33-40; also *Sharing Groups in the Church* (New York: Abingdon, 1970).

44. Bennett, "Project Laity: Groups and Social Action," p. 72.

Chapter III.

1. James Spickard, "On Ideology and Liberation." An unpublished paper presented at the Area IV Colloquium, Graduate Theological Union, Berkeley, California. This paper was originally developed in response to an earlier draft and presentation on the "Relational Self" by me.

2. George Herbert Mead, *Mind Self, and Society,* ed. Charles W. Morris (Chicago: The University of Chicago Press, 1934), p. 196.

3. Rubem A. Alves, *A Theology of Human Hope* (St. Meinrad, Indiana: Abbey Press, 1975), pp. 136-37.

4. Mead, *Mind Self, and Society,* p. 174.

5. Irving M. Zeitlin, *Rethinking Sociology* (New York: Appleton-Century-Crofts, 1973), p. 227.

6. Anselm Strauss, *George Herbert Mead on Social Psychology* (Chicago: University of Chicago Press, 1956), p. 233.

7. Edward E. Sampson, *Ego at the Threshold* (New York: A Delta Original, 1975), p. 196.

8. Mead, *Mind Self, and Society,* p. 134.

9. For a critical analysis of this viewpoint, see Richard J. Bernstein, *The Restructuring of Social and Political Theory* (New York: Harcourt Brace Jovanovich, 1976), pp. 208-13. And Thomas McCarthy, *The Critical Theory of Jurgen Habermas* (Cambridge, Mass.: The MIT Press, 1978).

10. Jurgen Habermas, "Toward a Theory of Communicative Competence," *Inquiry,* 13, 1970, p. 372.

11. Bernstein, *The Restructuring of Social and Political Theory,* p. 212.

12. Bertell Ollman, *Alienation* (Cambridge, Mass.: Cambridge University Press, 1973), p. 84.

13. Benjamin A. Reist, *Theology in Red, White, and Black* (Philadelphia: The Westminster Press, 1975), p. 26.

14. See John Francis Kavanough, *Following Christ in a Consumer Society: The Spirituality of Cultural Resistance* (Maryknoll, N.Y.: Orbis Books, 1981); John B. Cobb, Jr., *Theology and Pastoral Care* (Philadelphia: Fortress Press, 1977); and Gibson Winter, *Liberating Creation: Foundations of Religious Social Ethics* (New York: Crossroads, 1981).

Chapter IV.

1. See Don S. Browning, *The Moral Context of Pastoral Care* (Philadelphia: The Westminster Press, 1976). Browning addresses pastoral care and counseling in the context of contemporary, mainline Protestant churches. His concern to view pastoral care and counseling within a moral and ethical context has relevance for the praxis of the pastoral care of souls in the black church. The argument of this chapter on the dialogue of therapy: a black perspective parallels Browning's main concern, namely to view the personal dimension of human suffering with the context of larger social patterns and ethical questions.

2. William H. Grier, "When the Therapist Is Negro: Some Effects on the Treatment Process," in *American Journal of Psychiatry*, No. 123, Vol. 12 (June, 1967), p. 1587.

3. LaMaurice H. Gardner, "Psychotherapy Under Varying Conditions of Race," in Roderick W. Pugh, ed. *Psychology and the Black Experience* (Monterey, Calif.: Brooks/Cole Publishing Company, 1972), pp. 44-45.

4. In addition to the two references cited above, see: Martin Shane, "Some Subcultural Considerations in the Psychotherapy of a Negro Patient," in *The Psychiatric Quarterly* (January 1960), Vol. 34, 1-19; Harold Rosen, M.D., and Jerome Frank, M.D., "Negroes in Psychotherapy," in *American Journal of Psychiatry*, Vol. 119, No. 5 (November, 1962), pp. 456-60; George Banks, Bernard G. Berenson, and Robert R. Carkhuff, "The Effects of Counselor Race and Training upon Counseling Process with Negro Clients in Initial Interviews," in *Journal of Clinical Psychology*, 1967, Vol. 23, 70-72; Robert R. Carkhuff and Richard Pierce, "Differential Effects of Therapist Race and Social Class upon Patient Depth of Self-Exploration in the Initial Clinical Interview," in *Journal of Consulting Psychology*, 1967, Vol. 31, No. 6, pp. 632-34; Richard R. Waite, "The Negro Patient and Clinical Theory," in *Journal of Consulting and Clinical Psychology*, 1968, Vol. 32, No. 4, pp. 427-33; Maynard Calnek, "Racial Factors in the Countertransference: The Black Therapist and the Black Client," in *American Journal of Orthopsychiatry*, Vol. 40 (1) (January, 1970); William Grier and Price Cobbs, *Black Rage (New York: Basic Books, 1968); Jerome M. Sattler, "Racial Experimenter Effects in Experimentation, Testing, Interviewing, and Psychotherapy," in Psychological Bulletin*, 1970, Vol. 73, No. 2, pp. 137-60; Peter Cimbolic, "Counselor Race and Experience Effects on Black Clients," in *Journal of Counseling and Clinical Psychology*, 1972, Vol. 39, No. 2, pp. 328-32; Enrico E. Jones, "Effects of Race on Psychotherapy Process and Outcome: An Exploratory Investigation," *Psychotherapy: Theory, Research and Practice*, Vol. 15, No. 13 (Fall, 1978); Enrico E. Jones, "Psychotherapy Outcome as a Function of Client-Therapist Race." Unpublished paper. University of California, Berkeley, 1979.

5. Jerome D. Frank, in the introduction to C. B. Traux and R. R. Carkhuff, *Toward Effective Counseling and Psychotherapy* (Chicago: Adline Publishing Company, 1967), p. ix.

6. Alfred Schutz, *Collected Papers I* (The Hague: Martinus Nijhoff, 1971), pp. 104-5.

7. C. R. Stinnette, "Reflection and Transformation: Knowing and Change in Psychotherapy and in Religious Faith," in Peter

Homans, ed. *The Dialogue Between Theology and Psychology* (Chicago: University of Chicago Press, 1968), Vol. III, p. 85.

8. LaMaurice H. Gardner, "Psychotherapy Under Varying Conditions of Race," pp. 50-51.

9. Hilde Bruch, M.D., *Learning Psychotherapy: Rationale and Ground Rules* (Cambridge: Harvard University Press, 1974), pp. ix-x.

10. Anthony Barton, *Three Worlds of Therapy* (Palo Alto, Calif.: Mayfield Publishing Company, 1974), p. 33.

11. Also see Seymour L. Halleck, *The Politics of Therapy* (New York: Harper & Row, 1971); and Franz Fanon, *The Wretched of the Earth,* trans. C. Farrington (New York: Grove Press, 1963).

12. Fanon, *Ibid.,* pp. 250, 310.

13. Fanon might have diagnosed Samuel's response as a temporary "reactionary psychoses" and identified his response as a psycho-affective consequence of systemic oppression.

Chapter V.

1. J. Deotis Roberts, "Christian Liberation Ethics: The Black Experience," in *Religion in Life,* Vol. 48, Abingdon, 1979, p. 227.

2. Frederick S. Carney, "Theological Ethics," Warren T. Reich, ed. *Encyclopedia of Bioethics,* Vol. 1 (New York: The Free Press, 1978), p. 435.

3. Joseph Fletcher, *Situation Ethics* (Philadelphia: The Westminster Press, 1970), pp. 14, 30.

4. Joseph Fletcher, "Situation Ethics," Warren T. Reich, ed. *Encyclopedia of Bioethics,* Vol. 1 (New York: The Free Press, 1978), p. 422.

5. Albert R. Jonsen, *Responsibility in Modern Religious Ethics* (Washington: Corpus Books, 1968), p. 179f.

6. Libertus A. Hoedemaker, *The Theology of H. Richard Niebuhr* (New York: Pilgrim Press, 1970), p. 67.

7. H. Richard Niebuhr, *The Responsible Self* (New York: Harper & Row, 1963), p. 65.

8. John M. Swomley, Jr., *Liberation Ethics* (New York: The Macmillan Co., 1972), pp. 1, 34.

9. *Ibid.,* pp. 3-4, 5.

10. Enoch H. Oglesby, *Ethics and Theology from the Other Side: Sounds of Moral Struggle* (Washington, D.C.: University of America, Inc., 1979), p. 19.

11. Eugene D. Genovese, *Roll, Jordan, Roll: The World the Slaves Made* (New York: Vintage Books, 1972), p. 244.

12. J. Garfield Owens, *All God's Chillun: Meditations on Negro Spirituals* (Nashville: Abingdon, 1971), p. 43.

13. Melvin G. Talbert, "The Ministry of the Black Church in the 70s," James S. Gadsden, ed. *Experiences, Struggles, and Hopes of the Black Church* (Nashville: Tidings, 1975), pp. 5-6.

14. Joseph R. Washington, "How Black Is Black Religion?" *Quest for a Black Theology,* James J. Gardiner, SA, and J. Deotis Roberts, Sr., eds. (Philadelphia: Pilgrim Press, 1971), p. 38.

15. Gayraud S. Wilmore and James H. Cone, *Black Theology: A Documentary History* (Maryknoll, N.Y.: Orbis Books, 1979), pp. 347-48.

16. Howard Dodson, "Review to Review," in *The Witness* (March, 1978), pp. 8, 9, 12, 13.

17. Richard J. Bernstein, *Praxis and Action* (Philadelphia: University of Pennsylvania Press, 1971), p. IX.

18. Paulo Freire, *Pedagogy of the Oppressed* (New York: Herder and Herder, 1970), pp. 75, 77-78.

19. Bernard M. Loomer, "The Web of Life." An unpublished paper. The Graduate Theological Union, Berkeley, California, October, 1977, p. 1.

20. Allan Aubrey Boesak, *Farewell to Innocence* (Marknoll, N.Y.: Orbis Books, 1977), p. 152.

21. Douglas Henry Daniels, *Pioneer Urbanites: A Social and Cultural History of Black San Francisco* (Philadelphia: Temple University Press, 1980), p. 122.

22. James H. Cone, "A Black American Perspective on the Asian Search for a Full Humanity," Virginia Fabella, ed. *Asia's Struggle for Full Humanity* (Maryknoll, N.Y.: Orbis Books, 1980), p. 177.

23. *Ibid.,* pp. 178, 180, 182.

Chapter VI.

1. See Ervin Smith, *The Ethics of Martin Luther King, Jr.,* Vol. 2 (New York: The Edwin Mellen Press, 1981).

2. Allan Aubrey Boesak, *Farewell to Innocence* (Maryknoll, N.Y.: Orbis Books, 1977), p. 124.

3. See Joseph R. Washington, *The Politics of God* (Boston: Beacon Press, 1967).

4. See J. Deotis Roberts, *Liberation and Reconciliation* (Philadelphia: The Westminster Press, 1971); and "Christian Liberation Ethics: The Black Experience" in *Religion in Life,* Vol. 48, Abingdon, 1979.

5. See Gayraud Wilmore, *Black Religion and Black Radicalism* (Garden City, N.Y.: Doubleday & Co., 1973).
6. See Major J. Jones, *Christian Ethics for Black Theology: The Politics of Liberation* (New York: Abingdon, 1974).
7. See James H. Cone, *God of the Oppressed* (New York: The Seabury Press, 1975).
8. *Ibid.*, pp. 206, 208.
9. Joseph K. Washington, "How Black Is Black Religion?" James J. Gardiner, Sr., and J. Deotis Roberts, Sr., eds. *Quest for a Black Theology* (Philadelphia: Pilgrim Press, 1971), p. 40.
10. Robert K. Merton, "Foreword," *The Technological Society* by Jacques Ellul (New York: Vintage Books, 1964), p. viii.
11. Allan Aubrey Boesak, *Farewell to Innocence*, p. 148.
12. Richard J. Bernstein, *The Restructuring of Social and Political Theory* (New York: Harcourt Brace Jovanovich, 1976), p. 200.
13. Jerome D. Frank, *Persuasion and Healing* (New York: Schocken Books, 1963), pp. 2-3.
14. Theodor W. Adorno, "Sociology and Psychology," *New Left Review*, No. 46 (November-December 1967), p. 69.
15. Peter L. Berger, "Toward a Sociological Understanding of Psychoanalysis," *Facing Up to Modernity* (New York: Basic Books, 1977), p. 33.
16. Adorno, "Sociology and Psychology," pp. 76, 78. Also see Michael Glenn and Richard Kunnes, *Repression or Revolution? Therapy in the United States Today* (New York: Harper & Row, 1973). They have argued that therapy often serves to adjust people within the systems that oppress them. "Therapists are caught in a contradiction: on the one hand, wanting to help people, and on the other, oppressing them for the system and making a living from people's suffering," p. vii.
17. Talcott Parsons, "Psychoanalysis and the Social Structure," in *The Psychoanalytic Quarterly*, Vol. 19, No. 3 (1962), p. 376.
18. An exceptional treatment of the relationship between psychoanalysis and social structure is to be found in Nancy Chodorow, *The Reproduction of Mothering: Psychoanalysis and the Sociology of Gender* (Berkeley: University of California Press, 1978).
19. C. Wright Mills, "On Reason and Freedom," in Maurice Stein *et al.*, *Identity and Anxiety: Survival of the Person in Mass Society* (New York: The Free Press, 1960), pp. 116, 112.
20. Jacques Ellul, *The Technological Society* (New York: Vintage Books, 1964), p. xxv.
21. Mills, "On Reason and Freedom," p. 113.
22. *Ibid.*, pp. 114, 117.

23. Herbert Marcuse, *One-Dimensional Man* (Boston: Beacon Press, 1964), pp. xv, xvi. The opposite thesis to the one dimensional man is argued in James Ogilvy, *Many-Dimensional Man* (New York: Harper & Row, 1979).

24. *Ibid.*, pp. xi, xiii-xiv, x.

25. Paul Ricoeur, *Freud and Philosophy* (New Haven: Yale University Press, 1977), p. 367.

26. R. J. Bernstein, *The Restructuring of Social and Political Theory*, pp. 180-81.

27. P. Ricoeur, *Freud and Philosophy*, p. 366.

28. Charles E. Reagan and David Stewart, *The Philosophy of Paul Ricoeur: An Anthology of His Work* (Boston: Beacon Press, 1978), p. 191.

29. For a treatment of character ethics, see three important contributions by: James Wm. McClendon, Jr., *Biography as Theology* (Nashville: Abingdon, 1974); and Stanley Hauerwas, *Vision and Virtue* (Notre Dame: Fides Publishers, 1974); Stanley Hauerwas *et al.*, *Truthfulness and Tragedy* (Notre Dame: University of Notre Dame Press, 1977).

30. Joseph R. Washington, "How Black Is Black Religion?" pp. 37-38.

31. Gibson Winter, *Liberating Creation: Foundations of Religious Social Ethics* (New York: Crossroads, 1981), p. 219.

32. Frank, *Persuasion and Healing*, pp. 27, 29.

33. Winter, *Liberating Creation*, p. 132.

34. Howard J. Clinebell, Jr., *Basic Types of Pastoral Counseling* (Nashville: Abingdon, 1966), pp. 14, 71.

35. See Speed Leas and Paul Kittlaus, *The Pastoral Counselor in Social Action* (Philadelphia: Fortress Press, 1981); Harvey Seifert and Howard Clinebell, *Personal Growth and Social Change* (Philadelphia: The Westminster Press, 1969); Don Browning, *The Moral Context of Pastoral Care* (Philadelphia: The Westminster Press, 1976); and Daniel Day Williams, *The Minister and the Care of Souls* (New York: Harper & Brothers, 1961).

36. *Oh Freedom*, arranged by Paul Abels, in *Workers Quarterly*, Vol. 39, No. 1 (July 1967), p. 22.

Chapter VII.

1. Roy Bhaskar, *The Possibility of Naturalism: A Philosophical Critique of the Contemporary Human Sciences* (New York: Humanities Press, 1979), p. 27.

2. See Winter, *Liberating Creation*, especially pp. 54-90.

3. Bertell Ollman, *Alienation: Marx's Conception of Man in Capitalist Society* (Cambridge, Mass.: The University Press, 1973), p. 30.

4. Robin M. Williams, Jr., *American Society*, 3rd ed. (New York: Alfred A. Knopf, 1970), p. 115.

5. William Ernest Hocking, in the Foreword to *Reality as Social Process*, by Charles Hartshorne (New York: Hufner Publishing Company, 1971), p. 16.

6. Theodore W. Adorno, "Sociology and Psychology" in *New Left Review*, No. 46 (Nov.-Dec., 1967), p. 76.

7. Eli Zaretsky, *Capitalism, and the Family, and Personal Life* (New York: Harper & Row, 1973), p. 123.

8. *Ibid.*, p. 114.

9. Robert Zwier and Richard Smith, "Christian Politics and the New Right," *Christian Century* (October 8, 1980), p. 937.

10. David Edwin Harrell, Jr., "The Roots of the Moral Majority: Fundamentalism Revisited," *Occasional Papers* (Institute for Ecumenical and Cultural Research, No. 15 Collegeville, Minnesota, May 1981), p. 10.

11. James McBride and Paul M. Schwartz, "The Moral Majority and the Failure of Religious Legitimations." An unpublished paper. *The Graduate Theological Union* (Center for the Study of New Religious Movements, Berkeley, California, 1980), pp. 6-7.

12. Eldon G. Ernst, *Without Help or Hindrance: Religious Identity in American Culture* (Philadelphia: The Westminster Press, 1977), p. 63.

13. Karl Mannheim, *Ideology and Utopia* (New York: Harcourt, Brace and World, Inc., 1936), p. 58.

14. Louis Althusser, *Lenin and Philosophy* (New York: Monthly Review Press, 1971), p. 158.

15. Edward C. Banfield, "The Unheavenly City," ed. David M. Gordon, *Problems in Political Economy: The Urban Perspective* (Lexington, Mass.: D. C. Heath and Co., 1971), pp. 47-48.

16. Althusser, *Lenin and Philosophy*, p. 159.

17. Winter, *Liberating Creation*, p. 129. Also see Clifford Geertz, *The Interpretation of Cultures* (New York: Basic Books, 1973), pp. 194-233, 131.

18. Juan Luis Segundo, *The Liberation of Theology* (Maryknoll, N.Y.: Orbis Books, 1976), p. 132.

19. Rosalind Coward and John Ellis, *Language and Materialism* (Boston: Routledge & Kegan Paul, 1977), p. 67.

20. *Ibid.*, p. 77.

21. Edward E. Sampson, "Cognitive Psychology as Ideology," in *American Psychologist* [forthcoming] (March, 1981), pp. 7, 8.

22. *Ibid.*, p. 6.

23. Althusser, *Lenin and Philosophy*, pp. 172-73.
24. Coward and Ellis, *Language and Materialism*, p. 68.
25. *Ibid.*, p. 93.
26. Althusser, *Lenin and Philosophy*, p. 172.
27. Coward and Ellis, *Language and Materialism*, p. 94.
28. Herbert Marcuse, *Eros and Civilization* (Boston: Beacon Press, 1966), pp. 13, 15-16.
29. *Ibid.*, pp. 18-19.
30. Winter, *Liberating Creation*, p. 71.
31. *Ibid.*, p. 69.

Chapter VIII.

1. Marshall Kilduff and Ron Javers, *The Suicide Cult* (San Francisco: A Gantam Book, 1978); *Newsweek* (December 4, 1978); *New West Magazine* (December 18, 1978); *The Black Panther Intercommand News Service* (December 30, 1978); "Pictures of a Madman: The Secret Tapes of Jim Jones," by the I-Team. KPIX Eyewitness News, San Francisco (November 12-13, 1979).
2. Barbara Hargrove, "Informing the Public: Social Scientist and Reactions to Jonestown." Unpublished paper. The School of Theology at Illif. Denver, Colorado (1979); Doyle Paul Jonson, "Dilemmas of Charismatic Leadership: The Case of the Peoples' Temple," *Sociological Analysis*, Vol. 40, No. 4 (Winter, 1979), pp. 315-23; James T. Richardson, "Peoples' Temple and Jonestown: A Corrective Critique and Comparison." Unpublished paper. University of Reno, Reno, Nevada (June, 1979); James S. Wolf, "On the Causes and Cures of Cults: Reflections on Peoples' Temple." Unpublished paper (December, 1978); David Wiencek, "A Demographic Profile of Jonestown Victims," University of Virginia. Unpublished paper delivered at the annual meeting for the Sociology of Religion. Boston, Mass. (August, 1979).
3. Hugo, J. Zee, M.D., "The Guyana Incident: Some Psychoanalytic Considerations," in *Bulletin of the Menniger Clinic*, Vol. 44, No. 4 (July, 1980), pp. 345-63.
4. Mark Lane, *The Strongest Poison* (New York: Hawthorne Books, 1980).
5. Jeannie Mills, *Six Years with God* (New York: A & W Publishers Inc., 1979).
6. John Peer Nugent, *White Night* (New York: Rawson, Wade Publishers Inc., 1979); *The Assassination of Representative Leo J. Ryan and the Jonestown, Guyana, Tragedy*. Report of a staff investigative group to the Committee on Foreign Affairs. U.S. House of Representatives (May 15, 1979).
7. C. Eric Lincoln and Lawrence H. Mamiya, "Daddy Jones and

Father Divine," The Cult as Political Religion, in *Religion in Life* (Spring, 1980).

8. See Zee, "The Guyana Incident." This brief sketch of Jones' life draws upon Zee's account.

9. Kilduff and Javers, *The Suicide Cult,* pp. 15, 17.

10. Nugent, *White Night,* p. 19.

11. *Maine Sunday Telegram* (October 5, 1980), p. 1D.

12. Mills, *Six Years with God,* p. 13. On Wednesday, February 27, 1980, *The San Francisco Examiner* carried the first page headline, "2 Temple Opponents Murdered in Berkeley." Al Mills' mother found Jeannie Mills and her husband Al murdered in their bedroom, shot along with their sixteen-year-old daughter, Daphene. Berkeley police were unable to establish a connection between their murder and the Peoples' Temple.

13. *Main Sunday Telegram* (October 5, 1980), p. 1D.

14. See Lincoln and Mamiya, "Daddy Jones and Father Divine," pp. 6-23.

15. Kilduff and Javers, *The Suicide Cult,* p. 33.

16. *The Assassination of Representative Leo J. Ryan and the Jonestown, Guyana Tragedy,* p. 319.

17. Kilduff and Javers, *The Suicide Cult,* pp. 39-42.

18. *Ibid., p. 42.*

19. *Mills, Six Years with God,* p. 98.

20. Nugent, *White Night,* p. 6.

21. For an excellent interpretation and elaboration of this point, see Doyle Paul Johnson, "Dilemmas of Charismatic Leadership: The Case of the Peoples' Temple," in *Sociological Analysis,* Vol. 40, No. 4 (Winter, 1979), pp. 315-23.

22. New Religious Movement Newsletter, Graduate Theological Union, Berkeley, California, Vol. 1, No. 2 (March, 1979), p. 5.

23. *Newsweek* (December 4, 1978), p. 72.

24. Margaret Thaler Singer. Quoted in "Why People Join," *Time Magazine* (112 (22), 1978), p. 27.

25. Arthur H. Fauset, *Black Gods of the Metropolis: Negro Religious Cults of the Urban North* (Philadelphia: University of Pennsylvania Press, 1944), pp. 107-8.

26. Joseph R. Washington, Jr., *Black Sects and Cults* (New York: Doubleday & Co., 1972), pp. 1, 2.

27. The appeal of Jim Jones was not limited to one group, but cut across a wide section of the population. Religious cults such as the Moonies, Children of God and Hare Krishna tend to recruit young persons from white and middle-class backgrounds. Blacks tend not to join these groups—especially blacks who are elderly, single parents, welfare dependents, or wards of the state. The Peoples'

Temple did claim these and others. Its social base was much broader than most groups that have been referred to as "cults." Also see Figures 1 and 2 for a breakdown of race, age, and sex of the Jonestown victims.

28. Hart M. Nelsen and Ann Kusener Nelsen, *Black Church in the Sixties* (Lexington: The University Press of Kentucky, 1975), p. 99. Nelsen and Nelsen basically reject the conclusion reached in *Protest and Prejudice* by Gary Marx who argued that religion was a sedating influence rather than a stimulating drive toward social protest, reform, and radicalism among the black masses. Nelsen and Nelsen found that blacks, when compared to whites, were more likely to favor the church's speaking out on social and political questions. At least this was the case during the 1960s. This posture was consistent with black churches which were at the forefront of liberation struggles in the nineteenth century. However, *both* other worldly orientation and this worldly change have been a part of the black religious heritage in the United States.

29. Mills, *Six Years with God*, p. 26.

30. Paul Schwartz is a doctoral candidate at the Graduate Theological Union in Berkeley, California, and a research assistant in the New Religious Movement Program interviewing Temple defectors. His remarks were shared at a Graduate Theological Colloquium on April 10, 1979.

31. Sigmund Freud, *The Future of an Illusion* (New York: Doubleday & Co., 1975).

32. Zee, "The Guyana Incident," p. 358; also see Lincoln and Mamiya, "Daddy Jones and Father Divine."

33. *Ibid.* Zee's interpretation of Jonestown was an exception to this general criticism. He combined psychoanalytic considerations with group dynamics in order to interpret the interplay between Jones and his followers. Yet the larger social dimension was not treated in his interpretation.

34. *The New York Times* (December 1, 1978).

35. Mills, *Six Years with God*, introduction, p. 9.

36. Ernest Becker, *The Denial of Death* (New York: The Free Press, 1973), p. 136.

37. R. D. Laing, *Self and Others* (New York: Penguin Books, 1969), pp. 108-9, 111.

38. Lincoln and Mamiya, "Daddy Jones and Father Divine," p. 14.

39. *The Daily Californian* (January 9, 1979).

40. *Ibid.*

41. *The New York Times* (November 26, 1978).

42. Sydney E. Ahlstron, "From Sinai to the Golden Gate: The

Liberation of Religion in the Occident," eds. Jacob Needleman and George Baker, *Understanding the New Religions* (New York: The Seabury Press, 1978), pp. 21-22.

43. Theodore Roszak, *Unfinished Animal* (New York: Harper & Row, 1975), p. 5.

44. Richard K. Fenn, "Toward a Theory of Secularization." Mimeograph series number 1. Published by the Society for the Scientific Study of Religion, 1978.

45. Eldon G. Ernst, *Without Help or Hindrance: Religious Identity in American Culture* (Philadelphia: The Westminster Press, 1977), p. 75.

46. For an excellent discussion on pastoral care ministry in the black perspective, see Edward P. Wimberly's *Pastoral Care in the Black Church* (Nashville: Abingdon, 1979). Wimberly's discussion is focused around the black church community and is not intended as a discussion of the black community as a whole. This paper attempts to draw the implications for ministry to the comunity as a totality. Both Wimberly's work and this paper can be seen as complementary.

47. Sterling P. Lamprecht, *Our Philosophical Traditions* (New York: Appleton-Century-Crofts, 1955), pp. 210, 212.

48. Stuart Hampshire, *The Age of Reason* (New York: A Mentor Book, 1956), p. 15.

49. Peter Berger, *The Sacred Canopy* (New York: Doubleday & Co., 1969), pp. 107-8.

50. Bernard M. Loomer, "The Web of Life," The Graduate Theological Union, Berkeley, California (October, 1977). Unpublished paper, pp. 17, 27.

51. Charles Hartshorne, "Reality as Social Process," *Studies in Metaphysics and Religion* (New York: Hefner Publishing Company, Inc., 1954), p. 40.

52. See W. E. B. DuBois, *The Souls of Black Folk* (Greenwich, Conn.: Fawcett Publications, 1961); Melville J. Herskovits, *The Myth of the Negro Past* (Boston: Beacon Press, 1941); John W. Blassingame, *The Slave Community* (New York: Oxford University Press, 1972); Eugene D. Genovese, *Roll, Jordan, Roll* (New York: Vintage Books, 1976); Albert J. Raboteau, *Slave Religion: The "Invisible Institution" in the Antebellum South* (New York: Oxford University Press, 1978).

53. Henry H. Mitchell, *Black Belief* (New York: Harper & Row, 1975), pp. 59-60.

54. Bonjanjalo Goba, "Corporate Personality: Ancient Israel and Africa," *The Challenge of Black Theology in South Africa*, ed. Basil Moore (Atlanta: John Knox Press, 1973).

55. Allan Aubrey Boesak, *Farewell to Innocence* (Maryknoll, N.Y.: Orbis Books, 1977), p. 152.

56. Paul G. Pfuetze, *Self, Society, Existence* (New York: Harper & Brothers, 1954), p. 131.
57. C. Wright Mills, *The Sociological Imagination* (London: Oxford University Press, 1959), p. 3.
58. James H. Cone, "Where Do We Go from Here?" in *The Witness* (March, 1978), p. 6.
59. Eli Zaretsky, *Capitalism, the Family and Personal Life* (New York: Harper & Row, 1973), pp. 135-36.
60. Larry George Murphy Lee, "Equality Before the Law: The Struggle of Nineteenth-Century Black Californians for Social and Political Justice." Unpublished Ph.D. Dissertation presented to the Faculty of the Graduate Theological Union, Berkeley, California (May 16, 1973). Also see Philip S. Funer, "Reverend George Washington Woodley: Early Twentieth Century Black Socialist," in *The Journal of Negro History,* Vol. 61, No. 2 (April, 1976); Gayraud Wilmore, *Black Religion and Black Radicalism* (New York: Doubleday & Co., 1972); Benjamin E. Mays and Joseph W. Nichelson, *The Negro's Church* (New York: Russell, 1933); C. Eric Lincoln, *The Black Church Since Frazier* (New York: Schocken Books, 1974); Douglas Henry Daniels, *Pioneer Urbanites: A Social and Cultural History of Black San Francisco* (Philadelphia: Temple University Press, 1980).
61. Lawrence N. Jones, "They Sought a City: The Black Church and Churchmen in the Nineteenth Century," eds. Martin E. Marty and Dean G. Peerman, *New Theology No. 9* (New York: The Macmillan Co., 1972), pp. 172-73.
62. C. Eric Lincoln, "Faith and Socialization," in *The Journal of The Interdenominational Theological Center,* Vol. VI, No. 1 (Fall, 1978), p. 21.
63. From a conversation with a Temple participant who wished not to be identified.
64. John V. Moore, former pastor of First United Methodist Church, Reno, Nevada. November 19, 1978, sermon.
65. *New West Magazine* (December 18, 1978), p. 50.
66. Cornel West, "Black Theology and Socialist Thought," *The Witness,* Amber, Pa.: The Episcopal Church Publishing Company, Vol. 63, No. 4 (April, 1980), p. 18.
67. Mills, *Six Years with God,* p. 13.
68. DuBois, *The Souls of Black Folk,* p. 146.
69. Genovese, *Roll, Jordan, Roll,* p. 6.
70. *Ibid.,* p. 7.
71. Wimberly, *Pastoral Care in the Black Church,* pp. 20-21.
72. Gayraud A. Wilmore and James H. Cone, *Black Theology: A Documentary History, 1966-1979* (Maryknoll, N.Y.: Orbis Press, 1979), p. 347.

INDEX

251